State Parks
of the
SOUTH

Blair Howard

Hunter Publishing, Inc
300 Raritan Center Parkway,
Edison, NJ 08818
(908) 225 1900
Fax (908) 417 0482

ISBN 1-55650-655-4

© 1995 Blair Howard

Maps by Kim André
Cover Photo: Roanoke Sound, NC by Frederica Georgia
(Photo Network)
Photos courtesy of the author and the Department of Parks
for Alabama, Florida, Georgia, Kentucky and Tennessee

Contents

Introduction

Each year numerous families make the annual pilgrimage to one of the nation's coastal resort areas in search of sun, sand and sea. And each year many of them, after fighting the crowds and inflated prices, swear they'll never do it again, but they do. And it's understandable because a year of working hard and battling the pressures of everyday life can leave one a little stir-crazy. So once again they head for crowded shores, never knowing there's an alternative.

State parks offer a whole new world of vacation fun where all the comforts of the great resorts are readily available, but at a much lower cost. Crowds are minimal, the air is clean and invigorating and the scenery spectacular – a real opportunity for rest and relaxation. This alternative is often much closer to home than the nearest coastal hot-spot, so you won't even have to deal with hours of travel. Despite the fact that parks are open to everyone, most remain largely undiscovered by the vacationing public and it is there that the beauty lies.

Very few people are aware of the facilities offered within state parks – they rival even the most highly-acclaimed resorts: hotels with luxury suites and fine dining rooms, rustic cabins in the high country or on the banks of a river, great stone fireplaces and roaring fires, swimming pools, tennis courts, indoor and outdoor sports complexes, deserted beaches. Some parks even have private airstrips!

While smaller, in general, than their more famous counterparts in the National Parks System, they are certainly not lacking charm or beauty. There's nothing to compare with the majestic beauty of Yellowstone and Yosemite, but few national parks could rival the mystery and breathtaking views at Okefenokee Swamp at Stephen C. Foster State Park in Georgia, the magnificent waterfall at Fall Creek Falls State Park in Tennessee, or the spectacular water park at Lake Guntersville State Park in Alabama.

Some of the parks described in this book will be well known to you, others you will be less familiar with, and still more you may never have heard of. Regardless of your familiarity with them, it's likely you will have little idea of what or how much they have to offer. Some are very large and rich in facilities, others are smaller and offer nothing more than the beautiful countryside they strive to protect. All are unique.

State parks often have special significance for people with specific interests: beaches, fishing, hiking, boating, waterskiing, American history, etc., and these are identified throughout this book. All you need do is turn to the state of your choice and browse through the pages until you find exactly what you're looking for. And if you need more help it's always available; your nearest state park is only a phone call away, even on a Sunday.

Alabama

Alabama's state parks have plenty to offer the discerning vacationer, from the finest resorts and convention centers to the most primitive of mountain getaways. The state has 24 magnificent outdoor retreats that cater to a wide variety of individual tastes and needs. These range from a tastefully designed lodge complete with full-service restaurants and convention facilities, to lakefront cottages and ridge-top chalets, to rustic mountain cabins and primitive campsites. Their amenities vary considerably with the more exclusive establishments offering, among other things, a full-service marina and the campgrounds providing picnic tables and shelters.

But Alabama has more tucked away: sailing the clear blue waters of the Gulf of Mexico, camping beneath the stars, fishing some of the finest waters in the entire United States, golfing at the most challenging courses in the South and dining on freshly-caught seafood. Whether you're here for a long stay or simply a day out, spending time with the family or travelling alone, Alabama's state parks have something for you. Enjoy the sunshine, discover the great outdoors and let your cares float away in the tranquillity of the mountains.

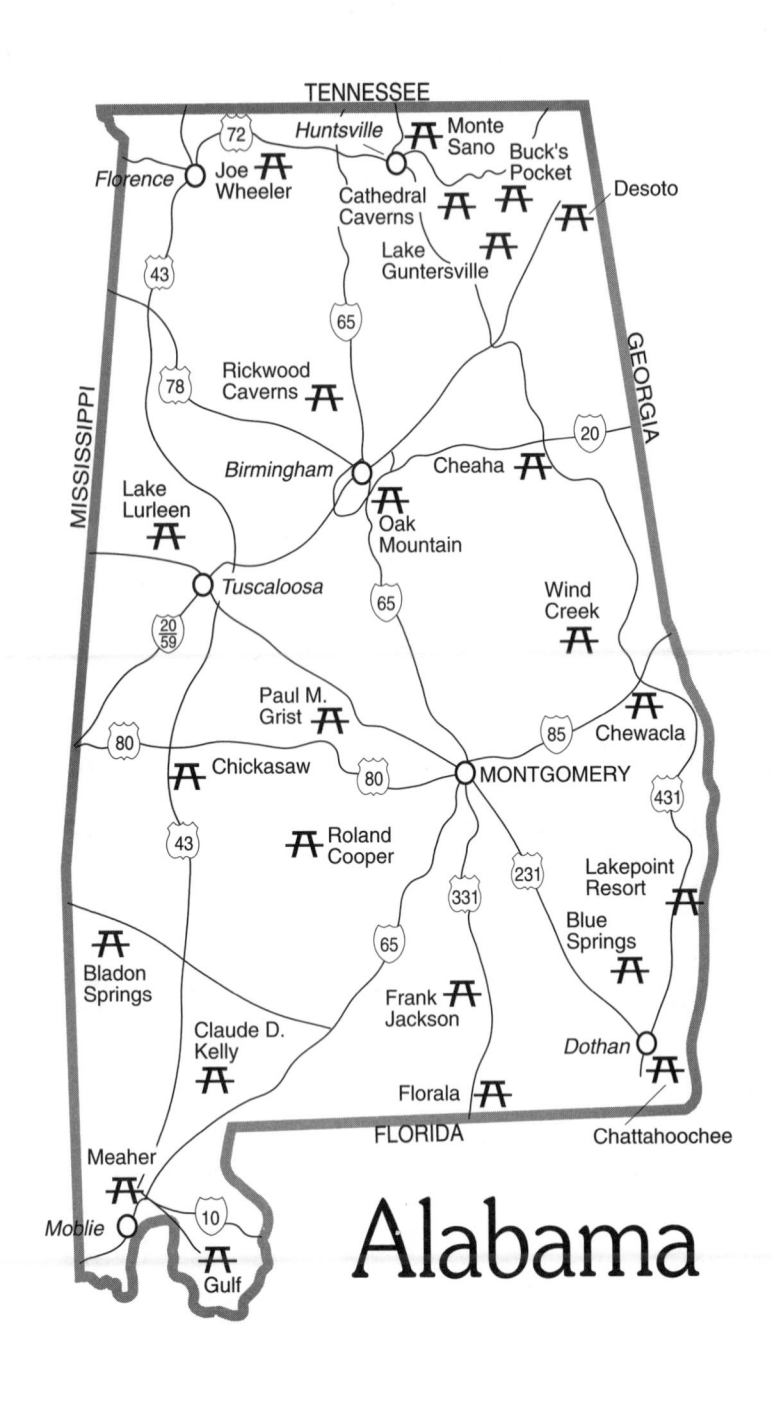

Alabama

Bladon Springs State Park

Bladon Springs is a small, day-use park of less than 400 acres. Its limited facilities are used mainly by families for small gatherings and reunions. There are several picnic shelters, a playground for the kids and a comfort station. The main feature of the park is the sulfur water springs.

INFORMATION: Bladon Springs State Park, Bladon Springs, AL 36902. Telephone 205-754-9479. The park is just one mile north of Bladon Springs off Alabama Highway 84.

Blue Springs State Park

Blue Springs is another of Alabama's smaller parks, about 103 acres, in the southeastern part of the state. It is well-known for its pure waters that are fed from an underground spring. The park has a swimming pool, 50 modern campsites, primitive camping, several tennis courts, a playground, picnic shelters, a comfort station, and refreshment facilities.

Camping fees are $11 per day (there is no fee for primitive camping) and reservations can be made up to a year in advance. The office is open to take reservations, either in person or by telephone, from 9 AM until 5 PM Monday through Friday.

A Labor Day celebration is held here in September.

NEARBY ATTRACTIONS: Lakepoint State Park, Shorter Mansion and Tom Mann's Fishing World (both in Eufala), Walter F. George Lock & Dam, Dothan, Frank Jackson State Park in Opp, Pike Pioneer Museum near Troy, Fort Mitchell National Cemetery in Phoenix City, the Old Russell County Courthouse in Seale and Lake Eufala.

INFORMATION: Blue Springs State Park, Route 1, Box 132, Clio, AL 36017. Telephone 205-397-8703. Bookings may also be made through the Central Reservation Service 1-800-ALA-PARK. The park is six miles east of Clio off County Highway 10.

Buck's Pocket State Park

Buck's Pocket, set in a secluded area in the Appalachian Mountains, is a naturalist's dream. The picnic area, located high on a ridge, affords a magnificent view of the pocket below.

Major features of the park are 45 modern campsites ($10 per day), primitive camping (free), a camp store, comfort stations, a picnic area with group shelters, five nature trails, fishing and boating facilities on Lake Guntersville, including a boat slip, refreshment facilities and a playground.

ACTIVITIES: Hiking and backpacking, fishing, boating, sailing, nature study, bird watching, and wildlife photography. There are more than 12 miles of backcountry trails and fishing at Morgan Cove on Lake Guntersville is said to be spectacular.

NEARBY ATTRACTIONS: DeSoto State Park, Little River Canyon, Looking Glass Caverns, Fort Payne, Lake Guntersville State Park, and Cathedral Caverns State Park.

INFORMATION: Buck's Pocket State Park, Route 1, Box 36, Grove Oak, AL 35975. Telephone 205-659-2000. Camping reservations can be made at the park office either in person or by telephone. It is open Monday through Friday from 9 AM until 5 PM. Alternatively, call the Central Reservation Service at 1-800-ALA-PARK. Bookings can be made up to a year in advance. The park is two miles north of Grove Oak just off County Highway 227.

Cathedral Caverns State Park

This is one of Alabama's newest parks. Here, more than 460 acres of rolling hills, valleys and scenic forests, along with the state's most beautiful backcountry, surround one of the finest cave systems in the United States. Amenities include a modern, full-service campground, a restaurant, several comfort stations, picnic areas, a play area and several hiking trails.

NEARBY ATTRACTIONS: Boaz Shopper's Paradise, Lake Guntersville Aero-Replica Fighter Museum, Lake Guntersville State Park and Buck's Pocket State Park.

INFORMATION: Alabama State Park Office in Montgomery (205-242-3333). Cathedral Caverns is eight miles north of Columbus City and seven miles south of Scottsboro on County Highway 79.

Chattahoochee State Park

Chattahoochee State Park is located at the extreme southeastern corner of the state. The 600-acre scenic park takes its name from the nearby Chattahoochee River where the fishing is reputedly excellent and the weather almost always warm.

Facilities at the park include primitive camping at no charge; extensive facilities for fishing and boating on the river; picnic tables and group facilities; and eight nature trails which between them offer more than seven miles of strenuous hiking.

NEARBY ATTRACTIONS: Farley Nuclear Visitor Center on Highway 95 South near Columbia, George W. Andrews Lock & Dam, Blue Springs State Park, Dothan, Landmark Park in Dothan, Boll Weevil Monument in Enterprise, the US Army Aviation Museum at Fort Rucker near Ozark and Lake Seminole in Florida.

INFORMATION: Chattahoochee State Park, Star Route, Box 108, Gordon, AL 36343. Telephone 205-522-3607. The park is situated 11 miles southeast of Gordon off County Highway 95.

Cheaha State Park

This park is set atop Cheaha Mountain in the northeast portion of Alabama. The 2,800-acre area, Alabama's highest mountain retreat, offers spectacular scenery. From season to season the vibrant colors of the countryside change from fresh greens and pastel colors in spring and early summer, to golden hues in fall and glittering white landscapes in winter. On warm summer evenings one can wander along more than seven miles of hiking and nature trails, and watch as the falling sun bathes the mountain top in the glow of a thousand spectral fires and turns the surface of the lake into a sea of burning metal.

Cheaha offers extensive facilities. There are 73 modern campsites, all with water, electrical and sewage hookups. Primitive camping is also available with the added advantage of a bathhouse, laundry room, comfort stations and a camp store close by. There are 15 chalets and stone cabins, each of which can accommodate from two to eight people. These are furnished with everything you might need for a comfortable vacation, including bed linens, cooking utensils, fireplaces and outdoor grills.

The park also features a resort lodge with 30 well-appointed guest rooms, each with two double beds, TV and telephone. The lodge's full-service restaurant is open throughout the year and has meeting and banquet facilities for up to 50 people. Another option, Bald Rock Group Lodge, accommodates up to 50 people in an old-fashioned stone building complete with a dining hall, large kitchen, ice machine and fireplace.

The park has hiking trails, picnic areas with pavilions and a playground, a lake where you can rent pedal boats and an observation tower.

ACTIVITIES: Camping, hiking, swimming, fishing, nature study, bird watching and photography.

The Civilian Conservation Corps Reunion in June and the AMA Motorcycle Show in October are held here annually.

NEARBY ATTRACTIONS: Oak Mountain State Park, Birmingham, Tuskegee National Forest, Montgomery, Chewacla State Park, Camp ASCCA in Jackson's Gap, Horseshoe Bend National Military Park, Fort Toulouse and Jackson Park close to Wetumpka and Jasmine Hill Gardens & Outdoor Museum, just north of Montgomery off Highway 231.

INFORMATION: Cheaha State Park Lodge, PO Box 546, Lineville, AL 36266. Telephone 205-488-5115. Cheaha is fairly close to Lineville, just south of I-20 off Highway 431.

Chewacla State Park

Chewacla lies on the fall line that separates the Piedmont plateau from the coastal plain. The entire area was once part of the ocean. Today the 700-acre park offers 36 modern campsites, five family cottages and primitive camping facilities for those who really want to get away from it all. There's a group pavilion, a bathhouse, comfort stations, picnic areas, a play area, refreshment facilities and rental boats on the lake where a lifeguard is on duty.

ACTIVITIES: Fishing, hiking (six trails total more than five miles), tennis, nature study and bird watching.

The Wet & Wild Triathlon is held here every May and the Banana Man Biathlon in October.

INFORMATION: Chewacla State Park, PO Box 447, Auburn, AL 36831. Telephone 205-887-5621. Chewacla is four miles south of Auburn on I-85.

Chickasaw State Park

Chickasaw State Park, with little more than 500 acres, is one of Alabama's smaller recreational areas. Even so, it provides most of the amenities offered by larger parks. There are only three modern, full-service campsites so be sure to make a reservation. There's plenty of room for primitive camping and the park is well served with comfort stations, picnic areas and playgrounds, as well as a hiking trail.

NEARBY ATTRACTIONS: Bluff Hall and Gainswood in Demopolis, Greene County Greyhound Park in Eutaw, Demopolis Lock and Dam, Armistead Lock and Dam, Magnolia Grove in Greensboro, Bladon Springs State Park and Moundville Archeological Park.

INFORMATION: Chickasaw State Park, Route #1, Box 430, Gallion, AL 36742 (205-295-8230). The park is four miles north of Linden off US 28.

Claude D. Kelly State Park

Claude D. Kelly State Park in Atmore is fast becoming known as something of a mecca for the freshwater fisherman. The lake here, though fairly small by some standards, offers quiet, lazy hours of drifting beneath towering pines where only non-powered boats are permitted.

The park has five modern campsites, three family cottages, facilities for primitive camping, a group pavilion, comfort stations, picnic areas, playgrounds for the children and conveniently located vending machines.

ACTIVITIES: Swimming, picnicking, boating, hiking along the six miles of nature trails, nature study, bird watching and, of course, fishing.

NEARBY ATTRACTIONS: Little River State Forest, William Rutherford Monument, Fort Mims Historic Site in Tensaw, Thomas E. Macmillan Museum in Brewton and Peacock Valley Winery in Perdido.

INFORMATION: Claude D. Kelly State Park, Route #2, Box 77, Atmore, AL 36502 (205-862-2511). The park is 12 miles north of I-65 in Atmore.

Desoto State Park

The focal point of this park, perched on the brow of Lookout Mountain close to Fort Payne, is Little River Canyon, claimed to be the deepest canyon east of the Rockies. The woodlands that surround it are home to a plethora of wildlife, several species of which are on the endangered list. These include the green salamander, the harparella, the Krals water plantain and the pitcher plant. Little River itself, sometimes gentle, often turbulent, but always inspiring, is unspoiled, sparkling clean and extraordinarily beautiful. It is said to be the only river in the United States that forms and flows its entire length on the top of a mountain.

As the seasons come and go in the canyon, so the environment changes and adjusts to suit the climate. In springtime the scent of fresh flowers fills the air. From May to June mountain laurel and rhododendron are in bloom, covering the area in a blanket of a hundred delicate shades of pink. Summer is a time to spend drifting on the lake above DeSoto Falls or strolling along the river bank deep in the canyon. In October the air turns crisp and the fall season paints a riot of color: bronze, amber, gold and red. By the time December arrives, winter has already turned the trees into stark woodland skeletons. Then the snow comes to the mountain top; not the deep drifts of Colorado, but a light covering of soft white powder that transforms the countryside into a winter fairyland.

Little River Canyon, Desoto State Park

ACTIVITIES: More than 100 miles of natural hiking trails wind their way along the canyon rim and through the 4,500 acres of the DeSoto State Park. They range in length from short walks around Little River Canyon Mouth Park to a challenging 12-mile hike along DeSoto Scout Hiking Trail. Tiny pathways meander back and forth across the canyon walls leading ever downward to the canyon floor. Spectacular views, unusual rock formations, rustic footbridges and an abundance of plant life are just a few of the wonders to be found along the way.

At the north end of the canyon is DeSoto Falls, where Little River cascades more than 100 feet to the canyon floor. High above the falls a beautiful lake provides clear water for swimming and fishing. The route down to the river is well defined, though somewhat rigorous, and the dedicated walker will enjoy the challenge.

DeSoto State Park, while maintaining the unique nature of the surrounding countryside, offers the following facilities: accommodation in the form of mountain chalets with fireplaces, sleeping lofts, heat, air conditioning and screened porches; rustic vacation cottages, modern in every way and equipped with all necessaries for light housekeeping. There is also a restaurant that features, along with wonderful country cooking, exposed beams and an extra large fireplace; a large modern bathhouse; an Olympic-size pool and two regulation-size tennis courts. A full-service Wilderness Camping Area is set in the forest away from traffic. It is complete with hookups, two comfort stations and a playground.

NEARBY ATTRACTIONS: Grace's High Falls – the highest waterfall in Alabama and very beautiful in spring and early summer – on the south side of Bear Creek Canyon on Rim Parkway (Highway 176) around Little River Canyon; Howard's Chapel, one of the most unusual churches in the world, is only a half-mile north of the park's information center; Weiss Lake, 20 miles from DeSoto, with more than 36,000 acres of water and at least 425 miles of shoreline, offers plenty of boating, fishing swimming and walking trails. While you're there be sure to visit Yellow Creek Falls, a spectacular waterfall that drops straight off the face of Lookout Mountain into Weiss Lake. If skiing is of interest, you can do that too. Yes, even in Alabama! On the banks of Little River, just a couple of miles from the park, is the 1,000-acre Cloudmont Ski and Golf Resort. Although it sounds quite grand it's really not. It does, however, have a fine golf course, where there's absolutely no waiting for a tee time, and some fairly extensive vacation facilities. The resort is a peaceful, rustic, hideaway that boasts access to more than 100 miles of bridleways and hiking trails. It has ski lifts that take you to an 1,800-foot elevation where, depending upon the season, you can shuss down the slope on snow or grass.

Annual special events at the park include the Little River Canyon Cleanup in March, a Wildflower Program in May, the Rhododendron Festival also in May and the Fall ColorFest in October.

INFORMATION: For camping, hiking and picnicking details call 205-845-0051, or write DeSoto State Park, Route 1, Box 210, Fort Payne, AL 35967. For accommodations and reservations call 205-

845-5380, or write DeSoto State Park, Route 1, Box 205, Fort Payne, AL 35967. Both the park and canyon are easily accessible from I-59, at Fort Payne, 50 miles south of Chattanooga, Tennessee and 80 miles north of Birmingham.

Florala State Park

Florala, at just 40 acres, is a very small park. The attraction here is its access to Lake Jackson, where the fishing is superb and the powerboat is the preferred mode of transportation. Visitors come from miles around to enjoy a day on the water, be it for fishing, swimming, waterskiing or sailing. The park offers 23 modern campsites, primitive camping, comfort stations and a community building with a meeting room. There are several boat ramps as well as fishing piers, picnic tables and play areas. The town's stores are only a short walk away along the shores of the lake.

INFORMATION: Florala State Park, PO Box 322, Florala, AL 36442-0322. Telephone 205-858-6425. The park is located in town.

Frank Jackson State Park

Once again it's a lake that makes this park such a big attraction. At the time of publication, camping facilities were still in the planning stage, but there were comfort stations. For the family outing there are picnic areas with group pavilions, play areas, refreshment facilities, swimming, boating and hiking along two nature trails. Fishing on the lake (they keep it well stocked) is excellent.

Jaycees Fireworks display on July 4th takes place each year and The Old Folks Day Arts & Crafts Festival also makes use of the park on an annual basis.

NEARBY ATTRACTIONS: Coffee County Lake, Conecuh National Forest, Lake Jackson and Florala State Park and Geneva State Forest.

INFORMATION: Frank Jackson State Park, Route #3, Box 73-C, Opp, AL 36467. Telephone 205-493-6988. The park is just outside Opp on Highway 331.

Gulf State Park

At 6,150 acres, Gulf is the second largest of Alabama's state parks and offers just about everything one could ask for. Seagulls, sea-shells, raging surf and more than 2.5 miles of white sand beach welcome you to Gulf State Park. The pride of the park is its outstanding convention complex that houses a modern 144-room beachfront hotel, 21 cabins, a superb restaurant overlooking the coast and a challenging 18-hole golf course.

The hotel offers rooms with ocean views, cable TV, telephones and air-conditioning. It also maintains a number of rooms accessible to guests with disabilities. There's a swimming pool, snack bar, lounge, two lighted tennis courts (rackets and balls may be rented) and in the summer there's an evening Luau. Meeting facilities for up to 1,000 persons for receptions and 600 for banquets are also available.

Stilted holiday cabins, Gulf State Park

Seventeen modern cabins overlook Lake Shelby, each comfortably furnished and fully equipped with blankets, linens, cooking utensils and dishes. Four rustic, one-room cabins are just to the north of the lake. These have all the comforts of modern cabins.

Whenever you visit this sub-tropical park you're almost sure to enjoy the best of weather. During spring and fall the days are warm and the evenings cool. Even in winter the weather is often warm. Summer days are almost always hot, but a cool sea breeze blowing in off the Gulf of Mexico keeps temperatures comfortable.

On the golf course, one of the most beautiful in Alabama, hotel guests receive a discount and rental clubs are available at the pro's shop. The course is a tough 6,563 yards and the tees are often shaded by huge moss-draped oaks, tall pines and magnolias. The greens are large and well kept, the bunkers well placed and filled with sand and several of the fairways are bordered by water. You can either walk the course or rent a golf cart.

There are 468 modern campsites at Middle Lake. Many of them have sewage hookups and all have access to picnic tables, grills, tennis courts, a laundromat, boat ramps, a camp store and comfort stations.

ACTIVITIES: Picnicking is a popular pastime at Lake Shelby where tables, grills, and pavilions are provided. Other outdoor activities include hiking the more than four miles of trails, fishing in the Gulf of Mexico from the 825-foot pier, freshwater fishing on Lake Shelby, and sunbathing and swimming on the beach.

Annual events at the park are a Valentine's Day Dinner/Dance Package, the Sea Oats Festival in May, a Motor Club Rally in June, the Surf, Turf, Golf & Fishing Classic in December, the Intercoastal Canal Christmas Lighted Boat Parade and a New Year's Eve Dinner/Dance Event.

NEARBY ATTRACTIONS: Baldwin Heritage Museum in Elberta, Waterville USA, Miss Collen's House at Point Clear, Easter Shore Arts Association Museum in Fairhope, Styx River Water World in Robertsdale, The American Sport Art Museum and Archives in Daphne, U.S.S. Alabama Battleship Memorial Park in Mobile and Blakely Historic Park near Spanish Fort.

INFORMATION: Gulf State Park, 20115 St. Highway 135, Gulf Shores, AL 36542. Telephone 205-948-7275 (Park Office & Cabin Information). For resort reservations write or call their office at PO Box 437, Gulf Shores, AL 36547. Telephone 800-544-4853. Gulf State Park is on State Highway 135 just off State Highway 59 which connects to US 98 and to Interstates 10 and 65.

Joe Wheeler State Park

Joe Wheeler certainly is a fisherman's paradise but, more than that, it's a backcountry resort of outstanding natural beauty. You can sail the deep green waters of the lake, enjoy a quiet afternoon disturbed only by the rustle of the breeze in the sail, have a home-cooked breakfast on the deck of a rustic cabin or set off on an invigorating hike along the woodland trails. You can spend your days fishing at the lake, enjoy fast afternoons of waterskiing and wake up to a round of golf or a couple of sets of tennis. For honeymooners it's a place to be alone, to stroll hand-in-hand along the landscaped shores of Lake Wheeler or to spend time together sunbathing in a secluded spot.

The park offers 116 improved campsites and several primitive campsites along with shower and laundry facilities. There are 23 vacation cabins at the Wheeler Dam facility, each accommodating four to eight people, and two group lodges: one at Elk River with capacity for 30 persons, and one at Wheeler Dam which can accommodate 20 more. There's also a resort lodge overlooking the lake at First Creek. The lodge has 74 luxury units, including nine suites, convention facilities, a meeting room that seats 400, full-service dining room, full-service marina, golf course, tennis courts and a swimming pool. It also has a store for canoe, fishing boat or pontoon rentals, groceries, fishing tackle and boating supplies. There's a gasoline island and several boat ramps. The golf course has its own pro shop with equipment rentals and a snack bar.

Resort Lodge at Joe Wheeler State Park

NEARBY ATTRACTIONS: Ivy Green in Tuscumbia (birthplace of Helen Keller); Alabama Music Hall of Fame also in Tuscumbia; General Joe Wheeler's Home in Hillsboro; the Animal House Zoological Park in Hatton; Lake Lurleen State Park; The Coon

Dog Graveyard (Key Underwood Memorial) in Colbert County, near Tuscumbia; Wheeler National Wildlife Refuge and Interpretive Center in Decatur.

INFORMATION: Joe Wheeler State Park, Route #4, Box 369A, Rogersville, AL 35652. Telephone 205-247-5466. For resort reservations and queries call or write the Resort Lodge & Convention Center, PO Drawer K, Rogersville, Alabama 35652. Telephone 800-544-5639. The park is in Lauderdale County, two miles west of Rogersville off US 72.

Lake Guntersville State Park

Covering more than 6,000 acres, this park is the third largest in the Alabama system. Of the 949 miles of lake shoreline, 50 lie within the boundaries of Lake Guntersville State Park. The lake is renowned for its fishing, but the park as a whole has much more to offer.

It has 322 improved campsites, primitive camping, a camp store, laundry facilities, boat docks and several comfort stations nearby. There are 15 lakeview cottages, each accommodating up to eight people, and 20 chalets with room for six people. All of the cottages and chalets have a fireplace, TV and telephone. They are set up for light housekeeping. Blankets, linens, and cooking and serving utensils are supplied.

The resort lodge, set high atop the bluff among the trees, has 94 well-appointed guest rooms, six luxury suites, a fine dining room, coffee shop, gift shop, tennis courts, pool and an art gallery. The convention center offers a range of facilities which can be tailored to the needs of nearly all private parties. It offers banqueting arrangements for up to 1,200 people. There's a fine golf course complete with pro shop and equipment rental.

The lake is a perfect spot for swimming and is within easy walking distance of the campground. There are two lighted tennis courts, picnic pavilions, tables and grills for a meal in the great outdoors. There are more than 12 miles of trails to hike and a nature center with a park naturalist in attendance to answer all your questions about the natural wonders found here and to keep both you and the kids amused.

Holiday cabin, Guntersville State Park

Wildlife in the park is abundant: deer, squirrel, rabbits, woodchucks, chipmunks, weasels, raccoon, opossum, muskrat, bobcats, cougar and fox. In the trees or wheeling high above the park you are likely to spot eagles, hawks, crows and even vultures. The 66,470-acre lake is ideal for sailing, boating, waterskiing and fishing for large- and smallmouth bass, crappie, bluegill, white bass and catfish.

Events helld annually at Lake Guntersville include Eagle Weekends in January, Peak Wildflower Blooming Season in April and Peak Color Autumn Foliage in October. All of these are well worth a weekend trip.

NEARBY ATTRACTIONS: DeSoto State Park, Little River Canyon, Looking Glass Caverns, Fort Payne, Buck's Pocket State Park and Cathedral Caverns State Park.

INFORMATION: Lake Guntersville State Park, 7966 Alabama Highway 227, Guntersville, Alabama 35976-9126. Telephone the park office 205-571-5444; the resort 800-548-4553; the campground 205-571-5455. The park is off Alabama Highway 227, six miles northeast of Guntersville.

Lake Lurleen State Park

Lake Lurleen is set in a quiet area of northwest Alabama and is named for the state's only female governor, Lurleen B. Wallace. The scenic 1,625-acre park is set along the shores of a 250-acre lake. Even though the park is known as a backcountry retreat, there's still plenty to see and do. More than five miles of hiking trails meander through the woodlands; you can fish and boat on the lake or enjoy a picnic in the park; there's a playground for the children, a place set aside for swimming and sunbathing and plenty of room to spread out, relax and enjoy the sunshine.

Facilities include 91 modern, full-service campsites, a camp store, several comfort stations, and a convention and meeting room complete with gift shop and refreshments.

NEARBY ATTRACTIONS: Tuscaloosa; Tom Bevill Visitor Center at Pickensville; Tannehill Historical State Park; Moundville Archeological Park in Moundville; and Talladega National Forest.

INFORMATION: Lake Lurleen State Park, Route 1, Box 479, Coker, AL 35452. Telephone 205-339-1558. The park is 12 miles northwest of Tuscaloosa off Alabama Highway 82.

Lake Point State Park

Lake Point is yet another of Alabama's great state parks located and focused on the water. It's a picturesque resort offering something special for everyone. The scenic outdoor setting and modern facilities provide numerous fun-filled activities along with a year-round schedule of recreational and educational programs run by the park's naturalist staff. These include environmental slide shows, guest speakers, bird watching and nature walks. A special summer camp provides an introduction to the world of conservation where specialists from the Alabama Department of Conservation share their expertise in the fields of wildlife, marine biology, fisheries management and natural resource conservation.

The park includes a deluxe resort inn, 29 rustic lakeside and woodland cottages, 244 woodland campgrounds (complete with hookups and comfort stations), a fine 18-hole golf course (with pro-shop and equipment rental), picnic areas with playgrounds, a swimming pool at the inn and a superb restaurant with spectacular views of Lake Eufala, "the Bass Capital of the World." The resort inn has 101 rooms, most with balconies overlooking the lake, and six luxury suites. The convention center features six meeting rooms and full-service facilities for up 500 people.

ACTIVITIES: Tennis, horseriding, sunbathing at the lakeside beach complex, golfing and hiking. There are almost five miles of woodland trails. For those who enjoy history, there are several nearby historic ante-bellum homes where you are greeted by lovely young ladies decked in period costumes of the pre-Civil War South.

NEARBY ATTRACTIONS: Shorter Mansion in Eufala, Tom Mann's Fishing World also in Eufala, Fort Mitchell National Cemetery in Phoenix City, the Old Russell County Courthouse in Seale and Lake Eufala.

The park has several annual events; Watchable Wildlife in January, the Eufala Pilgrimage in April and the 4-H National Wildlife Habitat Judging in August.

INFORMATION: Lakepoint State Park, Route 2, Box 94, Eufala, AL 36027-9202. Telephone 205-687-6676. The resort number is 800-544-5253. The park is seven miles north of Eufala off Highway 431.

Meaher State Park

Meaher State Park is nestled in the wetlands of Mobile Bay. Although it is a day-use-only park, it is rapidly expanding to become a full-service facility with a campground and comfort stations planned for the future. Already there is a picnic area and playground, two nature trails, which include a system of boardwalks over parts of the Mobile Delta, and there's an area set aside for swimming, boating and fishing.

NEARBY ATTRACTIONS: Baldwin Heritage Museum in Elberta, Waterville USA, Miss Collen's House at Point Clear, Easter Shore Arts Association Museum in Fairhope, Styx River Water World in Robertsdale, The American Sport Art Museum and Archives in Daphne, U.S.S. Alabama Battleship Memorial Park in Mobile and Historic Blakely Park near Spanish Fort.

INFORMATION: Call the office at 205-626-5529. The park is set on Mobile Bay close to I-10.

Monte Sano State Park

The big attraction here is Huntsville Space and Rocket Center. The 2,140-acre park was established in 1935 and combines the history of the Civilian Conservation Corps with the space technology of the future. The rocket center features all sorts of space technology from its beginnings in Germany with the V-2 rocket to the modern space shuttle. You can ride a space station simulator and see a mock-up of the Hubbell Space Telescope.

Overnight facilities include 89 modern campsites, primitive camping, modern full-service comfort stations with hot showers, a camp store and 14 family cottages all fully equipped. There are several picnic areas with tables and grills, play areas for the children, a group pavilion and refreshment facilities.

ACTIVITIES: An extensive system of hiking trails range from a casual stroll to some pretty strenuous climbs. The five trails total more than 14 miles.

Annual special events at the park include a Civilian Conservation Corps Reunion in June and the Monte Sano Race in October.

INFORMATION: Monte Sano State Park, 5105 Nolen Avenue, Huntsville, AL 35801. Telephone 205-534-3757.

Oak Mountain State Park

Oak Mountain offers over 10,000 acres of rolling hills and valleys and is one of Alabama's most picturesque parks. Located in the center of the state, it is a perfect park for a family vacation.

Getting close to nature is the focus of the vast Oak Mountain Park complex, and it really does provide you with the opportunity to escape, for a short while at least, the hustle and bustle of city life. The latest addition to the park is Oak Mountain Nature Center which is set in the foothills of the mountain. It displays both stuffed and living animals and houses a number of aquariums.

Options for those planning to stay overnight include 10 family cottages all fully equipped for housekeeping, 91 modern camp-sites with all the usual utilities, comfort stations with hot showers and restrooms, a camp store and a gift shop.

ACTIVITIES: There's a challenging 18-hole golf course, four beautiful lakes, picnic and play areas, refreshment facilities, a swimming center, boating and canoeing on the lake, a lakeside fishing center, tennis courts, group pavilions and an assortment of nature programs.

Oak Mountain has a number of outdoor recreational activities, not only for the general public, but for school groups, camping clubs, scout troops, group meetings and civic clubs. There are more than 35 miles of hiking trails. Guided hikes are conducted twice a month by Park Service volunteers. Of special interest is the Treetop Nature Trail, accessible via a boardwalk that winds upward for more than 600 feet to a hardwood valley. En route to the top you will have the chance to see, close-up, some of the mountain's resident birds of prey: hawks and owls. They are housed in six elevated treetop enclosures. The boardwalk is com-pletely accessible to the physically handicapped via a ground-level parking lot.

Annual events include the Cleanup in March, the City Triathlon in July, waterski tournaments, moto-cross races and the Bowhun-ters Convention.

INFORMATION: Oak Mountain State Park, PO Box 479, Pelham, AL 35124. Telephone the park office at 205-663-6783; the camp-ground at 205-663-3061; the golf pro shop at 205-663-6731; the cabin and pavilion at 205-663-6771. Oak Mountain State Park is just off I-65, 16 miles south of Birmingham.

Paul M. Grist State Park

This is the place where the sights and sounds of nature gently soothe away your cares and worries. Enjoy lazy weekends fish-ing, swimming, boating and sailing on the 100-acre lake or hiking along the scenic nature trail. Alternatively, simply while away the afternoon hours picnicking under the trees and let the kids enjoy themselves on the playground or splash happily in the shallow waters of the lake.

Overnight possibilities for a place to bed down are rather limited, with only six modern campsites and a few primitive campsites. There is, however, a camp store and a full-service comfort station with hot showers and restrooms. There are also several picnic areas with grills, play areas, refreshment facilities and group pavilions.

NEARBY ATTRACTIONS: Selma, Old Cahawba State Historical Park, Sturdivant Hall in Selma, Brown Chapel A.M.E. Church in Selma, Old Depot Museum in Selma, Smitherman Historic Building in Selma, Talladega National Forest, Robert Henry Lock and Dam, William Bill Dannelly Reservoir and Roland Cooper State Park.

INFORMATION: Paul M. Grist State Park, 1546 Grist Road, Selma, AL 36701. Telephone 205-872-5846. The park is 15 miles north of Selma close to Alabama Highway 22.

Rickwood Caverns State Park

Travel back some 260 million years to a time when dinosaurs roamed the earth and man had not yet made his appearance. Experience the thrills of Rickwood's miracle mile of underground caverns. See blind cave fish and silent underground pools where the reflections of the ceiling above give an impression of great depth and color, then marvel at the great limestone stalagmites and stalactites that have formed over millions of years. Above ground, you can spend a day or two relaxing in the sunshine and enjoying the facilities at one of Alabama's most beautiful backcountry parks.

It offers 13 improved campsites, facilities for primitive camping, a full-service comfort station with hot showers and restrooms, picnic areas with tables and grills, play areas, refreshments and a hiking trail.

NEARBY ATTRACTIONS: Ava Maria Grotto and St. Bernard Abbey in Cullman, Cullman County Museum, William B. Bankhead National Forest, Incident at Looney's Tavern in Double Springs, Smith Lake Cruises and Free State Lady in Double Springs and Lewis Smith Dam.

INFORMATION: Rickwood Caverns State Park, Route 3, Box 340, Warrior, AL 35180. Telephone 205-647-9692. To reach the park take Exit 289 off I-65.

Roland Cooper State Park

The focus of this 236-acre park is the impressive 22,000-acre Dannelly Reservoir and the fine hunting available in nearby woodlands. The fishing at Roland Cooper is claimed to be as good as anywhere in Alabama. Bass, crappie and bluegill inhabit the lake in large numbers and fishermen come from around the state to cast their lines. And if the fish aren't biting, why not enjoy a round or two of golf on the park's nine-hole golf course?

There are 41 modern campsites served by several full-service comfort stations and a camp store. Other accommodations include five fully-equipped family cottages and primitive camping facilities for those who really want to get away from it all. In addition to the golf course, the park has boat ramps, picnic areas with tables and grills, a group pavilion, play areas for the children, a swimming beach on the lake shore, refreshment facilities, a series of nature programs presented by the park staff and two hiking trails. The American Cancer Society Golf Tournament is held here each year.

NEARBY ATTRACTIONS: Selma, Old Cahawba State Historical Park, Sturdivant Hall in Selma, Brown Chapel A.M.E. Church in Selma, Old Depot Museum, Smitherman Historic Building in Selma, Talladega National Forest, Robert Henry Lock and Dam, William Bill Dannelly Reservoir, Clarke County Museum in Grove Hill and Paul M. Grist State Park.

INFORMATION: Roland Cooper State Park, Deer Run Dr., Camden, AL 36726. Telephone 205-682-4858.

Wind Creek State Park

Set on the shores of attractive Lake Martin, Wind Creek is the perfect place for family-oriented recreation, fun and relaxation. The park has something for just about everyone: swimming in sparkling waters, hiking the more than eight miles of nature trails and fishing for bass, catfish, crappie and bluegill.

ACTIVITIES: Watersports include sailing, power boating, canoeing and waterskiing. The park's interpretive programs offer art & craft shows, square dancing and bluegrass music. Guest speakers and experts on nature and the local environment present, among other things, a children's nature hour, clog dancing, slide shows and movies focusing on the environment. On-going recreational programs include an annual Civil War Living History presentation, monthly gospel singing and square dance programs, and a Guys & Dolls Fishing Tournament in February.

Facilities at the park are extensive. Many of the 669 modern campsites are set on the shores of the lake so you can fish, swim and boat directly from your personal picnic area. There's a camp store, several full-service comfort stations, a full-service marina, picnic and play areas for the day-use visitor, several group pavilions, refreshment facilities, boat ramps and two nature trails.

NEARBY ATTRACTIONS: Tuskegee National Forest, Montgomery, Chewacla State Park, Camp ASCCA at Jackson's Gap, Horseshoe Bend National Military Park, Fort Toulouse and Jackson Park close to Wetumpka and Jasmine Hill Gardens & Outdoor Museum just north of Montgomery off Highway 231.

INFORMATION: Wind Creek State Park, Route 2, Box 145, Alexander City, AL 35010. Telephone 205-329-0845. The park is seven miles southeast of Alexander City close to Highway 38.

General Information

Overnight Accommodation Rates

CAMPING: Camping fees vary, but range from $8 to $12 per night for improved sites, from $3 to $8 per night for primitive sites. A non-refundable deposit of one night's rental may be required to reserve a site. Telephone the park directly or call 1-800-ALA-PARK (Mon.-Fri. 8 AM-5 PM).

RESORT HOTELS/MODERN & RUSTIC CABINS: For details call the resort of your choice or the Central Reservation Service (see above).

Activities Fees

GOLF: Golf is offered at Gulf State Park, 18 holes; Lake Guntersville, 18 holes; Joe Wheeler, 18 holes; Oak Mountain, 18 holes; Roland Cooper, 9 holes. The fees for 18 holes range from $10 at Roland Cooper to $17 at Gulf and Lake Guntersville. For 9 holes prices range from $7 to $11. Cart rentals run $14 for 18 holes at Roland Cooper; $20 at Gulf State Park.

FISHING: Monthly fishing permits at all parks except Gulf are $7.50; annual permits $35. Senior citizen (65+) permits are just $17.50 annually. At Gulf pier-fishing permits start at $3 daily. A monthly permit is $30; $80 for the year. Permits for children (0-11yrs.) are $1.50 daily, $6 weekly, $20 monthly and $50 annually. Boat rental is offered at Chattahoochee, Chewacla, Claude D. Kelly, Gulf, Lake Guntersville, Joe Wheeler, Lake Lurleen, Meaher, Oak Mountain, Paul M. Grist, Roland Cooper and Wind Creek. Fees range from $5 per half-day to $12 for a full day. Canoes are available at most parks and fees range from $2 to $8 per hour.

INTERPRETIVE EVENTS: Usually free, but sometimes a small fee.

SWIMMING: Fees range from $1 to $2 per day.

GROUP PAVILION: Reserve via each park. Fees run between $10 and $125 depending upon the size of the party and type of accommodation.

TENNIS: $1 per hour, per court, but free to overnight guests.

CAVE TOURS AT RICKWOOD: $6 adult, $2.50 children (6 -11 yrs.).

AMPHITHEATER AT MONTE SANO: Fee is $50 for 2.5 hours.

SENIOR CITIZENS (62+) are eligible for 15% discount.

Florida

From Perdido Key in the extreme northwest of the Florida Panhandle, to Fort Zachary Taylor on Key West, Florida's 116 state parks and historical sites offer more than 13 million travelers each year a veritable cornucopia of outdoor, vacation, and recreational opportunities.

It is said that no single landscape can represent the natural diversity of Florida. From the distinctly southern flavor of the plantation country in the north, to the sub-tropical environment of the south, all surrounded by more than a thousand miles of sun-scorched sandy beaches and deep blue ocean, Florida is sure to offer something for almost every visitor.

The park system encompasses many environmental treasures and hides a wealth of natural wonders and a profusion of wildlife in diverse natural habitats. The parks offer everything from lush, sub-tropical forests, to glittering coral reefs, to crystal waters of a thousand inland lakes and windswept salt marshes of a lonely coastline.

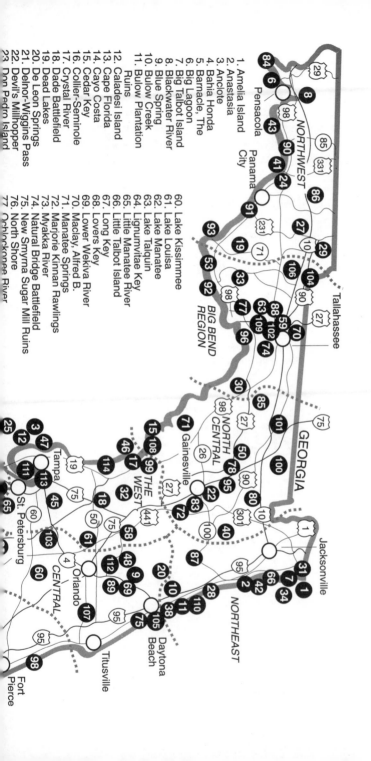

1. Amelia Island
2. Anastasia
3. Anclote
4. Bahia Honda
5. Barnacle, The
6. Big Lagoon
7. Big Talbot Island
8. Blackwater River
9. Blue Spring
10. Bulow Creek
11. Bulow Plantation Ruins
12. Caladesi Island
13. Cape Florida
14. Cayo Costa
15. Cedar Key
16. Collier-Seminole
17. Crystal River
18. Dade Battlefield
19. Dead Lakes
20. De Leon Springs
21. Delnor-Wiggins Pass
22. Devil's Millhopper
23. Don Pedro Island

60. Lake Kissimmee
61. Lake Louisa
62. Lake Manatee
63. Lake Talquin
64. Lignumvitae Key
65. Little Manatee River
66. Little Talbot Island
67. Long Key
68. Lovers Key
69. Lower Wekiva River
70. Maclay, Alfred B.
71. Manatee Springs
72. Marjorie Kinnan Rawlings
73. Myakka River
74. Natural Bridge Battlefield
75. New Smyrna Sugar Mill Ruins
76. North Shore
77. Ochlockonee River

Florida

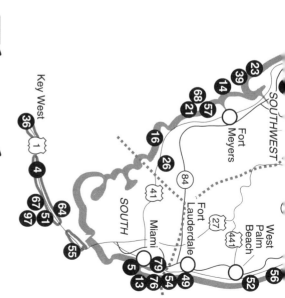

And even though Florida is the #1 tourist destination in the US, it's still possible to find romantic, out-of-the-way places where a couple can take a quiet walk along a moonlit beach, a gentle canoe ride beneath the shady tropical foliage, an afternoon boat ride down a secluded river, a private picnic on an isolated barrier island where the sun almost always shines and the sand is soft and sugar-white, or even a candlelight tour of a historic fort. Twelve of Florida's state parks are listed among the state's most romantic vacation spots.

The Florida State Park system is a big one, but it is organized into nine regions for easy access from the interstates: Northwest, Big Bend, North Central, Northeast, West, Central, Southwest, Southeast, and South. We have followed this organizational scheme in the pages that follow.

The Florida State Park Service recommends certain parks for particular activities and these are indicated as follows:

Best Hiking/Backpacking

Best Fishing

Best Birding

Best Snorkeling

In addition, a survey conducted annually by the Laboratory for Coastal Research at the University of Maryland selects the nation's Top 20 Beaches. Nine of these beaches are in Florida's state parks. They are rated on the natural quality of the beach, as well as the recreational value offered. Each of the nine best beaches is identified for you in the individual park listings by the following symbol:

Best Beaches

The Northwest

Big Lagoon State Recreation Area

Big Lagoon, complete with observation tower, is a bird watcher's paradise. The park provides habitats for many species of land and water birds: nuthatches, cardinals, the great blue heron, and many more. It's an area where wide sandy beaches and great salt marshes meld with the Gulf Islands National Seashore and the Intracoastal Waterway.

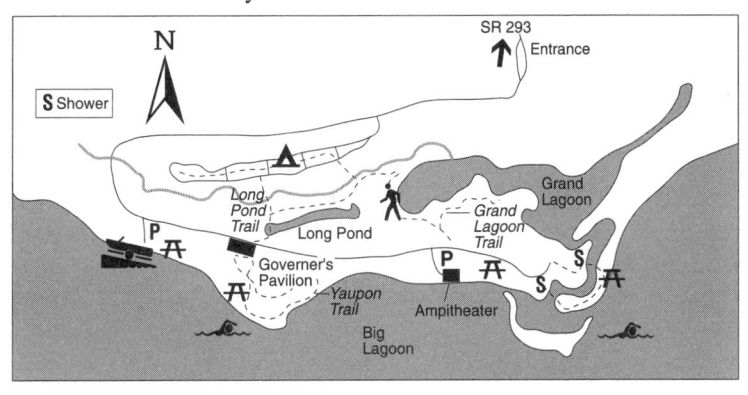

ACTIVITIES: Fishing, boating, camping, hiking, picnicking, canoeing, swimming and nature study.

The park offers full-service campsites with water and electric hookups, restrooms and hot showers. There are boat ramps, swimming areas, a large pavilion and a meeting room for rent, a picnic area and, of course, the observation tower.

NEARBY ATTRACTIONS: Gulf Islands National Seashore, the Zoo and Botanical Gardens at Gulf Breeze, The Art Center and Wentworth Museum at Pensacola, Gulf Shores and Fort Barrancas.

INFORMATION: Big Lagoon State Recreation Area, 12301 Gulf Beach Highway, Pensacola, FL 32507. Telephone 904-492-1592. The park is on CR 292A, about 10 miles southwest of Pensacola.

Blackwater River State Park

Blackwater River, still in a natural state for most of its length, is considered to be one of the finest and purest sand-bottom rivers in the world. It's a haven for nature lovers and watersports enthusiasts alike. The river itself offers some of the finest canoeing anywhere and the naturalist will delight in the diversity and abundance of wildlife to be found. Still something of a quiet little backwater, Blackwater River is one of Florida's jewels waiting to be discovered.

ACTIVITIES: Fishing, boating, camping, hiking, picnicking, canoeing, swimming and nature study.

Facilities at the park include full-service campsites with water and electric hookups, restrooms and hot showers. There's a boat ramp, swimming area and a place for picnics.

NEARBY ATTRACTIONS: Pensacola, Blackwater River State Forest, Armament Museum in Valparaiso, Gulf Islands National Seashore, Zoo and Botanical Gardens at Gulf Breeze, The Art Center and Wentworth Museum in Pensacola, Gulf Shores and Fort Barrancas.

INFORMATION: Blackwater River State Park, Route 1, Box 57-C, Holt, FL 32564. Telephone 904-623-2363. The park is 15 miles northeast of Milton off US 90.

Dead Lakes State Recreation Area

Dead Lakes is one of those semi-wild places where one goes to get close to nature. The area is said have been formed when great sand bars, thrown up by the current of the Apalachicola River, blocked the Chipola River. The waters of the Chipola rose creating a vast floodplain and killing thousands of trees – thus the area received its name.

Today the park is a naturalist's dream. Longleaf pines, sweetbay, magnolia and cypress abound throughout the area. The animal population includes the fox, cotton rat, raccoon, opossum, deer, rabbit, skunk, beaver, turtle, alligator, and a variety of snakes.

ACTIVITIES: Fishing, boating, camping, hiking, picnicking, canoeing and nature study.

Facilities at the park include full-service campsites with water and electric hookups, restrooms and hot showers. There's a boat ramp and a picnic area.

NEARBY ATTRACTIONS: St. Vincent Wildlife Refuge, St. Joseph Peninsula State Park, Constitution Convention State Museum, Apalachicola National Forest and John Gorrie State Museum.

INFORMATION: Dead Lakes State Recreation Area, PO Box 989, Wewahitchka, FL 32465. Telephone 904-639-2702. The park is just one mile north of Wewahitchka of SR 71.

Eden State Gardens

Eden State Gardens was once the Gulf Coast home of an affluent lumbering family. Today you can enjoy a tour of the house, grounds and gardens. While the house is only open from 9 AM to 4 PM Thursday through Monday, the grounds are open daily from 8 AM until sundown.

NEARBY ATTRACTIONS: Grayton Beach State Recreation Area, Rocky Bayou State Recreation Area, the dog track at Ebro and Santa Rosa Beach.

INFORMATION: Eden State Gardens, PO Box 26, Point Washington, FL 32454. Telephone 904-231-4214. Eden State Gardens is in Point Washington, off US 98 on CR 395.

Falling Waters
State Recreation Area

Interesting is a word one might use to describe Falling Waters, but it would be inadequate, for the main feature of the park is something of an anomaly. The 67-foot waterfall from which the area takes its name is natural enough. Waterfalls abound throughout the nation, but the Falling Waters Sink is something different. The Sink is a 100-foot-deep, 20-foot-wide cylindrical pit into which a small stream flows. Once in the pit the water simply disappears – it's quite a mystery.

ACTIVITIES: Camping, swimming, hiking, picnicking, canoeing, and nature study.

Facilities at the park include full-service campsites with water and electric hookups, restrooms, and hot showers. Youth camping is available, too. There's a swimming area at the Sink, a campfire circle, several nature trails and a picnic area.

NEARBY ATTRACTIONS: Ponce de Leon Springs State Recreation Area, the Florida Caverns, Dead Lakes State Recreation Area, and the dog track at Ebro.

INFORMATION: Falling Waters State Recreation Area, Route 5, Box 660, Chipley, FL 32428. Telephone 904-638-6130. The area is three miles south of Chipley, off SR 77A.

Grayton Beach
State Recreation Area

Great Beach is one of the oldest cities on Florida's Gulf Coast. The 356-acre recreation area offers plenty to do, whether it's for a day, a week, or a month. The beaches are wonderful (they are on the list of America's Best Beaches) and the sea is clear and warm.

ACTIVITIES: Fishing, boating, camping, hiking, picnicking, canoeing and swimming.

The park has full-service campsites with water and electric hookups, restrooms and hot showers. There's a boat ramp, swimming areas, a campfire circle, nature trail and picnic area.

NEARBY ATTRACTIONS: Eden State Gardens, Rocky Bayou State Recreation Area, the dog track at Ebro, and Santa Rosa Beach.

INFORMATION: Grayton Beach State Recreation Area, Route 2, Box 6600, Santa Rosa Beach, FL 32459. Telephone 904-231-4210. The area is near Grayton Beach on SR 30-A, south of US 98.

Henderson Beach
State Recreation Area

Located just east of Destin, Henderson Beach manages to escape the hustle and bustle of Florida's booming tourist areas on the Emerald Coast. The snow white sands, scrub oaks, southern magnolias, dune rosemary and deep green waters of the Gulf of Mexico all provide a natural backdrop for a variety of marine wildlife. Keep a sharp eye out for friendly gulls, black skimmers, sanderlings, brown pelicans and sea turtles.

Destin itself, once a sleepy little fishing village, is only now beginning to make its presence felt as one of Florida's premier tourist attractions. Fine seafood restaurants, deep sea fishing expeditions, and a variety of tiny shops selling everything from exquisitely made local crafts to suntan oil, are only a few of the local attractions. Henderson Beach offers the finest surf fishing, safe swimming, picnic areas and boardwalks that protect the dunes and fragile plant life and provide easy access to the beaches.

NEARBY ATTRACTIONS: Grayton Beach State Recreation Area, Eden State Gardens, Rocky Bayou State Recreation Area, the dog track at Ebro and Santa Rosa Beach.

INFORMATION: Henderson Beach State Recreation Area, 17000 Emerald Coast Parkway, Destin, FL 32541. Telephone 904-837-7550. The recreation area is east of Destin on US 98.

Perdido Key State Recreation Area

The Perdido Key State Recreation Area is a 247-acre park on a barrier island. These islands not only protect the Florida mainland from the great storms, but provide a wonderful natural habitat for sea birds and other marine life. They offer every visitor something very special. Perdido Key's wide, sugar-white beaches and rolling dunes have yet to be discovered by the great mass of vacationers that arrive every year on the Emerald Coast. For now at least, Perdido Key is a quiet little backwater where one can sit or swim in the sunshine and forget, for a moment or two, life in the fast lane.

NEARBY ATTRACTIONS: Big Lagoon State Recreation Area, Gulf Islands National Seashore, the Zoo and Botanical Gardens at Gulf Breeze, The Art Center and Wentworth Museum in Pensacola, Gulf Shores and Fort Barrancas.

INFORMATION: Perdido Key State Recreation Area, c/o Big Lagoon State Recreation Area, 12301 Gulf Beach Highway, Pensacola, FL 32507. Telephone 904-492-1595. Perdido Key State Recreation Area is 15 miles southwest of Pensacola, off SR 292.

Ponce De Leon Springs State Recreation Area

It is said that Ponce de Leon's fountain of youth was probably one of Florida's beautiful natural springs. And of all of them, it is certainly true that those at Ponce de Leon Park would qualify among the best. The main spring consists of two flows from a natural limestone cavity, one into the Choctawatchee River, and the other into the Gulf of Mexico. Between them, they produce more than 14 million gallons of the purest water each day. The temperature of the water remains constant at a refreshing 68° and provides a cooling refuge from the heat of the summer sun.

ACTIVITIES: Swimming in the waters of the spring, hiking nature trails, sunbathing and picnicking.

NEARBY ATTRACTIONS: Falling Waters State Recreation Area, the Florida Caverns, Dead Lakes State Recreation Area and the dog track at Ebro.

INFORMATION: Ponce de Leon Springs State Recreation Area, c/o Falling Waters State Recreation Area, Route 5, Box 660, Chipley, FL 32445. Telephone 904-836-4281. The Ponce de Leon Springs State Recreation Area is one half-mile south of US 90 on CR 181-A.

Rocky Bayou
State Recreation Area

Rocky Bayou is a quiet area just north of Fort Walton Beach on the Florida Panhandle. Bypassed by the steady, southbound stream of tourists from the north, the park offers a quiet refuge on the fringe of the Emerald Coast. The area is noted for its sand pine forest, diverse wildlife and for the nearby wetlands.

ACTIVITIES: Fishing, boating, camping, hiking, picnicking, swimming and nature study.

The park offers full-service campsites with water and electric hookups, restrooms and hot showers. There's a boat ramp, swimming areas, a campfire circle and picnic area.

NEARBY ATTRACTIONS: Grayton Beach State Recreation Area, Eden State Gardens, Henderson Beach State Recreation Area, the dog track at Ebro and Santa Rosa Beach.

INFORMATION: Rocky Bayou State Recreation Area, 4281 Highway 20, Niceville, FL 32578. Telephone 904-833-9144. Rocky Bayou is five miles east of Niceville on SR 20.

St. Andrews
State Recreation Area

St. Andrews is yet another state recreation area that rates as one of America's Best Beaches. For miles in either direction the shoreline stretches into the distance. White sand dazzling under the hot Florida sun and deep emerald waters of the Gulf of Mexico make St. Andrews a vacation spot that never will be forgotten. It's a place for families, children, lovers of the great outdoors and couples to walk barefoot in the moolight.

ACTIVITIES: Surf fishing, boating, camping, hiking, picnicking, swimming and nature study. There's also a nature trail where visitors may encounter all sorts of wild marine birds and animals, including alligators.

There are full-service campsites with water and electric hookups, restrooms and hot showers. In addition, you'll find a boat ramp, concession stand, swimming areas and a picnic area.

NEARBY ATTRACTIONS: Grayton Beach State Recreation Area, Henderson Beach State Recreation Area, Eden State Gardens, Rocky Bayou State Recreation Area, the dog track at Ebro and Santa Rosa Beach.

INFORMATION: St. Andrews State Recreation Area, 4415 Thomas Drive, Panama City, FL 32408. Telephone 904-233-5140. St. Andrews is three miles east of Panama City Beach, off SR 392.

St. Joseph Peninsula State Park

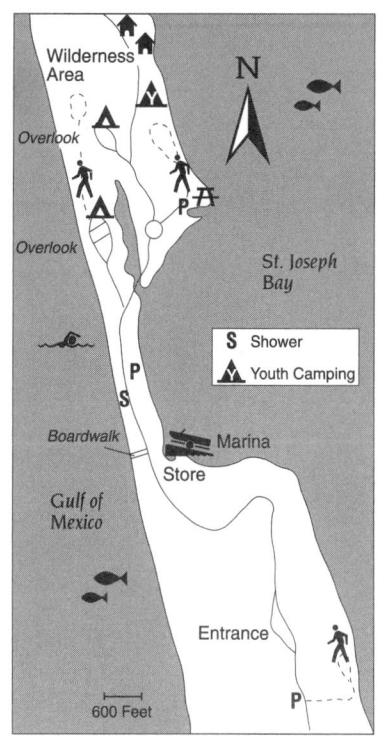

St. Joseph Peninsula State Park offers 2,500 acres of fun. Located on a thin strip of beach and surrounded on three sides by the Gulf of Mexico and St. Joseph's Bay, it's a park with a difference. St. Joseph is listed as one of America's Best Beaches and the pale green ocean has some of the best swimming and snorkeling anywhere in Florida.

ACTIVITIES: Hiking the many miles of trails and the Gulf beach, bird watching (more than 209 species of wild birds recorded), surf fishing, swimming, snorkeling, boating, canoeing, and camping. There's a park store where visitors can purchase fishing supplies and other sundry items. The Park Service also provides a variety of guided walks and campfire programs.

Accommodations include furnished rental cabins with all modern amenities; 119 full-service campsites with water and electric hookups, restrooms and hot showers; youth camping facilities and primitive camping, too. There's a boat ramp, boat basin, canoe rentals, concession stand, swimming areas with fresh-water showers and a picnic area for all to enjoy.

NEARBY ATTRACTIONS: St. Vincent Wildlife Refuge, Dead Lakes State Recreation Area, The Constitution Convention State

Museum, Apalachicola National Forest and the John Gorrie State Museum.

INFORMATION: St. Joseph Peninsula State Park, SR 1, Box 200, Port St. Joe, FL 32456. Telephone 904-227-1327.

The Big Bend Region

Florida Caverns State Park

Florida Caverns State Park offers something more than the usual recreational attractions. It includes a natural and interesting series of connecting caves containing limestone stalactites, stalagmites, columns, rimstone, flowstones and draperies. All the formations are composed of calcite, which is dissolved from the limestone when the surface water containing carbolic acid percolates through the rock and into the cave. Guided tours of the caves are quite fascinating. They are run daily by knowledgeable Park Service guides.

ACTIVITIES: Fishing, horseriding (with overnight facilities for horses), canoeing, boating, camping, hiking, picnicking, swimming and nature study.

Facilities include a visitor center, full-service campsites with water and electric hookups, restrooms and hot showers. Youth camping facilities are also available. There's a boat ramp, swimming areas, hiking trails, horse trails and a picnic area.

NEARBY ATTRACTIONS: Falling Waters State Recreation Area, Ponce de Leon Springs State Recreation Area, Dead Lakes State Recreation Area and the dog track at Ebro.

INFORMATION: Florida Caverns State Park, 3345 Caverns Road, Marianna, FL 32446. Telephone 904-482-9598. The park is three miles north of Marianna on SR 167.

Forest Capital State Museum

This unique museum is dedicated to the timber that built Florida. Almost everything you will see here is made from woods indigenous to the state's forests and the industries that grew up around them. The long-leaf pines which grow on the museum grounds are especially important to timbering. More than 5,000 products are manufactured from them. The center of the museum is a geodesic dome made mostly from cypress and featuring many other woods unique to Florida, including buttonwood, the wood that burns hottest and is virtually smokeless; leadwood or black iron wood, the heaviest wood; and lignumvitae, the hardest wood. All of the museum's display cases are made from one or more woods native to Florida, and contain hundreds of interpretive exhibits.

The Cracker Homestead, adjacent to the museum, is typical of the dwellings throughout the forest regions of North Florida at the end of the 19th Century.

The museum includes a visitor center and a picnic area. Every October the museum is host to the Florida Forest Festival, an extravaganza which celebrates the state's timber industry and attracts thousands of visitors.

INFORMATION: Forest Capital State Museum, 204 Forest Park Drive, Perry, FL 32347. Telephone 904-584-3227. The museum is located south of Perry, on US 19.

Fort Gadsden State Historic Site

Fort Gadsden was a coastal fortress built by the British to blockade the approaches to US territory, some 50 miles to the north of the fort, during the War of 1812. It was also used by them as a base from which to recruit Indians for the war. In order to protect the approaches the American commander in the field ordered the fort to be destroyed. This was to be done by gunfire from American gunboats. At about five o'clock on the morning of July 27, 1816, the ships opened fire on the fort with devastating effect. The fifth shot hit the powder magazine and in a single tumultuous explosion the fort was totally destroyed. Of the 300 men, women, and children inside, only 30 survived. It was one of the shortest battles in naval history.

Today, on the original site, there's a miniature replica of the fortifications and several other interesting exhibits that offer visitors a look at the way things might have been during the time of the British occupation. The site is open from 8 AM until sundown.

NEARBY ATTRACTIONS: Constitution Convention State Museum, John Gorrie State Museum, Apalachicola National Forest, St. Joseph Peninsula State Park, Dead Lakes State Recreation Area, Lake Talquin and Lake Talquin State Forest and the city and beaches of Apalachicola.

INFORMATION: Fort Gadsden State Historic Site, PO Box 157, Sumatra, FL 32335. Telephone 904-670-8988. The site is off SR 65, six miles southwest of Sumatra.

John Gorrie State Museum

John Gorrie was a physician and sometime postmaster in Apalachicola during the early 1880s. An extreme concern for the welfare of his many yellow fever patients and a desire to cool their rooms, lead to his invention of an ice-making machine. This machine became the forerunner of the air-conditioners and refrigerators we see today. A replica of Gorrie's machine is on display in the museum.

NEARBY ATTRACTIONS: The Constitution Convention State Museum, Apalachicola National Forest, St. Joseph Peninsula State Park, Dead Lakes State Recreation Area, Lake Talquin and Lake Talquin State Forest and all that Apalachicola offers.

INFORMATION: John Gorrie State Museum, PO Box 267, Apalachicola, FL 32320. Telephone 904-653-9347. The museum is set on Sixth Street in Apalachicola.

Lake Jackson Mounds State Archaeological Site

Lake Jackson is located just to the north of Florida's state capital, Tallahassee. It is in an area once inhabited by a tribe of Indians who, according to the evidence, participated in a socio-religious cult. It seems the community was a thriving one, reaching the peak of its prosperity sometime around 1200 A.D.

The complex itself consists of a series of seven mounds; six of them are thought to be temple mounds, the other a burial mound. Only a part of the original settlement and two of the mounds are located within the state site. The largest mound is some 36 feet high and its base covers an area of over 86,000 square feet – a massive construction project considering what tools were available at the time.

NEARBY ATTRACTIONS: Maclay Gardens, Natural Bridge Battlefield State Historic Site, Lake Talquin State Recreation Area, the dog track near Monticello, San Marcos de Apalache State Historic Site, Apalachicola National Forest, the city and beaches of Apalachicola, and Wakulla Springs State Recreation Area and Lodge.

INFORMATION: Lake Jackson Mounds State Archaeological Site, 1022 DeSoto Park Drive, Tallahassee, FL 32301. Telephone 904-922-6007. The site is in Tallahassee, two miles off I-10.

Lake Talquin
State Recreation Area

Lake Talquin is a place of rugged landscapes, ravines, forests and an abundance of wildlife. The lake was formed in 1927 when the Jackson Bluff Dam was built across the Ochlockonee River to produce hydroelectric power. Today, anglers converge on the lake from far and wide in the hope of catching largemouth bass or speckled perch.

ACTIVITIES: Hiking (there are many nature trails through woods and ravines), bird watching for wild turkey, osprey and bald eagles, picnicking and boating. The park has picnic areas and a boat ramp.

NEARBY ATTRACTIONS: Lake Jackson Mounds State Archaeological Site, Maclay Gardens, Natural Bridge Battlefield State Historic Site, John Gorrie State Museum, the dog track near Monticello, San Marcos de Apalache State Historic Site, Apalachicola National Forest, Apalachicola and Wakulla Springs State Recreation Area and Lodge.

INFORMATION: Lake Talquin State Recreation Area, 1022 DeSoto Park Drive, Tallahassee, FL 32301. Telephone 904-922-6007. The lake is 20 miles west of Tallahassee on Vause Road, off SR 20.

Maclay State Gardens

Alfred B. Maclay was a man with a dream. In 1923, while on a visit to Tallahassee, Maclay and his wife, Louise, bought this piece of real estate with the idea of creating an ornamental garden for the public to enjoy. Unfortunately, Alfred Maclay died in 1944 before his dream was fulfilled. Louise took up the dream and in 1953 she donated the land to State of Florida.

The park is open to the public year-round, but the high blooming season is from January 1 until April 10. To catch the most spectacular colors, you should visit mid-to-late March, although it is pretty at any time.

ACTIVITIES: Canoeing, fishing, swimming and hiking. There's a boat ramp available for public use and a concession for gifts and refreshments.

NEARBY ATTRACTIONS: Lake Jackson Mounds State Archaeological Site, Lake Talquin State Recreation Area, Natural Bridge Battlefield State Historic Site, St. George Island State Park, John Gorrie State Museum, the dog track near Monticello, San Marcos de Apalache State Historic Site, the national forest, beaches and city of Apalachicola, and Wakulla Springs State Recreation Area and Lodge.

INFORMATION: Maclay State Gardens, 3540 Thomasville Road, Tallahassee, FL 32308 (tel. 904-487-4556). The gardens are a half-mile north if I-10 on US 319.

Natural Bridge Battlefield State Historic Site

Tallahassee was the only Confederate state capital east of the Mississippi River never to suffer the ignominy of falling to Union forces. Only by an assortment of good luck, high intelligence and courage was this happy situation made possible.

During the final weeks of the war, in March 1865, a large force of Union troops arrived by sea hoping to take the defenders at Tallahassee by surprise. They landed on the shores of Apalachee Bay and began working their way northward to the city. Confederate observers sent warning of the approach. A call for volunteers to reinforce the meager garrison was made and, almost within hours, the numbers began to swell. It was a somewhat rag-tag force of Confederate regulars, old men, and boys that faced the

Union Army at Natural Bridge on St. Marks River. Rag-tag they might have been, but they were more than a match for the Union forces opposing them. Three times the Federals hurled themselves against the Confederate defenders, and three times they were repulsed.

FEATURES: Park Service employees and local volunteers offer a program of Living History and military reenactments for your enjoyment and education.

NEARBY ATTRACTIONS: Lake Jackson Mounds State Archaeological Site, St. George Island State Park, Maclay Gardens, Lake Talquin State Recreation Area, John Gorrie State Museum, the dog track near Monticello, San Marcos de Apalache State Historic Site, Apalachicola National Forest, the city and beaches of Apalachicola and Wakulla Springs State Recreation Area and Lodge.

INFORMATION: Natural Bridge Battlefield State Historic Site, 1022 DeSoto Park Drive, Tallahassee, FL 32301. Telephone 904-922-6007. Natural Bridge is six miles east of Woodville, off SR 363.

Ochlockonee River State Park

This 392-acre park is an area of outstanding natural beauty on the banks of the Ochlockonee River, at the edge of Apalachicola National Forest and less than 10 miles from the shores of the Gulf of Mexico. As close as it is to some of Florida's most sophisticated and densely populated areas, the park offers the visitor a feeling of remoteness, of a land time forgot. The shallow grassy wetlands, small ponds, and an amalgam of hard and softwood thickets provide habitats for a diverse mixture of wildlife, including deer, bobcats, foxes and a wide variety of marine and land-based birds. This park is another of Florida's gems awaiting discovery.

Facilities at the park include full-service campsites with water and electric hookups, restrooms and hot showers. Youth camping is also available. There's a swimming area, nature trails, a boat ramp, showers for public use and a picnic area.

ACTIVITIES: Boating, canoeing, hiking, bird watching and salt-water and freshwater fishing for largemouth bass, bream, catfish, speckled perch, redfish and speckled trout.

NEARBY ATTRACTIONS: St. Joseph Peninsula State Recreation Area, the Convention State Museum, Lake Jackson Mounds State Archaeological Site, Maclay Gardens, Natural Bridge Battlefield State Historic Site, John Gorrie State Museum, the dog track near Monticello, Dead Lakes State Recreation Area, Lake Talquin State Recreation Area, St. George Island State Park, the city, beaches and national forest of Apalachicola and Wakulla Springs State Recreation Area and Lodge.

INFORMATION: Ochlockonee River State Park, PO Box 5, Sopchoppy, FL 32358 (tel. 904-962-2771). The park is four miles south of Sopchoppy on US 319.

River Bluff State Picnic Site

The River Bluff State Picnic Site is nestled on the shores of beautiful Lake Talquin. The lake was formed in 1927 when the Jackson Bluff Dam was constructed on the Ochlockonee River to produce hydroelectric power. The lake is famous throughout Florida and the fishing world for its largemouth bass, speckled perch, bream, catfish, redfish and speckled trout. Much of the lake's waters are shallow and the abundance of dead and rotting tree stumps provide a natural habitat for fishy monsters. Heavily forested hills and valleys of the surrounding countryside provide homes for a vast spectrum of wildlife, including migrating waterfowl during the winter months, and often for the bald eagle and osprey. In spring the entire area turns into a wonderland of wildflowers as the flowering dogwood, redbud and red buckeye, all burst into bloom.

The deep ravines along the edge of the lake give you a peek at the tiny world-within-a-world where orange azalea, pyramid magnolia, rare heartleaf, and dogtooth violets grow. With good luck you may even glimpse a four-toed salamander.

Facilities at the picnic site include a fishing dock, pavilion and barbecue pit, picnic tables and a 45-minute loop walking trail.

The trail provides a closer view of the animal and plant life than you will see from the boardwalk.

NEARBY ATTRACTIONS: St. Joseph Peninsula State Recreation Area, the Convention State Museum, Lake Jackson Mounds State Archaeological Site, Maclay Gardens, Natural Bridge Battlefield State Historic Site, John Gorrie State Museum, the dog track near Monticello, Dead Lakes State Recreation Area, Lake Talquin State Recreation Area, Apalachicola National Forest and other attractions, St. George Island State Park or Wakulla Springs State Recreation Area and Lodge.

INFORMATION: River Bluff State Picnic Site, 1022 DeSoto Park Drive, Tallahassee, FL 32301. Telephone 904-922-6007. It is on Jack Vause Road off SR 20, about 10 miles west of Tallahassee.

San Marcos De Apalache
State Historic Site

The history of San Marcos dates back to 1528 when Panfilo de Narvaez arrived in the area bringing with him a force of 300 men. It was not until 1679, however, that a fort was constructed by the Spanish Governor at the junction of the Wakulla and St. Marks River. That fort is, unfortunately, long gone. Today, a museum that sits on the old fort site houses fine displays of the pottery, tools and artifacts unearthed in and around the area. The site is open from 8 AM until noon, and from 1 PM until 5 PM. It is closed on Tuesdays and Wednesdays, and on Thanksgiving, Christmas and New Year's Day. The park also has a visitor center and hiking trails.

NEARBY ATTRACTIONS: Lake Jackson Mounds State Archaeological Site, Maclay Gardens, Natural Bridge Battlefield State Historic Site, St. George Island State Park, John Gorrie State Museum, the dog track near Monticello, Lake Talquin State Recreation Area, Apalachicola National Forest and beaches and Wakulla Springs State Recreation Area and Lodge.

INFORMATION: San Marcos de Apalache State Historic Site, 1022 DeSoto Park Drive, Tallahassee, FL 32301. Telephone 904-922-6007. The site is in St. Marks, off State Route 363.

St. George Island State Park

St. George is another of Florida's Gulf Coast barrier islands and probably one of the best recreational locations that the park system has to offer. Set to the east of St. Joseph Peninsula and St. Vincent Wildlife Refuge, and to the southeast of Apalachicola, across the Apalachicola Bay, St. George Island is one Florida's premier nature centers. The sometimes wild and desolate environment offers the local bird and marine life the best of habitats. Nine miles of sandy shoreline and grassy flats provide nesting grounds for plovers, willets, terns, black skimmers and many other shore birds.

ACTIVITIES: Surf fishing, swimming and snorkeling, hiking the miles of sandy beaches, nature study and boating.

The park offers full-service campsites with water and electric hookups, restrooms and hot showers. Youth and primitive camping is another option. There's a swimming area, nature trails, a boat ramp, showers for public use and a picnic area.

NEARBY ATTRACTIONS: St. Joseph Peninsula State Recreation Area, the Constitution Convention State Museum, Ochlockonee River State Park, Lake Jackson Mounds State Archaeological Site, Maclay Gardens, Natural Bridge Battlefield State Historic Site, Lake Talquin State Recreation Area, John Gorrie State Museum, the dog track near Monticello, Dead Lakes State Recreation Area, Lake Talquin State Recreation Area, Apalachicola and Wakulla Springs State Recreation Area and Lodge.

INFORMATION: St. George Island State Park, Box 62, Eastpoint, FL 32328 (telephone 904-927-2111). The park is 10 miles southeast of Eastpoint, off US 98.

Tallahassee-St. Marks
Historic Railroad State Trail

From the early 1800s almost to the beginning of the 20th Century, the Tallahassee-St. Marks Railroad provided a means of commercial transportation from south Georgia and north Florida and the port of St. Marks on the Gulf Coast. The railroad was founded and paid for by the merchants whose goods, including the staple of the South, King Cotton, flowed in a steady stream southward and onward.

Today the glistening steel ribbons are gone, torn up and sold for scrap when the railroad's fortunes declined, until it eventually fell into disuse. New life, however, was breathed into a 16-mile section of the old way when it was cleared and improved for use as a hiking, bicycling and horseriding trail that now follows the historic route from Tallahassee into St. Marks. Rental bicycles are available at the north end of the trail.

NEARBY ATTRACTIONS: St. Joseph Peninsula State Recreation Area, the Convention State Museum, Ochlockonee River State Park, Lake Jackson Mounds State Archaeological Site, Maclay Gardens, Natural Bridge Battlefield State Historic Site, Lake Talquin State Recreation Area, John Gorrie State Museum, the dog track near Monticello, Dead Lakes State Recreation Area, Lake Talquin State Recreation Area, Apalachicola National Forest, the city and beaches of Apalachicola and Wakulla Springs State Recreation Area and Lodge.

INFORMATION: Tallahassee-St. Marks Historic Railroad State Trail, 1022 DeSoto Park Drive, Tallahassee, FL 32301. Telephone 904-922-6007. The parking lot and entrance to the trail are just to south of Tallahassee on SR 363.

Three Rivers State Recreation Area

The tri-state location, the hardwood and pine forests, the hilly terrain, Lake Seminole, the Flint, the Apalachicola, and the Chattahoochee Rivers, all contribute to a setting of unparalleled natural beauty for Florida's Three Rivers State Recreation Area. It is home to a variety of wildlife, thus making it a mecca for nature lovers. White-tailed deer and gray foxes roam the woodlands while squirrels and birds inhabit the treetops. It's a place to retreat from the rigors of daily life, a place to dream and become one with the wonders of nature. If ever there was a place to get away from it all, this is it.

ACTIVITIES: The fishing, both on lakes and rivers, is excellent. Lake Seminole is one of the Bass Capitals of the nation: largemouth and smallmouth bass, catfish, bluegill, speckled perch and bream are only a few of the species that anglers can expect to find here. From waterskiing to canoeing, from hiking to picnicking, there's something to do for just about everyone.

Full-service campsites with water and electric hookups, restrooms and hot showers are available. Youth camping is available, too. There's a swimming area, nature trails, boat ramp and a picnic area.

NEARBY ATTRACTIONS: Lake Seminole, Quincy, Florida Caverns State Park, Falling Waters State Recreation Area and Lake Talquin State Recreation Area.

INFORMATION: Three Rivers State Recreation Area, Route 1, Box 15-A, Sneads, FL 32460. Telephone 904-482-9006. The park is on SR 271, two miles north of Sneads.

Torreya State Park

The rare Torreya tree (from which the park gets its name), the extraordinary high bluffs along the Apalachicola River and the deep ravines carved into the rocks by thousands of years of water erosion, make the area around Torreya State Park a very special place. Sometimes rising to more than 150 feet, the densely forested bluffs provide a natural refuge for many rare and beautiful species of wildlife. The Torreya tree, once plentiful throughout the area, was, for the most-part, destroyed by disease. It is now found only on the high bluffs along the Apalachicola River. There are other rare trees and plants here too, including the Florida yew tree and the US Champion winged elm, along with a great variety of shrubs and wildflowers.

ACTIVITIES: Hikers and backpackers will enjoy the seven-mile loop trail, the Apalachicola Bluffs Trail and the National Recreational Trail, while those less active will find the Weeping Ridge Trail a pleasant, but less strenuous walk.

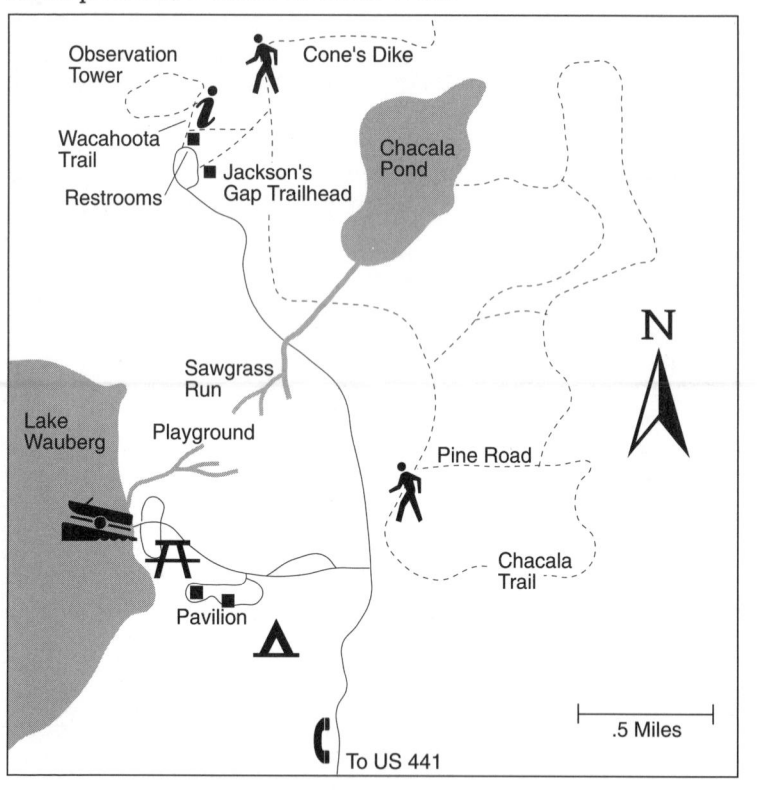

Campers will appreciate the extensive facilities at what is claimed to be one of Florida's most peaceful and scenic campgrounds. It includes a full-service campsite with water and electric hookups, restrooms and hot showers; two primitive campsites for those who prefer to do it all for themselves; youth camping is also available. There's also a picnic area with covered shelters.

NEARBY ATTRACTIONS: Lake Seminole, Bristol, Dead Lakes State Recreation Area, Apalachicola National Forest, Florida Caverns State Park, Falling Waters State Recreation Area and Lake Talquin State Recreation Area.

INFORMATION: Torreya State Park, Route 2, Box 70, Bristol, FL 32321. Telephone 904-643-2674. The park is on SR 12, just 13 miles north of Bristol and about eight miles south of I-10.

Wakulla Springs State Park, Lodge And Conference Center

The Edward Ball Wakulla Springs complex is one of the premier locations of the Florida State Park System. The highlight of the 2,860-acre park is one of the world's largest and deepest fresh water springs. Seven underground rivers are the source of the great spring and they push more than 400,000 gallons of water per minute into the lake above. On April 11, 1973, scientists measured a record peak flow of 14,325 gallons of water per second, some 1.2 billions of gallons per day. In 1958 explorers made the first attempt to map the ever-widening caverns beneath the spring; lately, divers have penetrated them to a distance of more than 6,000 feet. Beyond that point, and at depths of more than 250 feet, their lights revealed the walls of the cavern stretching away into the darkness and the unknown.

You can take to the lake in a glass-bottomed boat and gaze down

into the crystal clear waters to a depth of 120 feet where you will clearly see the entrance to a cavern. Alternatively, enjoy a boat trip downstream through ancient cypress groves and observe many species of Florida's wildlife, including alligators, white-tail

Wakulla Springs State Park

deer, raccoon, opossum, wild turkey, nine different species of herons and egrets; black vultures, turkey vultures, bald eagles, kites and osprey. During the winter months the park is host to thousands of migrating water fowl, including the hooded merganzer, the American widgeon, the American coot and the lesser scaup. The park is included in the nationwide Audubon Christmas Bird Count. So, taking everything into consideration, it's not without reason that Wakulla Springs is a mecca without equal for bird watchers and wildlife photographers.

ACTIVITIES: The temperature of the water is a constant 70° which makes it perfect swimming (designated areas only). Other activities include hiking a six-mile trail along the park service roads and ranger-led snorkeling programs during the summer months.

The Wakulla Lodge and Conference Center, operated by Florida State University's Center for Professional Development and Public Service, offers overnight accommodations. The lodge, built in 1937, is only 20 minutes from downtown Tallahassee and features marble floors, antique furniture and an ornate lobby ceiling. It has spacious guest rooms with private marble bathrooms, six conference rooms and a fine dining room with facilities for banquets and receptions. In winter great log fires burn in the lobby fireplace creating a cozy and secure atmosphere. Most people would agree that the park and lodge offer something that's a little different from the usual Florida seaside and sunshine vacation.

NEARBY ATTRACTIONS: St. Joseph Peninsula State Recreation Area, the Convention State Museum, Ochlockonee River State Park, Lake Jackson Mounds State Archaeological Site, Maclay Gardens, Natural Bridge Battlefield State Historic Site, Lake Talquin State Recreation Area, John Gorrie State Museum, the dog track near Monticello, Dead Lakes State Recreation Area, Lake Talquin State Recreation Area and the national forest and beaches of Apalachicola.

INFORMATION: Wakulla Springs State Park, 1 Spring Drive, Wakulla Springs, FL 32305. Telephone 904-222-7279. For conference center and lodge reservations call 904-224-5950. The park is 14 miles south of Tallahassee on SR 267.

North Central

Cedar Key State Museum

Cedar Key is a tiny island off the Florida Gulf Coast some 50 miles west of Gainsville. Back in the early 1860s, after the cross-state railroad was completed, it was a thriving sea port. Unfortunately, newer ships grew in size and draft, thus needing deep-water ports, and Cedar Key slowly lost its sea-going traffic until it finally became a sleepy, but picturesque, backwater. Fortunately, the history here and the key's importance to Florida's burgeoning industries, early and modern, is well preserved at the Cedar Key State Museum. The exhibits tell a colorful and interesting story of times gone by and include the tools, utensils and artifacts of an age that otherwise might have been forgotten. It is a tiny window through which to look at how life must have been here when it was a bustling sea port.

NEARBY ATTRACTIONS: St. Clair Whitman Museum, Waccasassa Bay State Preserve/Cedar Key Scrub State Reserve, Manatee Springs State Park, Crystal River State Archaeological Site, Hart Springs and the Lower Suwannee National Wildlife Refuge.

INFORMATION: Cedar Key State Museum, 1710 Museum Drive, Cedar Key, FL 32625. Telephone 904-543-5350. The museum is on Museum Drive, off SR 24.

Devil's Millhopper State Geological Site

Devil's Millhopper is a natural geological formation that has fascinated a host of people from as far back as the early 1880s. It is a huge sink hole created by the collapse of a large underground cavern. Water from tiny streams tumbles 120 feet down the steep sides of the great basin to disappear through the cracks and crevices into the unknown. Travellers in the Gainsville area will find the site an interesting side-bar to their vacation and well worth a visit.

NEARBY ATTRACTIONS: Paynes Prarie State Preserve, San Felesco Hammock State Preserve, Newman's Lake, Orange Lake, Marjorie Kinnan Rawlings State Historical Site and Ocala National Forest.

INFORMATION: Devil's Millhopper Geological Site, 4732 Millhopper Road, Gainsville, FL 32606 (telephone 904-336-2008). The site is two miles to the northwest of Gainsville, off SR 232.

Gold Head Branch State Park

Mike Roess Gold Head Branch State Park can offer the casual vacationer something just a little different, a little more secluded, definitely more relaxing, and perhaps a whole lot more interesting, than the usual hustle and bustle of Florida's conventional seaside vacation hot-spots. The 1,562-acre park is on an area known as the Central Ridge. It's pretty remote (six miles from the nearest community) and set among rolling sandhills, marshes, lakes and cleft by a deep ravine. It is overflowing with wildlife and offers a variety of outdoor activities for all the family.

Facilities include 14 fully furnished rental cabins complete with all conveniences, three separate full-service campsites, 74 units, with water and electric hookups, restrooms, hot showers, picnic tables and grills. Primitive and youth camping is also available. There's a boat ramp, swimming area, campfire circle, bicycling trail, picnic area, concession area where refreshments are available as well as rental canoes and bicycles.

ACTIVITIES: Camping, swimming, fishing for bass, bream, and speckled perch, nature study, hiking, canoeing and picnicking.

Hikers will enjoy the nature trails: There are four marked trails within the park. The Florida Trail is a two-hour hike recommended for experienced hikers. It begins at the park entrance and winds its way through the high country. The Ravine Ridge Trail

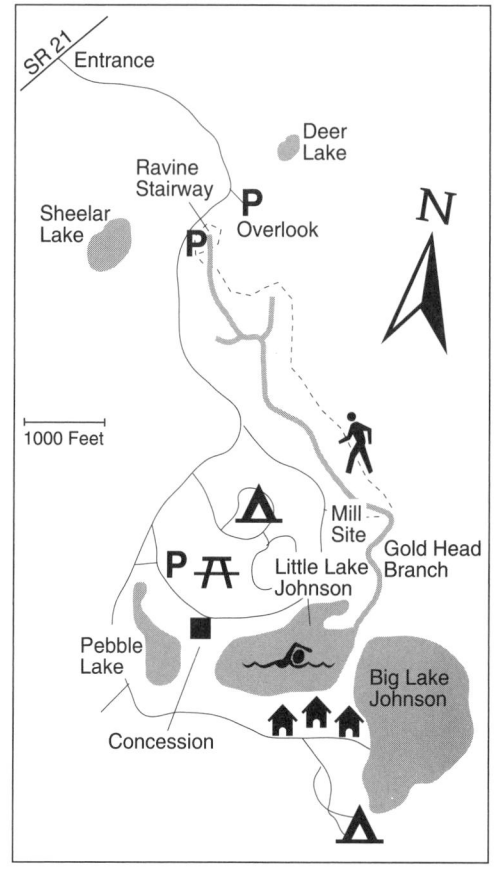

follows the upper ridge from the ravine stairway to the mill site. Loblolly Trail is a loop that begins and ends at the mill site taking in the largest loblolly pines in the park along the way. The shortest trail in the park is Fern Loop. It starts at the ravine stairway and passes by the head springs of the Gold Head Branch.

INFORMATION:
Gold Head Branch State Park, 6239 SR 21, Keystone Heights, FL 32656. Telephone 904-473-4701. The park is six miles northeast of Keystone Heights on SR 21.

Ichetucknee Springs State Park

Some 233 million gallons of sparkling water flow each day from a series of springs to form the Ichetucknee River. After a journey of six miles or so through hammock and swamp, this river flows into the Santa Fe River. The same hammock and swamplands, together with the softwood and hardwood forests of the park, are home to a variety of wildlife and birds. The river's head spring was declared a National Natural Landmark by the US Department of the Interior in 1972.

ACTIVITIES: Swimming, canoeing, snorkeling, picnicking and hiking. The Park Service also allows a certain amount of tubing on the river from June 1st to Labor Day. Tubers are encouraged to use the south entrance to the park and make use of the free in-park shuttle service. There's a picnic area available for public use, concessions and several hiking and nature trails.

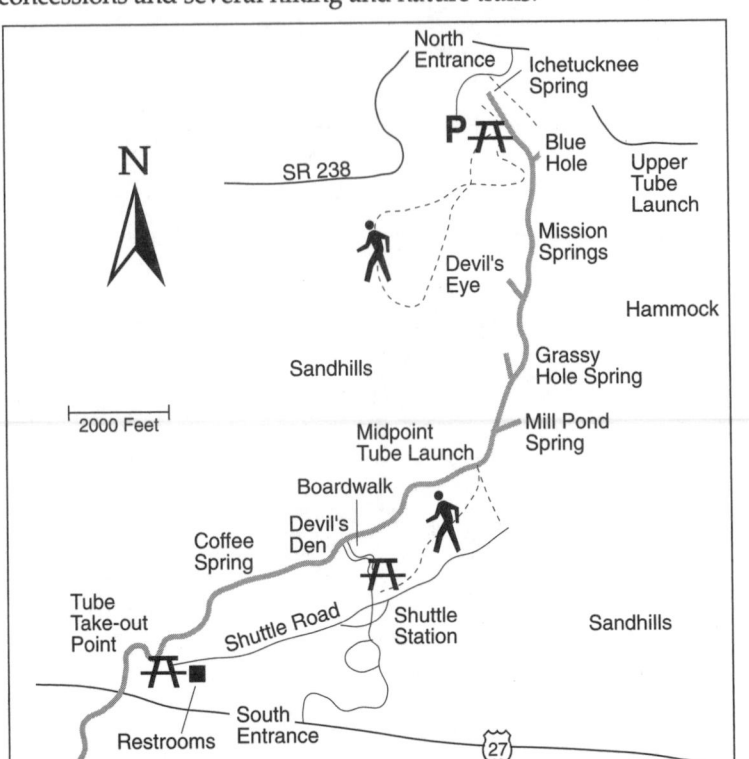

NEARBY ATTRACTIONS: Fort White, Olustee Battlefield State Historic Site, O'Leno State Park, Ocean Pond and Olustee Beach, Lake City, Ocala National Forest, the Stephen Foster Memorial, the Old Telford Hotel, the "For The People" radio talk show at White Springs, and the Stephen Foster State Folk Culture Center also at White Springs.

INFORMATION: Ichetucknee Springs State Park, Route 2, Box 108, Fort White, FL 32038. Telephone 904-497-2511. The springs

are situated four miles northwest of Fort White, off State Roads
47 and 238.

Manatee Springs State Park

Manatee Springs is yet another of Florida's northern state parks
where the focus is on the flow of water from an underground
natural spring. More than 116 million gallons of crystal water
flows upward, out into the sunshine, onward through the cypress
swamps, hammock and sandhill, and into the Suwannee River

Boardwalk winding through Manatee Springs

until eventually it
finds its way to the
Gulf of Mexico some
23 miles down-
stream. The 2,000
acres of park feature
a variety of unusual
trees and an abun-
dance of wildlife, in-
cluding the manatee
that makes rare ap-
pearances around the
mouth of the spring
run.

ACTIVITIES: Hiking and bicycling (the Park Service has just
added a new 8.5-mile trail), fishing, swimming, canoeing, picnicking and snorkeling. There's also a picnic area and refreshments are available.

NEARBY ATTRACTIONS: Cedar Key State Museum, the St.
Clair Whitman Museum, Crystal River State Archaeological Site,
Hart Springs and Lower Suwannee National Wildlife Refuge.

INFORMATION: Manatee Springs State Park, Route 2, Box 617,
Chiefland, FL 32626 (telephone 904-454-1853), for more details.
The park is at the end of SR 320, off US 98, six miles west of
Chiefland.

Marjorie Kinnan Rawlings
State Historical Site

The Marjorie Kinnan Rawlings home is one of Florida's most popular attractions. The cracker-style home is where she wrote her Pulitzer prize-winning novel, *The Yearling*. The house has been preserved as one of Florida's Historic Sites and is dedicated to her life and times, and to her memory. Florida Park Service conducts tours of the home, but, as the house is a small one, groups are limited to 10 people at a time. This can, on busy days, lead to delays so please be patient, the experience is well worth the short wait. The house is open to the public from 10 AM until 11:30 AM, and from 1 PM until 4:30 PM, Thursday through Monday. It is closed on Tuesday, Wednesday, Thanksgiving, Christmas, and New Year's Day.

NEARBY ATTRACTIONS: Paynes Prairie State Preserve, San Felesco Hammock State Preserve, Newman's Lake, Orange Lake, Devil's Millhopper State Geological Site or Ocala National Forest, all in the vicinity.

INFORMATION: Marjorie Kinnan Rawlings State Historical Site, Route 3, Box 92, Hawthorne, FL 32640. Telephone 904-466-3672. The house is located at Cross Creek, off SR 325.

O'Leno State Park

Hardwood hammocks, sink holes, a river swamp and a sandhill community all go toward the making of this, one of the oldest of Florida's State Parks. It was developed in the early 1930s by the Civilian Conservation Corps; the Corps' suspension bridge, one of the park's unique features, still spans the river. O'Leno is nestled on the banks of the scenic Santa Fe River. The river, a tributary of the Suwannee, enters the park only to disappear into one of the several sinkholes. It then flows underground for several miles before appearing again.

ACTIVITIES: There are two scenic nature trails in the park. The Santa Fe Trail takes hikers along the river bank to the sink where the river disappears underground, and the Limestone Trail, a shorter but very scenic walk. Nature-lovers may catch sight of alligators or turtles here, as the park is home to a wide range of wildlife and birds. Other activities include fishing for bass, bream, and catfish in the Santa Fe, or swimming, canoeing and horseback riding.

Facilities at the park include a group camp with 18 cabins (available with cots and mattresses, but no pillows or bed linens), dining hall, meeting room and a pavilion. The group camp can accommodate up to 140 persons and, along with the kitchen and dining hall, is fully equipped with cooking utensils, dishes and flatware. The park also offers the usual primitive camping and full-service campsites complete with water and electric hookups, restrooms, hot showers, picnic tables and grills. There's a general store selling food and drinks, as well as a variety of local crafts and gifts.

NEARBY ATTRACTIONS: Fort White, Olustee Battlefield State Historic Site, Ichetucknee Springs State Park, Ocean Pond and Olustee Beach, Lake City, Ocala National Forest, the Stephen Foster Memorial, the Old Telford Hotel and the "For The People" radio talk show at White Springs, and the Stephen Foster State Folk Culture Center also at White Springs.

INFORMATION: O'Leno State Park, Route 2, Box 1010, High Springs, FL 32643. Telephone 904-454-1853 for further information. The park is on US 441, six miles north of High Springs.

Olustee Battlefield State Historic Site

This site commemorates the largest battle fought in Florida during the Civil War. On February 7th, 1864, a large force of Union soldiers under the command of General Truman A. Seymore landed at Jacksonville with the intent to occupy the city and disrupt the Confederate line of supply. Moving westward on February 20, Seymore's troops, a force of 5,500 men and 16 pieces of artillery, encountered little opposition until they reached a point some 2.5 miles from Olustee.

In the meantime the fortunes of the Confederate State of Florida had been placed in the capable hands of Brigadier Generals Joseph Finegan and Alfred Colquit. On hearing that the federal forces were on the move, Finegan began looking for a defensible position. He found it here. The position was a strong one. With Ocean Pond to the left and heavy swampland to the right acting as natural defenses, only a narrow passage remained open. Finegan sent out a call for troops and Colquit responded bringing fresh troops from Savannah, Georgia. By the time the armies met at Olustee on the afternoon of February 20, they were almost equal in numbers. The battle lasted for more than five hours before the Union forces began withdrawing. They left behind 1,861 casualties, one third of the entire force, on the field. Confederate casualties were 946. The battle was an unqualified victory for the Confederacy.

The interpretive center at the site offers a variety of exhibits that interpret the battle. A seven-minute recorded presentation describes the battle from a Confederate soldier's point of view. The battle is reenacted in February each year. The interpretive center is open Thursday through Monday from 9 AM until 5 PM, and is closed on Tuesdays and Wednesdays.

NEARBY ATTRACTIONS: Fort White, Ichetucknee Springs State Park, O'Leno State Park, Ocean Pond and Olustee Beach, Lake City, Ocala National Forest, the Stephen Foster Memorial, the Old Telford Hotel and the "For The People" radio talk show at White Springs, and the Stephen Foster State Folk Culture Center also at White Springs.

INFORMATION: Olustee Battlefield State Historic Site, PO Box 2, Olustee, FL 32072. Telephone 904-752-3866. The site is two miles east of Ulustee on US 90.

Paynes Prairie State Preserve

Paynes Prairie is an 18,000-acre preserve in one of the most important and historically significant areas in Florida. Within its boundaries are some 20 distinct biological communities that provide habitats for a wide variety of wildlife and birds. The preserve is still one of the state's best kept secrets and is, as yet, an undiscovered recreational paradise.

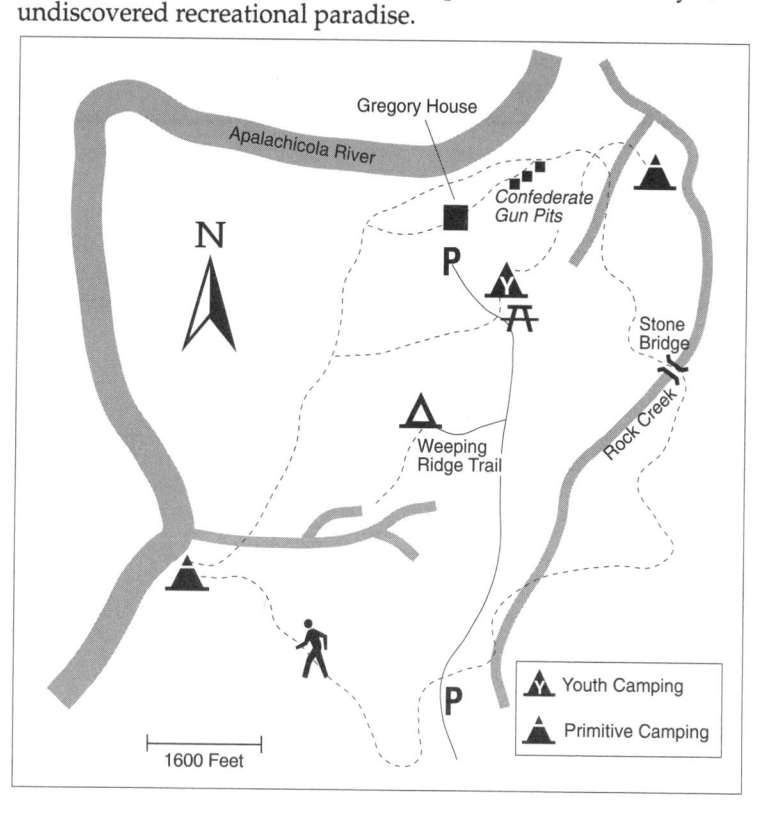

ACTIVITIES: Nature lovers will enjoy Paynes Prairie for the excellent bird and nature watching opportunities. Visitors can expect to see the sandhill crane, eagles, hawks, a wide variety of waterfowl and wading birds, alligators, otters, and many other species of marine life.

Other recreational activities at the preserve include bicycling, hiking, canoeing, fishing, horseback riding, and picnicking. There's a boat ramp available for small boats with electric motors only, canoes, and sailboats.

The visitor center is open from 9 AM until 5 PM daily, and displays a variety of exhibits, along with an audio visual program that interprets the preserve, its culture and natural history. Park Service rangers conduct a program of weekend guided hikes from October through March. You can call 904-466-4100 for details.

Other facilities at the park include the usual full-service campsites complete with water and electric hookups, restrooms, hot showers, picnic tables and grills. Primitive camping is also available and there are several hiking trails and a picnic area.

NEARBY ATTRACTIONS: Devil's Millhopper Geological Site, San Felesco Hammock State Preserve, Newman's Lake, Orange Lake, Marjorie Kinnan Rawlings State Historical Site and Ocala National Forest.

INFORMATION: Paynes Prairie State Preserve, Route 2, Box 41, Micanopy, FL 32667. Telephone 904-466-3397. The preserve is located 10 miles south of Gainsville, on US 441.

Peacock Springs
State Recreation Area

Once again it's a natural spring, or rather it's two of them, that are the focus here. There are two major springs in the park area, a major spring run, a number of sinks and a vast underwater cave system. The cave system, the largest underwater system in the United States, has only been partially explored. Over the years, divers have surveyed some 18,000 feet of caverns and passages. How much of the system remains unexplored is unknown.

On the surface the recreation area itself remains a largely undisturbed natural habitat for a diverse cross-section of plant life, animals and birds.

There are no overnight facilities at Peacock Springs. The park is intended only for day use. Activities include picnicking and swimming. Diving is also popular, but is restricted to certified divers.

INFORMATION: Peacock Springs State Recreation Area, Route 4, Box 370, Live Oak, FL 32060. Telephone 904-497-2511. The park is 16 miles west of Live Oak on SR 51, two miles east of Luraville on Peacock Springs Road.

San Felasco Hammock State Preserve

Hikers and horseback riders will enjoy this 6,500-acre preserve. Located close to Gainsville, San Felasco Preserve incorporates one of the finest examples of a natural hammock remaining in Florida. The park is home to many species of birds and animals, but it's the plant life that makes San Felasco unique. The extreme changes in elevation and the geological structure provide an environment wherein a diverse cross-section of plant life is able to flourish.

The preserve is intended for day use only, so there are no overnight facilities. San Felasco rangers offer a program of group hikes and nature walks. Self-guided hiking and horseback riding is encouraged.

NEARBY ATTRACTIONS: Devil's Millhopper State Geological Site, Paynes Prairie State Preserve, Newman's Lake, Orange Lake, Marjorie Kinnan Rawlings State Historical Site and Ocala National Forest.

INFORMATION: San Felasco Hammock State Preserve, c/o Devil's Millhopper State Geological Site, 4732 Millhopper Road,

Gainsville, FL 32601. Telephone 904-336-2008. The preserve is four miles northwest of Gainsville on SR 232.

Silver River State Park

This is one of the latest additions to Florida's extensive park system. The 2,300-acre park incorporates 14 distinct plant communities, several miles of river front and the inevitable couple of dozen natural springs. Silver Springs itself, a nearby attraction, is the head spring of the Silver River which flows into Olawaha River and on to the St. Johns River. The park is a natural habitat for an assortment of wildlife and birds, and for a diverse range of plant life, all of which offer naturalists and the recreation-seeking public alike a unique and interesting experience.

NEARBY ATTRACTIONS: Ocala National Forest, Silver Springs, Lake George, Lake Griffin, Paynes Prairie State Preserve, Lake Weir. The Early American Museum, Silver Springs Wildwater and the Reptile Institute are worth a trip and are in Silver Springs.

INFORMATION: Silver River State Park, c/o Rainbow Springs State Park, 19158 S. W. 81st Place Road, Dunnellen, FL 32630. Telephone 904-489-8503. The park is accessible only by boat. There is a boat ramp available for public use on SR40.

Stephen Foster State Folk Culture Center

The Stephen Foster State Folk Culture Center is set on the banks of the Suwannee River. It is dedicated to the memory of the famous composer and one of his most famous works, *Old Folks at Home*. Florida Department of State's Folklife program sponsors a variety of special events throughout the year, including the old-fashioned Fourth of July celebration and the Florida Folk Festival on Memorial Day. There's a visitor center, youth camping facilities, canoeing on the river and picnic facilities with tables and grills.

Carillon Tower, Stephen Foster

NEARBY ATTRACTIONS: Fort White, Ichetucknee Springs State Park, O'Leno State Park, Ocean Pond and Olustee Beach, Lake City, Ocala National Forest, the Stephen Foster Memorial, Olustee Battlefield State Historic Site, the Old Telford Hotel and the "For The People" radio talk show at White Springs.

INFORMATION: Stephen Foster State Folk Culture Center, Post Office Drawer G, White Springs, FL 32096. Telephone 904-397-2733 for more details about the park and its facilities. The center is located in White Springs, off US 41 North.

Suwannee River State Park

Here, where the scenic Withlacoochee River joins the Suwannee River, naturalists and lovers of the great outdoors will find a great deal to enjoy. The park encompasses more than 1,800 acres of wild and natural habitat from sandhill to river swamp, and includes many diverse plant communities. On a good day nature watchers might catch a glimpse of the great horned owl, wild turkeys, red tailed hawks, otters, gopher turtles, woodpeckers, beavers, and, of course, alligators. Also of interest are the earthworks built during the Civil War by Confederate soldiers to protect the railroad bridge across the Suwannee; an important link in the supply line that took beef, salt, sugar and other essential supplies to the Confederate armies fighting in Virginia, Tennessee and Georgia. Of interest, too, is the cemetery and the landing that once serviced the river boats as they carried goods and passengers back and forth along the river.

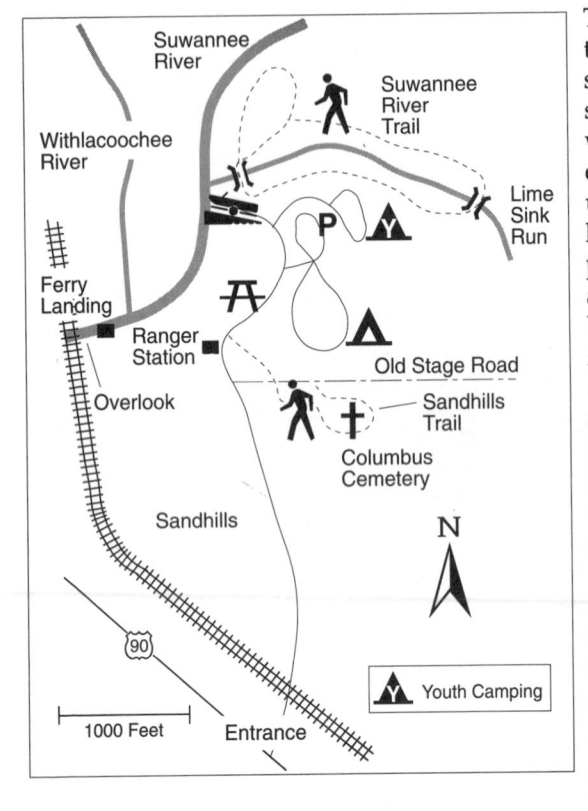

The park offers the usual full-service campsites, complete with water and electric hook-ups, restrooms, hot showers, picnic tables and grills. Youth camping facilities are also available and there are several hiking trails, a boat ramp and a picnic area.

ACTIVITIES: Bird watching, nature study, camping, fishing, canoeing, picnicking, and hiking.

INFORMATION: Suwanee River State Park, Route 8, Box 297, Live Oak, FL 32060. Telephone 904-362-2764. The park is 13 miles southwest of Live Oak, off US 90.

Waccasassa Bay State Preserve/ Cedar Key Scrub State Reserve

Waccasassa Bay State Preserve is a vast tract of wetlands and salt marshes, more than 30,000 acres in all, and interlaced by dozens of tiny tidal creeks. The rich environment, the tidal waters, and the marshlands provide ideal conditions for the spawning of hundreds of species of saltwater fish and shellfish. Many of the preserve's wily inhabitants are on the endangered species list, including the manatee. You may catch a glimpse of a black bear or, on rare occasions, the bald eagle, but nature lovers are sure to enjoy an outstanding experience observing all of the wildlife.

Enjoyable activities here include fishing, hiking, canoeing, wildlife photography and nature watching.

The Cedar Key Scrub State Reserve is a 4,000-acre tract of diverse natural habitats which includes salt marshes, pine flatwoods and sand pine scrub. It's a wild and rugged area, home to a wide variety of wildlife and birds.

ACTIVITIES: Fishing, hiking, canoeing, wildlife photography and nature watching. From September through December the Florida Game and Freshwater Commission allows hunting here.

NEARBY ATTRACTIONS: Cedar Key State Museum, St. Clair Whitman Museum, Manatee Springs State Park, Crystal River State Archaeological Site, Hart Springs and the Lower Suwannee National Wildlife Refuge.

INFORMATION: Waccasassa Bay State Preserve/Cedar Key Scrub State Reserve, PO Box 187, Cedar Key, FL 32625. Telephone 904-543-5567. The adjacent parks are nine miles east of Cedar Key on SR 24.

The Northeast

Amelia Island State Recreation Area

Amelia Island State Recreation Area is a 200-acre stretch of undeveloped sea island. The pristine beaches offer an unspoiled vacation spot where the sun shines and the kids can enjoy the sea.

Concessions, snacks and soft drinks are available and the Sea-horse Stable conducts guided horseback rides along the beaches. Other things to do here include fishing, hiking, bird watching and sunbathing.

NEARBY ATTRACTIONS: Amelia Island, Fort Clinch, Fort George, Huguenot Historic Museum at Fort George, Fernandina Beach, Guana River State Park, Little Talbot Island State Park, Big Talbot Island State Park, Jacksonville, the dog track at Orange Park, Fort Caroline National Memorial, Ponte Vedra Beach, Atlantic Beach, Neptune Beach and Jacksonville Beach.

INFORMATION: Amelia Island State Recreation Area, c/o the Talbot Islands GEOpark, 11435 Fort George Road East, Fort George, FL 32226. Telephone 904-251-2320. For reservations with Seahorse Stables call 904-261-4878. This recreation area is seven miles north of Little Talbot Island State Park on SR A1A, or eight miles south of Fernandina Beach on SR A1A.

Anastasia State Recreation Area

The Spanish first settled St. Augustine in 1565, making it the first city to be established in America, and this is where you will find Anastasia State Recreation Area. The Spaniards, in search of building materials, crossed the Matanzas River and established quarries for "coquina," a durable material ideal for their purposes. The same rock was used to build the nearby Castillo de San Marcos, the nation's oldest masonry fortress. Today, those same quarries are a part of the recreation area. This is the region where Juan Ponce de Leon landed and was so taken with the abundance of plant life and wildflowers that he called it Florida and claimed the land for Spain.

A variety of shorebirds, such as gulls, terns, sandpipers, pelicans, egrets and herons inhabit the park. During spring and fall all sorts of migratory birds visit the marshes and wooded areas on their journeys to and from their natural habitats in the northern United States.

Anastasia has plenty to offer its visitors. Facilities include coastal camping on modern, full-service campsites, complete with water and electric hookups, restrooms, hot showers, picnic tables and grills. There are also a variety of concessions, including sailboard lessons and rentals on Salt Run, while bicycles, umbrellas, paddle cruisers and beach chairs all can be rented on the beach.

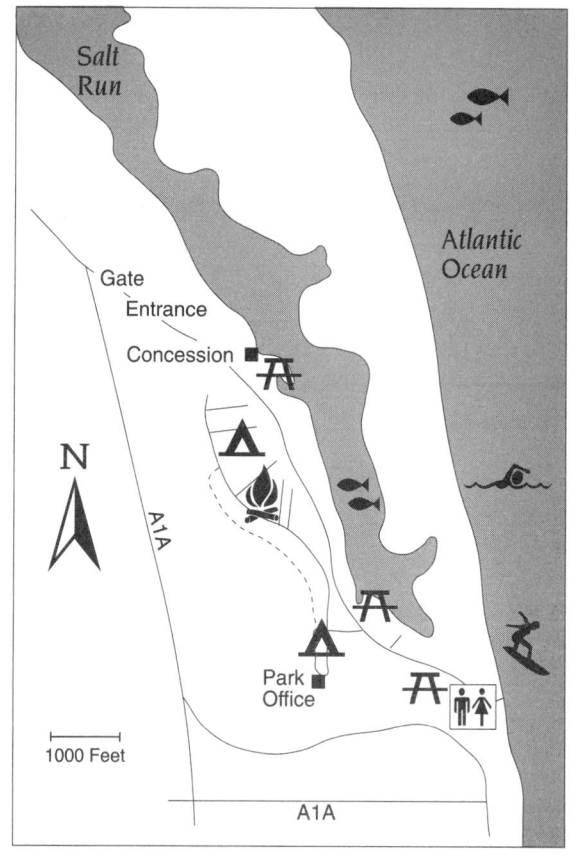

ACTIVITIES: Bird watching; camping; fishing in the surf or the lagoon for sea trout, bluefish, pompano, whiting, redfish and flounder; canoeing; hiking along the Atlantic beaches; and picnicking (there are three separate areas located along the main drive).

NEARBY ATTRACTIONS: Historic St. Augustine, St. Augustine Beach, Guana River State Park, Crescent Beach, the dog track at Orange Park, Jacksonville, the St. John River, Flagler Beach, Fort Matanzas National Monument, Washington Oak State Gardens and Castillo de San Marcos.

INFORMATION: Anastasia State Recreation Area, 1340-C A1A South, St. Augustine, FL 32084. Telephone 904-461-2033. The recreation area is on St. Augustine Beach, off A1A at SR 3.

Big Talbot Island State Park

This park is set on one of the unique sea islands northeast of Florida. It is a picturesque hammock of sand dunes and troughs covered with sea oats, morning glories, and a wide range of other ground-covering plant life and wildflowers, grasses, sedges, willows, slash pines and red cedars. During the fall and spring months, a variety of migrating birds stop off to enjoy this remote and often wild sea island.

At the southwest of the island is the river mouth at Fort St. George, to the east the Atlantic Ocean and its magnificent beaches, still largely undiscovered and certainly unspoiled. Big Talbot Island is one of Florida's best days out.

ACTIVITIES: Canoe routes interlace the salt marshes, and hikers may spend hours wandering the historic trails, sunbathing and swimming. There are also nature study and bird watching, wildlife photography, and fishing the surf, river and creeks for striped bass, speckled trout, bluefish, redfish, flounder, mullet, sheephead and whiting.

NEARBY ATTRACTIONS: Amelia Island, Fort Clinch, Fort George, Huguenot Historic Museum at Fort George, Fernandina Beach, Guana River State Park, Little Talbot Island State Park, Jacksonville, the dog track at Orange Park, Fort Caroline National Memorial, Ponte Vedra Beach, Atlantic Beach, Neptune Beach and Jacksonville Beach.

INFORMATION: Big Talbot Island State Park, c/o the Talbot Islands GEOpark, 11435 Fort George Road East, Fort George, FL 32226. Telephone 904-251-2320. The park is 20 miles east of downtown Jacksonville on A1A North, immediately north of Little Talbot Island State Park.

Bulow Creek State Park

The pivotal point of interest at Bulow Creek is an 800-year-old Fairchild oak tree. The tree, along with two water cisterns that once were a part of the plantations, have survived to become a monument to the people who pioneered the land and gave Florida its heritage. Today, Bulow Creek is one of Florida's premier day-use parks, a mecca for hikers and nature lovers alike. Trails interlace the magnificent hammocks, which provide natural habitats for a wide and diverse range of plant, animal and bird life.

NEARBY ATTRACTIONS: Bulow Plantation Ruins State Historic Site, Ormond Beach, Daytona Beach, Flagler Beach, Faver-Dykes State Park, Marineland of Florida, Gamble Rogers Memorial State Recreation Area, Fort Matanzas National Monument, Daytona International Speedway, Sugar Mill Gardens, Turtle Mound State Archaeological Site, Canaveral National Seashore, New Smyrna Sugar Mill Ruins State Historic Site, Lake George and Crescent Lake, to name just a few.

INFORMATION: Bulow Creek State Park, 3351 Old Dixie Highway, Ormond Beach, FL 32174. Telephone 904-677-4645. The park is near the Gamble Rogers Memorial State Recreation Area just off A1A.

Bulow Plantation Ruins State Historic Site

This historic site was a prosperous Southern plantation producing cotton, rice and indigo. What little remains of the once proud plantation tells the sad story of its fall as a result of the Second Seminole Indian War.

Facilities here include canoeing routes and canoe rentals, a boat ramp, fishing areas, a walking trail to the ruins of the sugar mill and an interpretive center where visitors can learn all about the plantation's history.

NEARBY ATTRACTIONS: Bulow Creek State Park, Ormond Beach, Daytona Beach, Flagler Beach, Faver-Dykes State Park, Marineland of Florida, Gamble Rogers Memorial State Recreation Area, Fort Matanzas National Monument, Daytona International Speedway, Sugar Mill Gardens, Turtle Mound State Archaeological Site, the Canaveral National Seashore, New Smyrna Sugar Mill Ruins State Historic Site, Lake George and Crescent Lake.

INFORMATION: Bulow Plantation Ruins State Historic Site, PO Box 655, Bunnell, FL 32010 (telephone 904-439-2219), for information. The historic site is located three miles west of Flagler Beach on SR 100, south on CR 2001.

Faver-Dykes State Park

Faver-Dykes is a full-service park with plenty to see and do for the entire family. The park incorporate some 750 acres of pine and hardwood forests, hammocks, pinelands, bayheads, swamps and marshes. The wild environment presents an illusion of remoteness, reminiscent of the landscape as it must have been when the Spanish explorers landed on Florida's shores in the late 1560s.

The diverse plant life provides habitats for an abundance of wildlife, including all sorts of wading birds, waterfowl, alligators and otters. Deer, turkeys, hawks, owls, squirrels, bobcats, foxes and opossums make their homes in the uplands close to Pellicer Creek and are often seen along the creek itself.

The park has 30 modern campsites complete with water and electric hookups, restrooms, hot showers, picnic tables and grills. Youth camping facilities are also available. There are two loop hiking trails. One begins near the picnic area and winds through the pinelands; the other at the camping area takes hikers through a mature hardwood hammock. A boat ramp gives access to Pellicer Creek and a picnic area overlooks the creek.

ACTIVITIES: Bird watching, wildlife photography, camping, boating, fishing in Pellicer Creek for speckled trout, redfish, sheephead, and flounder, canoeing, picnicking and hiking.

NEARBY ATTRACTIONS: Bulow Creek State Park, Bulow Plantation Ruins State Historic Site, Ormond Beach, Daytona Beach, Flagler Beach, Marineland of Florida, Gamble Rogers Memorial State Recreation Area, Fort Matanzas National Monument, Daytona International Speedway, Sugar Mill Gardens, Turtle Mound State Archaeological Site, Canaveral National Seashore, New Smyrna Sugar Mill Ruins State Historic Site, Lake George and Crescent Lake.

INFORMATION: Faver-Dykes State Park, 1000 Faver-Dykes Road, St. Augustine, FL 32086. Telephone 904-794-0997. The park is situated 15 miles south of St. Augustine at the intersection of I-95 and US 1.

Fort Clinch State Park

This park incorporates some 1,121 acres at the north end of Amelia Island, Florida's most northerly barrier island. Fort Clinch offers a wide variety of sea island recreational opportunities just beyond the popular tourist and residential areas of Amelia Island. The pristine beaches, unspoiled by the thousands of holiday makers that flee southward during peak vacation periods, make it a place that has something for the entire family to enjoy, where the sun shines most of the time and the kids can enjoy fun times in the sand.

Fort Clinch was named for General Duncan L. Clinch, an important figure in the Seminole War of the 1830s. It was constructed in 1847 and during the Civil War was occupied by a Confederate garrison. It was then occupied by Federal forces when General Robert E. Lee ordered a withdrawal in 1862. When the Civil War ended it was abandoned, but was reoccupied briefly in 1898 during the Spanish American War. Today, the fort remains in remarkably good condition. Park Rangers dress in Civil War Union uniforms and carry out the daily chores, cooking, sentry duty, and so forth, of a busy Civil War garrison. Candlelight tours can be arranged at the ranger station and there are annual reenactments of the fort's occupation by Confederate and Union troops during the months of May and October. The visitor center contains many exhibits, tools, utensils and artifacts that explain the history of the fort.

Facilities at the park include coastal camping at modern, full-service campsites, complete with water and electric hookups, restrooms, hot showers, picnic tables and grills. There's a primitive campsite for those who like to do everything themselves and get close to nature. There's also a picnic area for public use, a campfire circle, several hiking trails and fresh water showers at the beach. Concessions: snacks and soft drinks, are available near the beach.

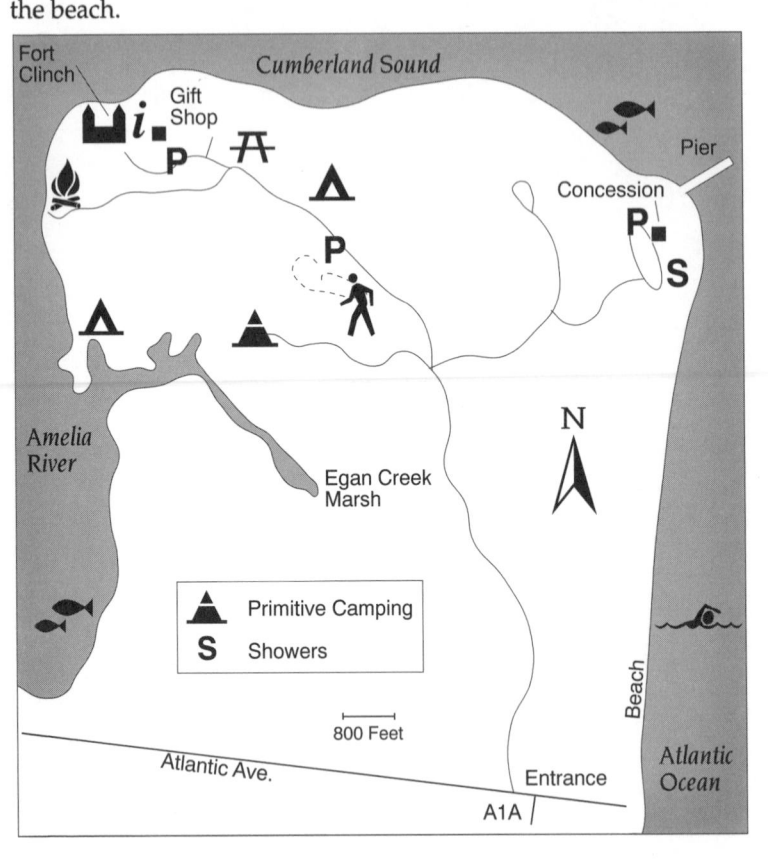

ACTIVITIES: Hiking along the nature trail or the beach, swimming in the ocean, spending lazy days sunbathing. For the nature lover there's a wealth of wildlife to observe, including wading birds. Many species of marine birds and mammals make their homes in the hammocks and dunes on the east side of the park. Anglers can enjoy fishing from the beach or the pier on the

Amelia River, the Cumberland Sound or the Atlantic Ocean for speckled trout, striped bass, redfish or bluefish.

NEARBY ATTRACTIONS: Amelia Island, Fort George, Huguenot Historic Museum at Fort George, Fernandina Beach, Guana River State Park, Little Talbot Island State Park, Big Talbot Island State Park, Jacksonville, the dog track at Orange Park, Fort Caroline National Memorial and numerous beaches.

INFORMATION: Fort Clinch State Park, 2601 Atlantic Avenue, Fernandina Beach, FL 32034. Telephone 904-261-4212. The park is close to Fernandina Beach, off A1A.

Fort George State Cultural Site

Moss-draped laurel and live oaks provide a lush canopy for visitors to yet another part of Florida's Talbot Islands GEOpark complex. Fort George Island has been continuously occupied for more than 5,000 years. The complex includes Mount Cornelia, highest point on the Atlantic coast south of Sandy Hook, New Jersey, and several plant species surviving far outside their normal range. Fort George is an interesting and educational experience, well worth a visit if you happen to be in the area.

NEARBY ATTRACTIONS: Amelia Island, Fort Clinch, Fort George, Huguenot Historic Museum at Fort George, Fernandina Beach, Guana River State Park, Little Talbot Island State Park, Jacksonville, the dog track at Orange Park, Fort Caroline National Memorial, Ponte Vedra Beach, Atlantic Beach, Neptune Beach and Jacksonville Beach.

INFORMATION: Fort George Island State Cultural Site, c/o Talbot Islands GEOpark, 11435 Fort George Road East, Fort George, FL 32226, telephone 904-251-2320, for details. Fort George Island State Cultural Site is located some 16 miles east of downtown Jacksonville on SR A1A North, or three miles south of Little Talbot Island State Park.

Gamble Rogers Memorial State Recreation Area At Flagler Beach

Gamble Rogers is bordered by the Atlantic on one side and the Intracoastal Waterway on the other. The 144-acre park offers a quiet place to spend a little time sunning on the beach while the kids enjoy themselves in the water. It's a place for bird watching, for chasing the tiny crabs as they bury themselves in the fine wet sand, or to watch the sea turtles in the summer months when they come ashore to lay their eggs.

ACTIVITIES: Hiking along the beach front; fishing in the surf for sea trout, bluefish, pompano, whiting, redfish and flounder; nature study; picnicking; swimming; camping; and boating.

Coastal camping is available on modern, full-service campsites, complete with water and electric hookups, restrooms, hot showers, picnic tables and grills. There's also a picnic area for public use and a boat ramp.

NEARBY ATTRACTIONS: Bulow Creek State Park, Bulow Plantation Ruins State Historic Site, Ormond Beach, Daytona Beach, Flagler Beach, Marineland of Florida, Faver-Dykes State Park, Fort Matanzas National Monument, Daytona International Speedway, Sugar Mill Gardens, Turtle Mound State Archaeological Site, Canaveral National Seashore, New Smyrna Sugar Mill Ruins State Historic Site, Lake George and Crescent Lake.

INFORMATION: Gamble Rogers Memorial State Recreation Area at Flagler Beach, 3100 South A1A, Flagler Beach, FL 32136. Telephone 904-439-2474. The recreation area is set on Flagler Beach, off A1A.

Guana River State Park

Guana River is a wild and remote 2,400-acre area of coastal river channels, salt water creeks and marshes, tidewater pools, undulating sand dunes and tide water forests. The park is home to a vast range of plant life, seabirds and mammals. High sand dunes, some more than 40 feet high, rise above a shoreline that stretches away like a great yellow ribbon between the deep blue of the Atlantic Ocean and the grassy hillocks of the dunes. The dunes act as a natural barrier against the sometimes furious action of the ocean. The tidal waters infiltrate the surrounding countryside in the form of hundreds of tiny saltwater creeks, streams, pools and the Guana River itself. In 1957 a dam was built across the river to flood the marshes and river channel, forming the half-mile-wide, 10-mile-long Guana Lake. It is thought that Guana River might have been Ponce de Leon's first landing place, but that is only speculation. Today, the park's visitors include holiday makers and nature lovers from all across the United States, Canada, Europe and Asia.

ACTIVITIES: Hiking along the beach, swimming and surfing; fishing the Atlantic surf for redfish, bluefish, drum, sheephead, flounder, whiting and pompano; fishing Guana Lake, Guana River or Tolomato River for sea trout, flounder or croaker. Nature watching is especially popular here. Other amusements are canoeing the rivers and creeks; boating on the lake (there's a boat ramp available for public use); sunbathing; and picnicking. Local inhabitants of the park, though difficult to find, include alligators, otters, deer, foxes, flying squirrel and bobcats.

NEARBY ATTRACTIONS: Historic St. Augustine, St. Augustine Beach, Anastasia State Recreation Area, Crescent Beach, the dog track at Orange Park, Jacksonville, St. John River, Flagler Beach, Fort Matanzas National Monument, Washington Oak State Gardens, Castillo de San Marcos, Amelia Island, Fort Clinch, Fort George, Huguenot Historic Museum at Fort George, Fernandina Beach, Guana River State Park, Little Talbot Island State Park, Fort Caroline National Memorial, Ponte Vedra Beach, Atlantic Beach, Neptune Beach and Jacksonville Beach.

INFORMATION: Guana River State Park, 2690 South Ponte Vedra Blvd., Ponte Vedra Beach, FL 32082, telephone 904-825-5071. The park is just off SR A1A, north of St. Augustine.

Little Talbot Island State Park

Little Talbot Island is another unique sea island northeast of Florida. The park encompasses more than 2,500 acres and over five miles of glistening sandy beaches. It's a picturesque, undisturbed hammock of sand dunes and troughs covered with live oak, southern magnolia, American holly, sea oats and morning glories. During the fall and spring months, a variety of migrating birds stop off to enjoy this remote island.

Nature lovers will enjoy wandering the dunes and forests, where there is an abundance of animal and bird life. River otters, marsh rabbits, bobcats and a selection of sea and shore birds inhabit the island. It is also on the list as one of the nation's "Best Beaches," so it's no surprise that the island offers some of the best swimming, surfing and sunbathing to be found anywhere in the United States.

Facilities at the park include coastal camping on modern, full-service campsites, complete with water and electric hookups, restrooms, hot showers, picnic tables and grills. There's also a picnic area for public use, youth camping facilities and most facilities are accessible to the handicapped.

ACTIVITIES: Canoe routes interlace the salt marshes, rivers and creeks. There's also hiking on the beaches, sunbathing, surfing, swimming, nature study and bird watching, wildlife photography and plenty of fishing in the surf, river and creeks.

NEARBY ATTRACTIONS: Amelia Island, Fort Clinch, Fort George, Huguenot Historic Museum at Fort George, Fernandina Beach, Guana River State Park, Little Talbot Island State Park, Jacksonville, the dog track at Orange Park, Fort Caroline National Memorial, Ponte Vedra Beach, Atlantic Beach, Neptune Beach and Jacksonville Beach.

INFORMATION: Little Talbot Island State Park, c/o the Talbot Islands GEOpark, 11435 Fort George Road East, Fort George, FL 32226, or call 904-251-2320, for information. Little Talbot Island

State Park is 17 miles northeast of downtown Jacksonville on SR A1A, immediately south of Big Talbot Island State Park.

New Smyrna Sugar Mill Ruins State Historic Site

This was only one of 10 sugar mills that once thrived along the eastern coast of Florida. During the early 1800s, New Smyrna was the heart of a great southern plantation and, producing a variety of products for export to the northern states and Europe, was operated by slave labor. It was attacked and burned by Seminole Indians during the second Seminole War in 1835.

NEARBY ATTRACTIONS: Bulow Plantation Ruins State Historic Site, Bulow Creek State Park, Ormond Beach, Tomoka State Park, Ravine State Gardens, Daytona Beach, Flagler Beach, Faver-Dykes State Park, Marineland of Florida, Gamble Rogers Memorial State Recreation Area, Fort Matanzas National Monument, Daytona International Speedway, Sugar Mill Gardens, Turtle Mound State Archaeological Site, Canaveral National Seashore, New Smyrna Beach, Lake George and Crescent Lake.

INFORMATION: New Smyrna Sugar Mill Ruins State Historic Site, PO Box 861, New Smyrna, FL 32170. Telephone 904-428-2126. The site is in New Smyrna Beach, west of SR 44, south on Mission Drive.

Ravine State Gardens

This park is the result of nature's constant forming and reforming of the Florida peninsula. The deep ravine was created by the action of water flowing beneath the sandy ridges that flank the western shore of St. Johns River. Slowly the steep slopes became inundated by a wide variety of grasses, shrubs, trees, small mammals and songbirds. The gardens were created in 1933 by the Federal Works Progress Administration. The peak flowering period is during March and April, which coincides with the Palatka Azalea Festival.

The gardens provide a very beautiful spot to hike and bicycle.

NEARBY ATTRACTIONS: Bulow Plantation Ruins State Historic Site, Bulow Creek State Park, Ormond Beach, Daytona Beach, Tomoka State Park, Flagler Beach, Faver-Dykes State Park, Marineland of Florida, Gamble Rogers Memorial State Recreation Area, Fort Matanzas National Monument, Daytona International Speedway, Sugar Mill Gardens, Turtle Mound State Archaeological Site, Canaveral National Seashore, New Smyrna Sugar Mill Ruins State Historic Site, Lake George and Crescent Lake.

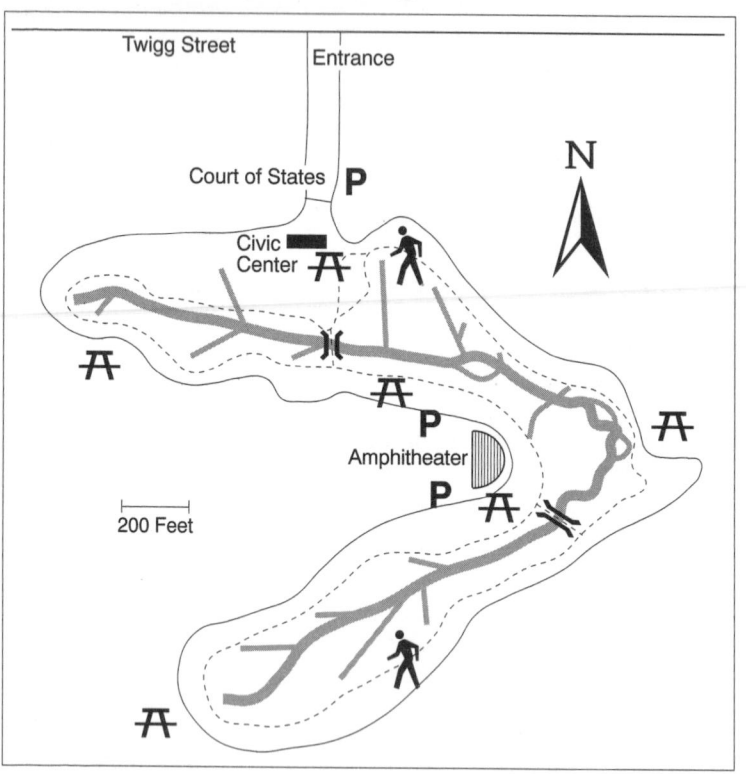

INFORMATION: Ravine State Gardens, PO Box 1096, Palatka, FL 32178. Telephone 904-329-3721. The gardens are in Palatka, just off Twigg Street.

Tomoka State Park

Tomoka State Park is near the junction of the Tomoka and Halifax rivers. Although it offers scenic beauty, creeks, rivers and lagoons, it is largely by-passed by the vacationing public. It has the official 'Gem' designation from the state of Florida.

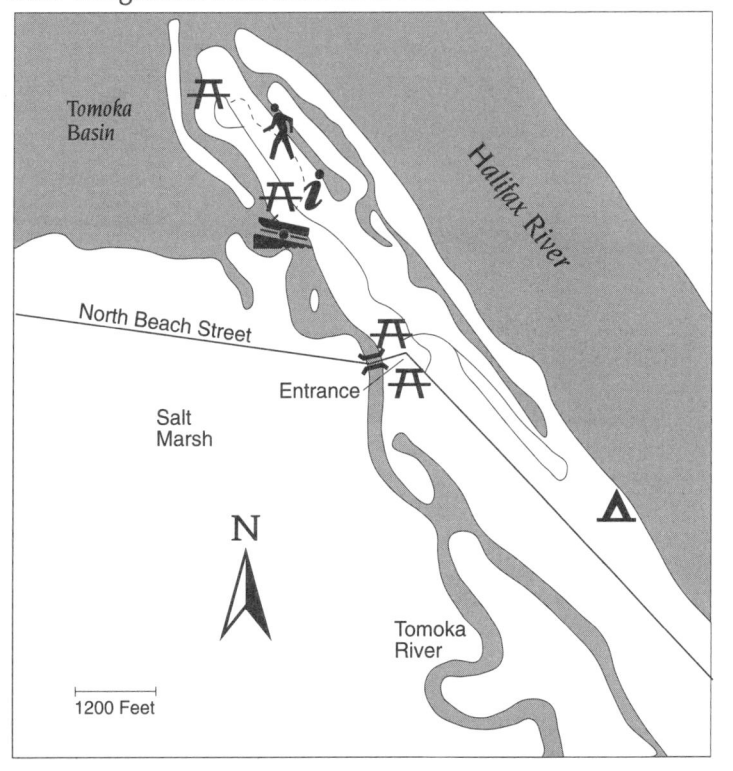

Facilities here include coastal camping at modern, full-service campsites, complete with water and electric hookups, restrooms, hot showers, picnic tables and grills. There are also facilities available for youth camping, a boat ramp, a nature trail and a park museum where you can buy real Florida gifts, food and drink and rent canoes. Most of the park's facilities are accessible to the handicapped.

ACTIVITIES: Picnicking; canoeing the lagoons, rivers and creeks; hiking the nature trail; nature study and bird watching, wildlife photography; fishing for striped bass, speckled trout, bluefish, redfish, flounder, mullet, sheephead and whiting.

NEARBY ATTRACTIONS: Bulow Plantation Ruins State Historic Site, Ormond Beach, Daytona Beach, Flagler Beach, Faver-Dykes State Park, Marineland of Florida, Gamble Rogers Memorial State Recreation Area, Fort Matanzas National Monument, Daytona International Speedway, Sugar Mill Gardens, Turtle Mound State Archaeological Site, Canaveral National Seashore, New Smyrna Sugar Mill Ruins State Historic Site, Lake George and Crescent Lake.

INFORMATION: Tomoka State Park, 2099 North Beach Street, Ormond Beach, FL 32174. The park is three miles north of Ormond Beach on North Beach Street.

Washington Oak State Gardens

The sometimes wild Atlantic Ocean to the east, and the scenic Matanzas River to the west, are the natural boundaries of the 389-acre Washington Oaks State Gardens. At low tide the coquina rock shoreline, tranquil tidal pools and boulder-strewn beaches provide a haven and a vast feeding ground for a multitude of sea and shore birds.

Visitors to the park can enjoy a quiet picnic on a sunny afternoon, or a stroll through the ornamental gardens, along the beach or the river bank. For the anglers among us, this is a wonderful place to take in an hour or two fishing for speckled trout, bluefish, redfish and flounder.

NEARBY ATTRACTIONS: Bulow Plantation Ruins State Historic Site, Ormond Beach, Daytona Beach, Flagler Beach, Faver-Dykes State Park, Marineland of Florida, Gamble Rogers Memorial State Recreation Area, Fort Matanzas National Monument, Daytona International Speedway, Sugar Mill Gardens, Turtle Mound State Archaeological Site, Canaveral National Seashore, New Smyrna Sugar Mill Ruins State Historic Site, Lake George and Crescent Lake.

INFORMATION: Washington Oak State Gardens, 6400 North Ocean Blvd., Palm Coast, FL 32137. Telephone 904-445-3161. The gardens are two miles south of Marineland, off SR A1A.

The West

Anclote Key State Preserve

The six distinct biological communities at Anclote Key State Preserve provide habitats for a wide variety of plant life, wild animals and birds, including the bald eagle and piping plover. It's a remote place where tall pines offer a nesting place for the osprey and where the federal lighthouse at the southern end of the island still stands, a lonely, though nowadays obsolete link with the past. It's a place where the blue waters of the Gulf of Mexico lap gently upon more than four miles of pristine beaches populated only by crabs and birds that spend their days endlessly fishing and foraging for food. It's no small wonder, then, that Anclote Key is one of those places where the air is clear, the breeze fresh and the harassed inhabitants of the city can spend a quiet afternoon relaxing in the sunshine.

There are no facilities at Anclote Key. That means no fresh water and no concessions, so be sure to plan your visit well and bring all you need along with you.

ACTIVITIES: Primitive camping, swimming, fishing, nature study (the preserve offers outstanding study opportunities), bird watching, wildlife photography and picnicking.

NEARBY ATTRACTIONS: Caladesi Island State Park, Honeymoon Island State Recreation Area, St. Petersburg Beach, Treasure Island, Little Manatee River State Recreation Area, Braden Castle Ruins at Bradenton, Spongeorama Large Sponge Fisheries, Madeira Beach, Indian Rocks Beach, Gamble Plantation State Historic Site, Captain Nemo's Pirate Cruise at Clearwater, the marina at Clearwater and the Marine Science Center, also at Clearwater.

INFORMATION: Anclote Key State Preserve, c/o Caladesi Island State Park, #1 Causeway Blvd., Dunedin FL 34698. Telephone 813-469-5918. The preserve is three miles off Tarpon Springs and is accessible only by boat.

Caladesi Island State Park

Caladesi Island is another of Florida's large, yet essentially undeveloped, Gulf Coast barrier islands. It's a fairly remote area, one of Florida's romantic hideaways where couples can walk hand-in-hand along the miles of balmy beaches or take a walk to secret places by way of one of the island's unspoiled nature trails. Visitors with private boats can tie up at one of the 99 slips at the bay-side marina or simply drop anchor in the clear blue waters and swim ashore for an afternoon of picnicking and romance.

The park offers camping at modern, full-service campsites, complete with water and electric hookups, restrooms, hot showers, picnic tables and grills. There are also concession facilities, a boat ramp and freshwater showers, all available at the beach.

ACTIVITIES: Shelling is popular here, along with picnicking, boating (overnight docking is available, but limited to 20 vessels from March through Labor Day), hiking the extensive system of nature trails, nature study, bird watching, wildlife photography, and fishing for bluefish, redfish, flounder, mullet, sheephead, and whiting, to name just a few.

NEARBY ATTRACTIONS: Little Manatee River State Recreation Area, the Florida Suncoast Dome, Madira Bickell State Archaeological Site, DeSoto National Memorial, Anclote Key State Preserve, Honeymoon Island State Recreation Area, Treasure Island, Braden Castle Ruins at Bradenton, Spongeorama Large Sponge Fisheries, Madeira Beach, Indian Rocks Beach, Gamble Plantation State Historic Site, Captain Nemo's Pirate Cruise at Clearwater, the marina at Clearwater and the Marine Science Center, also at Clearwater. Saint Petersburg has a number of interesting sites, including the Sunken Gardens, Mirror Lake Park, Great Explorations Museum and a beach.

INFORMATION: Caladesi Island State Park, #1 Causeway Blvd., Dunedin FL 34698. Telephone 813-469-5918. The park is located west of Dunedin off the Gulf Coast. It can only be reached by boat, but a scheduled passenger ferry runs from nearby Honeymoon Island State Recreation Area and from Clearwater.

Crystal River State Archaeological Site

For more than 1,600 years this 14-acre site was home to over 7,500 Indians. It is thought to be the longest continuously occupied site in Florida. The six-mound complex was built by a cultural group that archaeologists call pre-Columbian mound builders. At its conception, the Crystal River complex was an important religious and ceremonial center. Indians travelled great distances to bring their dead here for burial, to join in the ceremonies and to trade

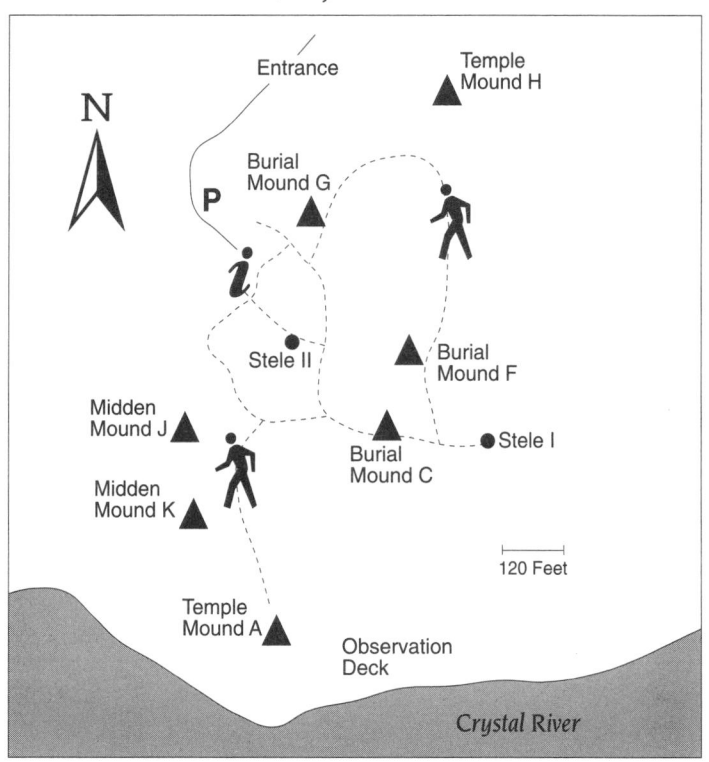

with local Indians. Crystal River State Archaeological Site is a National Historic Landmark.

NEARBY ATTRACTIONS: Cedar Key State Museum, St. Clair Whitman Museum, Waccasassa Bay State Preserve/Cedar Key Scrub State Reserve, Manatee Springs State Park, Vulee Sugar Mill Ruins State Historic Site, Dade Battlefield State Historic Site, Withlacoochee State Forest, Lake Panasoffkee, Homosassa Springs State Wildlife Park, Silver Lake, Ft. Cooper and Lower Suwannee National Wildlife Refuge.

INFORMATION: Crystal River State Archaeological Site, 3400 N. Museum Point, Crystal River, FL 32629, telephone 904-795-3817. The Archaeological Site sits on Museum Point in Crystal River.

Dade Battlefield State Historic Site

This site commemorates the battle that marked the beginning of the Second Seminole Indian War, and the brave stand made by Major Francis L. Dade and his company of 108 soldiers. It was early morning on December 28, 1835: "Have good heart," he said to his men, cold and tired after many hours of marching through the forests. "Our difficulties and dangers are over now and as soon as we arrive at Fort King you'll have three days to rest and keep Christmas gaily." Alas, it was not to be. The Indians attacked without warning. Only three men survived the savage eight-hour battle.

The story of the battle is told at the visitor center. You can tour the battlefield and enjoy a picnic surrounded by the quiet beauty that belies the horrors that took place upon the site more than 150 years ago. The site is open daily from 8 AM until sundown, and the visitor center open daily from 9 AM until 5 PM.

NEARBY ATTRACTIONS: Cedar Key State Museum, St. Clair Whitman Museum, Waccasassa Bay State Preserve/Cedar Key Scrub State Reserve, Manatee Springs State Park, Vulee Sugar Mill Ruins State Historic Site, Crystal River State Archaeological Site, Withlacoochee State Forest, Lake Panasoffkee, Homosassa Springs State Wildlife Park, Silver Lake, Ft. Cooper State Park and Lower Suwannee National Wildlife Refuge.

INFORMATION: Dade Battlefield State Historic Site, PO Box 938, Bushnell, FL 33513. Telephone 904-793-4781. The site is situated off I-75 and SR 48, west of Highway 301.

Egmont Key State Park

Egmont Key is a tiny, 440-acre island that sits at the mouth of Tampa Bay. The island has enjoyed a somewhat colorful and perhaps stormy history. It was a prison camp for captured Seminole Indians during the Third Seminole War, a Union naval base during the Civil War, and is today the site of the only fully-manned lighthouse in the United States. Egmont Key is a joint venture operated by the Florida Department of Natural Resources, the US Fish and Wildlife Service and the US Coast Guard.

ACTIVITIES: Swimming, boating and fishing. Because of its inaccessibility, Egmont Key is one of those quiet spots where it's easy to find a place to spend a few undisturbed hours.

NEARBY ATTRACTIONS: Anclote Key State Preserve, Honeymoon Island State Recreation Area, Treasure Island, Braden Castle Ruins at Bradenton, Spongeorama Large Sponge Fisheries, Madeira Beach, Indian Rocks Beach, Gamble Plantation State Historic Site, the Florida Suncoast Dome, Little Manatee River State Recreation Area, Madira Bickell State Archaeological Site, DeSoto National Memorial, Captain Nemo's Pirate Cruise at Clearwater, The Marina at Clearwater, and the Marine Science Center, also at Clearwater. St. Petersburg offers a beach, the Sunken Gardens, Mirror Lake Park and the Great Explorations Museum.

INFORMATION: Egmont Key State Park, Slip 656, 4801 37th Street South, St. Petersburg, FL 33711, telephone 813-893-2627. The park is located at the mouth of Tampa Bay, southwest of Fort DeSoto Beach. It is accessible only by private boat.

Fort Cooper State Park

Fort Cooper and beautiful Lake Holathikaha are more of Florida's undiscovered areas. The swamps, marshlands, a hardwood hammock and the sandhills around the lake provide habitats for a number of Florida's abundant wildlife. It's an area of wild and scenic beauty where the trees are festooned with moss and more than 10 miles of self-guided nature and hiking trails thread their way through the trees. Nature still rules here and the hand of man has been laid only lightly. The state of Florida designated Ft. Cooper a 'Gem.'

ACTIVITIES: Hiking, nature study and bird watching, wildlife photography, swimming in the spring-fed lake, fishing, horseback riding and picnicking.

The site has primitive camping sites, canoe and paddleboat rentals, pavilions and a picnic area.

NEARBY ATTRACTIONS: Cedar Key State Museum, St. Clair Whitman Museum, the Waccasassa Bay State Preserve/Cedar Key Scrub State Reserve, Manatee Springs State Park, Vulee Sugar Mill Ruins State Historic Site, Dade Battlefield State Historic Site, the Withlacoochee State Forest, Lake Panasoffkee, Homosassa Springs State Wildlife Park, Silver Lake, Crystal River State Archaeological Site, and Lower Suwannee National Wildlife Refuge.

INFORMATION: Ft. Cooper State Park, 3100 South Old Floral City Road, Inverness, FL 32650. Telephone 904-726-0315.

Hillsborough River State Park

Hillsborough River is one of the first state parks established in Florida. It was developed by the Civilian Conservation Corps in 1936 and opened to the general public two years later. Of special interest is Fort Foster, a pioneer fort where Park Service personnel run history programs and act out the everyday lives and duties of the early settlers, much as they might have been in 1837. Other activities at the 2,990-acre park include camping on modern, full-service campsites, complete with water and electric hookups, restrooms, hot showers, picnic tables and grills. There are also facilities for primitive and youth camping, concession stands selling gifts, food and drink, and canoes for rent. There are more than eight miles of nature trails intertwined among the hammocks, oaks, sabal palms, magnolias, and hickories along the banks of the Hillsborough River.

ACTIVITIES: Hiking, nature study, bird watching, wildlife photography, swimming, fishing, horseback riding, and picnicking.

NEARBY ATTRACTIONS: Florida Suncoast Dome, Caladesi State Park, Great Explorations Museum at St. Petersburg, Madira Bickell State Archaeological Site, Little Manatee River State Recreation Area, the Sunken Gardens at St. Petersburg, Mirror Lake Park at St. Petersburg, DeSoto National Memorial, Anclote Key State Preserve, Honeymoon Island State Recreation Area, St. Petersburg Beach, Treasure Island, Braden Castle Ruins at Bradenton, Spongeorama Large Sponge Fisheries, Madeira Beach, Indian Rocks beach, Gamble Plantation State Historic Site, Captain Nemo's Pi-

Ranger-led Canoe Trips on Hillsborough River

rate Cruise at Clearwater, The Marina at Clearwater, and the Marine Science Center, also at Clearwater.

INFORMATION: Hillsborough River State Park, 15402 U.S Highway 301 North, Thonotosassa, FL 33592. Telephone 813-986-1020. The park is 12 miles north of Tampa or six miles south of Zephyrhills on US 301.

Homosassa Springs
State Wildlife Park

Homosassa Springs is one of those rare places in the world where you can experience something very special. The gentle and endangered Florida manatee is hardly ever seen by the vacationing public, but here it's an everyday occurrence. You can walk "underwater" to view not only the manatee, but many of Florida's other aquatic species in the Spring of 10,000 Fish.

There are the many wildlife exhibits, including a Florida black bear, bobcats, alligators, and an extensive collection of wild birds.

A series of educational and interpretive programs provided by the Park Service focus on the manatees, alligators, and other wildlife. The Animal Encounters Arena features, among other things, Florida's snakes. This is another of Florida's 'Gems.'

Lucifer the Hippo, Homosassa Springs

ACTIVITIES: Hiking, nature study, wildlife photography, and boat tours.

NEARBY ATTRACTIONS: Cedar Key State Museum, St. Clair Whitman Museum, Ft. Cooper State Park, Waccasassa Bay State Preserve/Cedar Key Scrub State Reserve, Manatee Springs State

Park, Vulee Sugar Mill Ruins State Historic Site, Dade Battlefield State Historic Site, Withlacoochee State Forest, Lake Panasoffkee, Silver Lake, Crystal River State Archaeological Site, and Lower Suwannee National Wildlife Refuge.

INFORMATION: Homosassa Springs State Wildlife Park, 9225 West Fish Bowl Drive, Homosassa, FL 32646. Tel. 904-628-2311. Homosassa Springs State Wildlife Park is in Homosassa Springs, 75 miles north of Tampa off US 19.

Honeymoon Island
State Recreation Area

Honeymoon Island. The name conjures up all sorts of romantic images: deserted tropical islands, sugar white beaches, sea breezes blowing gently in from the ocean and day after day of perfect weather. For the most-part Honeymoon Island is all this and more. It's a place for those who want to find a perfect little hideaway. The sun-drenched miles of beaches are an open invitation to lazy days far away from the hustle and bustle of the regular honeymoon establishments. But Honeymoon Island is not just for lovers. It's a place where the entire family can enjoy quiet days swimming in the ocean or simply lounging in the sunshine. There's even a "Pet Beach" where you and your animal friends can enjoy a stroll together.

ACTIVITIES: Swimming, fishing the surf for bluefish, redfish, flounder, mullet, sheephead and whiting, nature study, bird watching, wildlife photography, hiking and picnicking.

For nature lovers there are two bird observatories. Naturalists will find plenty to interest them, including osprey nests and a wide variety of shorebirds and marine life. Along the island's northern loop trail hikers can enjoy one of Florida's few remaining stands of virgin slash pine.

Facilities include picnic areas and concessions, along with freshwater showers on the beach.

NEARBY ATTRACTIONS: The Sunken Gardens in St. Petersburg, Little Manatee River State Recreation Area, Mirror Lake Park in St. Petersburg, Florida Suncoast Dome, Caladesi State Park, Great Explorations Museum in St. Petersburg, The Madira Bickell State Archaeological Site, DeSoto National Memorial, Anclote Key State Preserve, Hillsborough River State Park, St. Petersburg Beach, Treasure Island, Braden Castle Ruins at Bradenton, Spongeorama Large Sponge Fisheries, Madeira Beach, Indian Rocks Beach, Gamble Plantation State Historic Site, Captain Nemo's Pirate Cruise in Clearwater, The Marina at Clearwater, and the Marine Science Center, also at Clearwater.

INFORMATION: Honeymoon Island State Recreation Area, #1 Causeway Blvd., Dunedin, FL 34698. Tel. 813-469-5942. The recreation area is situated at the extreme west end of SR 586, north of Dunedin.

Lake Griffin
State Recreation Area

Along with superb bass fishing, Lake Griffin, less than an hour from Florida's major commercial attractions, strives to offer something for all the family. It's an outdoor attraction that compares favorably with any of Florida's other parks.

ACTIVITIES: Camping, fishing, boating, canoeing, swimming, and picnicking.

Facilities include modern, full-service campsites, complete with water and electric hookups, restrooms, hot showers, picnic tables and grills. There's a boat ramp, and concessions selling gifts, food and drink. Canoes are available for rent on an hourly basis for those who want to get away from it all.

NEARBY ATTRACTIONS: Lake Griffin, Lake Harris, Lake Eustis, Lake Apopka, Walt Disney World in Orlando, Wikiwa Springs State Park, Rock Springs Run State Reserve, Dade Battlefield State Historic Site, Fort Mellon Historic Site, Ben White

Raceway in Orlando, Lake Louisa State Recreation Area, Mead Botanical Gardens in Orlando, Clearwater Lake, Ocala National Forest, the Early American Museum in Silver Springs, the Reptile Institute at Silver Springs, Silver Springs Wildwater, and Hontoon Island State Park.

INFORMATION: Lake Griffin State Recreation Area, 103 Highway 441/27, Fruitland Park, FL 34731. Telephone 904-787-7402. The site is two miles north of Leesburg.

Lake Louisa State Park

Lake Louisa State Park offers more than 1,790 acres of outdoor fun and recreational activities. As one of a chain of 13 lakes connected by the Palatlakaha River, it offers some of the finest freshwater fishing anywhere in Florida.

ACTIVITIES: Fishing, swimming, picnicking, canoeing, nature study, bird watching and wildlife photography.

NEARBY ATTRACTIONS: Lake Griffin, Lake Harris, Lake Eustis, Lake Apopka, Walt Disney World in Orlando, Wikiwa Springs State Park, Rock Springs Run State Reserve, Dade Battlefield State Historic Site, Fort Mellon Historic Site, Ben White Raceway in Orlando, Mead Botanical Gardens in Orlando, Lake Griffin State Recreation Area, Clearwater Lake, Ocala National Forest, the Early American Museum in Silver Springs, the Reptile Institute, also in Silver Springs, Silver Springs Wildwater, Hontoon Island State Park, and Orlando.

INFORMATION: Lake Louisa State Park, 12549 State Park Drive, Cleremont, FL 32711. Telephone 904-394-3969. The park is located 10 miles south of SR 50, off CR 561.

Little Manatee River State Park

The origins of Little Manatee River are in a swampy area near Fort Lonesome, a tiny spot on the map of Florida about eight miles southeast of Bradley Junction. From there the river flows westward almost 40 miles, passing through Little Manatee River State Park along the way, until it eventually reaches the sea at Tampa Bay. The river, which flows for more than four miles through the park, has been designated an "Outstanding Florida Water" and is a part of the Cockroach Bay Aquatic Preserve.

ACTIVITIES: Nature study, bird watching, wildlife photography, hiking, horseback riding, canoeing, picnicking, fishing and camping.

Facilities at the 1,600-acre park include provision for primitive camping, and youth camping. There are several miles of hiking trails and bridleways, and a picnic area for the family to enjoy.

NEARBY ATTRACTIONS: The Sunken Gardens in St. Petersburg, Mirror Lake Park also in St. Petersburg, Florida Suncoast Dome, Caladesi State Park, Honeymoon Island State Recreation Area, the Great Explorations Museum in St. Petersburg, The Madira Bickell State Archaeological Site, DeSoto National Memorial, Anclote Key State Preserve, Hillsborough River State Park, St. Petersburg Beach, Treasure Island, Braden Castle Ruins at Bradenton, Spongeorama Large Sponge Fisheries, Madeira Beach, Indian Rocks beach, Gamble Plantation State Historic Site, Captain Nemo's Pirate Cruise in Clearwater, The Marina in Clearwater, and the Marine Science Center, also at Clearwater.

INFORMATION: Little Manatee River State Recreation Area, 215 Lightfoot Road, Wimauma, FL 33598. Telephone 813-671-5005. The area is four miles south of Sun City, off US 301 on Lightfoot Road.

Weedon Island State Preserve

Weedon Island State Preserve is one of the few remaining mangrove swamps in the Tampa Bay area, one of Florida's most densely populated regions. The island has had an interesting, though somewhat turbulent, history. Over the years, as Florida's interests changed, so did the 1,000-acre park. In the early days there were citrus groves on the island. Then, as Florida's fledgling tourist industry began to grow, a roaring 1920s nightclub, a motion picture studio, and one of Florida's first airports sprang up. Today, the Weedon Island State Preserve is one of Tampa Bay's most popular outdoor recreation areas and is only a mile or two from the major cities of St. Petersburg and Tampa.

The nightclub, airport, and the studio are long gone, as are the high times of the 1920s. Visitors to the preserve, instead of drinking and dancing, now enjoy the great outdoors; hiking, canoeing, swimming, fishing, picnicking, nature study, bird watching, or simply relaxing under the hot Florida sunshine.

NEARBY ATTRACTIONS: Little Manatee River State Recreation Area, the Sunken Gardens in St. Petersburg, Mirror Lake Park also in St. Petersburg, Florida Suncoast Dome, Caladesi State Park, Honeymoon Island State Recreation Area, the Great Explorations Museum in St. Petersburg, The Madira Bickell State Archaeological Site, DeSoto National Memorial, Anclote Key State Preserve, Hillsborough River State Park, St. Petersburg Beach, Treasure Island, Braden Castle Ruins at Bradenton, Spongeorama Large Sponge Fisheries, Madeira Beach, Indian Rocks Beach, Gamble Plantation State Historic Site, Captain Nemo's Pirate Cruise in Clearwater, The Marina and the Marine Science Center, both in Clearwater.

INFORMATION: Weedon Island State Preserve, 1500 Weedon Island Drive, St. Petersburg, FL 33702. Telephone 813-570-5146. The preserve is located off Gandy Boulevard, just south of Gandy Bridge.

Ybor City State Museum

Ybor City is named for Don Vicente Martinez Ybor. He came to the frontier near Tampa Bay and "turned it into a city for thousands of immigrants," and the "Cigar Capital of the World." From the opening of the first cigar factory in 1886 until the 1930s, Ybor City was a thriving community, offering homes and opportunity to one and all. Then, as Florida's interests began to change Tampa began to grow, and Ybor City was slowly but surely absorbed into the urban sprawl that became the Tampa Bay we know today. The story of how and why this happened is related through the exhibits, tools and artifacts housed in the Ybor City State Museum. The museum, in a building that once housed the Ferlita Bakery, is open from 9 AM until noon, and from 1 PM until 5 PM, Tuesday through Saturday. La Cista, once a cigar worker's home, has been extensively restored and is open to the public from 10 AM until noon, and from 1 PM until 3 PM, Tuesday through Saturday.

NEARBY ATTRACTIONS: Weedon Island State Preserve, Florida Suncoast Dome, Caladesi State Park, Little Manatee River State Recreation Area, the Sunken Gardens in St. Petersburg, Mirror Lake Park also in St. Petersburg, Honeymoon Island State Recreation Area, the Great Explorations Museum in St. Petersburg, Indian Rocks Beach, Gamble Plantation State Historic Site, Captain Nemo's Pirate Cruise at Clearwater, The Marina at Clearwater, and the Marine Science Center, also at Clearwater, Madira Bickell State Archaeological Site, DeSoto National Memorial, Anclote Key State Preserve, Hillsborough River State Park, St. Petersburg Beach, Treasure Island, Braden Castle Ruins at Bradenton, Spongeorama Large Sponge Fisheries, and Madeira Beach.

INFORMATION: Ybor City State Museum, 1818 9th Avenue, Tampa, FL 33605. Telephone 813-247-6323. The museum is set at the corner of 9th Ave. and 19th St. in Tampa.

Yulee Sugar Mill Ruins State Historic Site

The Yulee Sugar Mill Ruins were once part of a thriving, 5,100-acre sugar plantation owned by David Levy Yulee. Yulee was a member of the Territorial Legislative Council and served in the US House of Representatives and US Senate after Florida attained statehood. The great plantation was operated for 13 years by more than 1,000 slaves and was a major supplier of sugar products for southern troops during the Civil War.

NEARBY ATTRACTIONS: Cedar Key State Museum, St. Clair Whitman Museum, Waccasassa Bay State Preserve/Cedar Key Scrub State Reserve, Manatee Springs State Park, Crystal River State Archaeological Site, Dade Battlefield State Historic Site, Withlacoochee State Forest, Lake Panasoffkee, Homosassa Springs State Wildlife Park, Silver Lake, Ft. Cooper, and Lower Suwannee National Wildlife Refuge.

INFORMATION: Yulee Sugar Mill Ruins State Historic Site, c/o Crystal River State Archaeological Site, 3400 N. Museum Point, Crystal River, FL 32629. Telephone 904-795-3817. The ruins are on SR 490, west of U.S Highway 19 in Homosassa.

The Central Region

Blue Spring State Park

This park is well known as a winter home for the endangered manatee, a large sea cow with big sad eyes and a gentle disposition. Manatees gather in the warm waters of the spring during the winter months, seeking refuge from the cold waters of St. Johns River.

It was in January of 1766, some three years after England acquired Florida from Spain, that a prominent English botanist named John Bartram explored St. Johns River and Blue Spring in search of resources that might be of value to his government.

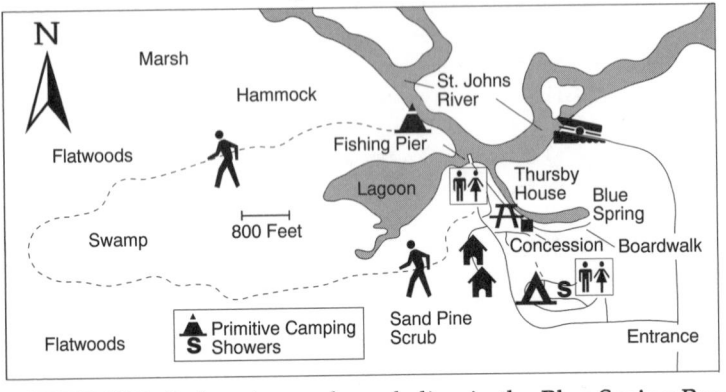

ACTIVITIES: Swimming and snorkeling in the Blue Spring Run, hiking, canoeing, boating and fishing. St. Johns River is known for its abundance of largemouth bass, shellcrackers, speckled perch, bluegill, and channel catfish. There's also plenty of opportunity for nature study, bird watching, photography, and picnicking.

Facilities include modern, full-service campsites, complete with water and electric hookups, restrooms, hot showers, picnic tables and grills; family vacation cabins with kitchens and bathrooms; a boat ramp and docks on St. Johns River; a picnic area; and a concession stand where you can buy gifts, camping supplies, food and drink, and rental canoes.

NEARBY ATTRACTIONS: Clearwater Lake, Bulow Plantation Ruins State Historic Site, Bulow Creek State Park, Ormond Beach, Tomoka State Park, Ravine State Gardens, Daytona Beach, Flagler Beach, Faver-Dykes State Park, Marineland of Florida, Gamble Rogers Memorial State Recreation Area, New Smyrna Sugar Mill Ruins State Historic Site, Fort Matanzas National Monument, Daytona International Speedway, Sugar Mill Gardens, Turtle Mound State Archaeological Site, De Leon Springs State Recreation Area, Canaveral National Seashore, New Smyrna Beach, Lake George, and Crescent Lake.

INFORMATION: Blue Springs State Park, 2100 West French Avenue, Orange City, FL 32763. Telephone 904-775-3663. The park is in Orange City, two miles west on French Avenue.

De Leon Springs
State Recreation Area

De Leon Springs is another of Florida's many state parks that focuses on a major natural spring system. At peak periods more than 19 million gallons of water gush daily into the spring, making it the centerpiece of an outstanding outdoor facility.

The area has a long and sometimes violent history. It was home to Native Americans as far back 8,000 B.C. By the early 1500s the

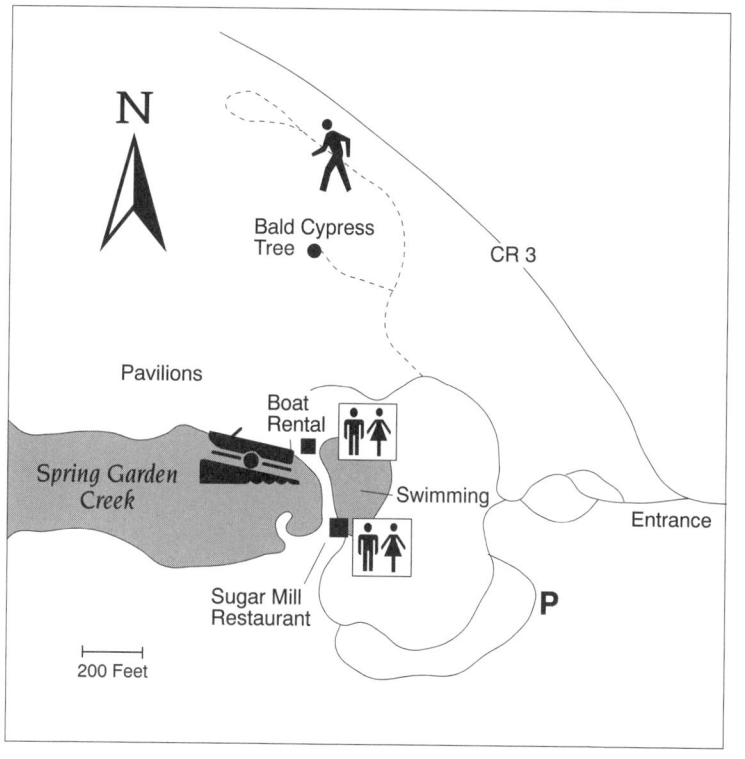

area belonged to Spain, then to the English in the mid-1700s. By 1783 it belonged once again to Spain. In 1832 American artist John James Audubon visited Spring Garden, a plantation owned by one Colonel Orlando Rees. The plantation was sacked during the Second Seminole War. During the Civil War it was an important supply center until Union troops eventually captured it and destroyed most of its facilities. In the late 19th century it became a winter tourist resort and in 1982 the State of Florida acquired the land and turned it into one of the state's finest recreation areas. Today, De Leon Springs is a place to get out into the open air and relax.

ACTIVITIES: Walking, swimming (the water remains steady at 72° year-round), canoeing (canoe rentals and other concessions are available), snorkeling, nature study, bird watching, and picnicking.

NEARBY ATTRACTIONS: New Smyrna Sugar Mill Ruins State Historic Site, Fort Matanzas National Monument, Daytona International Speedway, Sugar Mill Gardens, Turtle Mound State Archaeological Site, Canaveral National Seashore, New Smyrna Beach, Lake George, Crescent Lake, Clearwater Lake, Blue Springs State Park, Bulow Plantation Ruins State Historic Site, Bulow Creek State Park, Ormond Beach, Tomoka State Park, Ravine State Gardens, Daytona Beach, Flagler Beach, Faver-Dykes State Park, Marineland of Florida, and Gamble Rogers Memorial State Recreation Area.

INFORMATION: De Leon Springs State Recreation Area, PO Box 1338, De Leon Springs, FL 32130. Telephone 904-985-4212. The recreation area is in De Leon Springs, at the corner of Ponce De Leon and Burt Parks Road.

Highlands Hammock State Park

When Florida's Park Service was created in 1935 Highlands Hammock became one of its first areas of responsibility. Even before that, as far back as 1931, the 4,694-acre area of outstanding natural beauty had, through the efforts of concerned local citizens, been saved from being turned into farm land. By the time the Park Service took it over it had been open to the public for almost five years. Today, the dreams of the local citizens of the early 1930s have been respected and even expanded upon, to a point where their park has become not only a place where people can observe conservation at its best, but a natural refuge for many types of wildlife, including white-tailed deer, alligators, otters, bald eagles, the rare Florida panther, and many species of wild birds. This is one of Florida's 'Gems'.

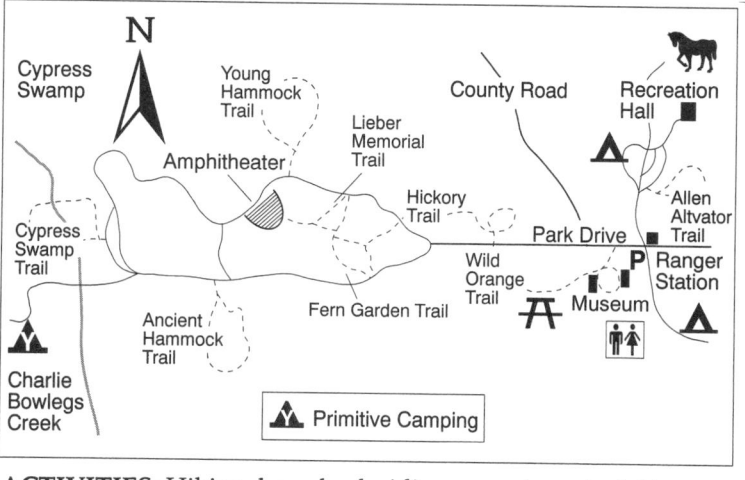

ACTIVITIES: Hiking, horseback riding, camping, picnicking, nature study, bird watching, and wildlife photography.

The Park Service also offers guided walks, campfire programs, and a ranger-led tram tour to the more remote areas of the park, where visitors often get the opportunity to observe the wildlife at its best.

Amenities at the park, many of them developed by the Civilian Conservation Corps, include modern, full-service campsites, complete with water and electric hookups, restrooms, hot showers, picnic tables and grills; facilities for youth camping; eight separate nature and hiking trails; a day-use horseback riding trail available to guests with their own horses; a paved loop trail for cyclists (bicycles are not allowed on the nature trails). Bicycles can be rented at the ranger station. There's also an interpretive center with exhibits that explain the park's wildlife, plant community, and history.

NEARBY ATTRACTIONS: Sebring, Sebring Race Track, Lake Istokpoga, Lake Okeechobee, Paynes Creek State Historic Site, Pioneer Park at Zolfo Springs, and Lake Arbuckle State Forest.

INFORMATION: Highlands Hammock State Park, 5931 Hammock Road, Sebring, FL 33872. Telephone 813-385-0011. The park is on SR 623, four miles west of Sebring.

Hontoon Island State Park

Hontoon Island is accessible only by private boat or passenger ferry. Before its purchase by the State of Florida in 1967 it had seen service as a home for the Timucuan Indians (their mounds can be viewed from the nature trail), a pioneer homestead, a cattle ranch, and a boatyard.

The island, bordered by St. Johns River and Huntoon Dead River, is one of Florida's lesser-known, though better appointed, state recreational areas. The park is a microcosm of Floridian habitats and wetlands, where the wildlife is as varied as the scenery. There are pine flatwoods, palm and oak hammocks, cypress swamps, marshes, river tributaries, even a lagoon. Hontoon Island is officially designated a 'Gem' by the state of Florida.

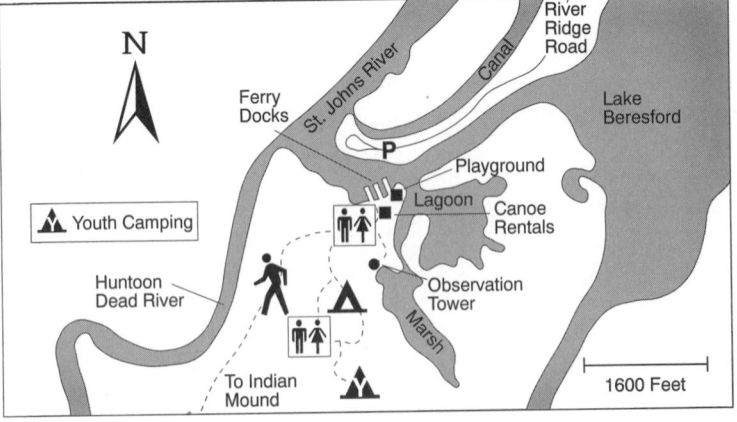

ACTIVITIES: Camping, canoeing (rentals are available), hiking, nature study and bird watching, picnicking, boating, and fishing for largemouth bass, bluegill, speckled perch, and channel catfish.

Facilities at the park include six rustic cabins set alonside a primitive camping site just a quarter-mile from the docks. There are also 48 boat camping slips, and youth camping. There's a self-guided hiking trail that provides visitors with a two-hour walk beginning at the ranger station and following Huntoon Dead River to a large Indian mound at the southwest corner of the park. An 80-foot-high observation tower set near the picnic area provides a breathtaking view over most of the island. And, of course, there's a picnic area for all the family to enjoy.

NEARBY ATTRACTIONS: Lake Louisa State Recreation Area, Mead Botanical Gardens in Orlando, Lake Griffin, Lake Harris, Lake Eustis, Lake Apopka, Walt Disney World in Orlando, Wikiwa Springs State Park, Rock Springs Run State Reserve, Dade Battlefield State Historic Site, Lake Griffin State Recreation Area, Fort Mellon Historic Site, Ben White Raceway in Orlando, Clearwater Lake, Ocala National Forest, the Early American Museum in Silver Springs, the Reptile Institute, also in Silver Springs, Silver Springs Wildwater, and Orlando.

INFORMATION: Hontoon Island State Park, 2390 River Ridge Road, Deland, FL 32720. Telephone 904-736-5309. The park is six miles west of Deland, off SR 44. It can be accessed only by private boat or by passenger ferry, which operates free of charge from 9 AM until one hour before sundown. A parking area is provided on the mainland.

Lake Kissimmee State Park

Lake Kissimmee State Park is some 40 miles as the crow flies south of Orlando in central Florida on the shores of Lakes Kissimmee, Tiger, and Rosalie. You will find no crowds, only the quiet sounds of the countryside. It's a fairly remote area, though extremely well served by the park's amenities. Here you can leave the rigors of city life behind and become one with nature. For the avid angler the three lakes offer some of the finest sport in Florida. Another of Florida's 'Gems' waiting to be discovered.

ACTIVITIES: Fishing, boating, canoeing, nature study and bird watching (the park is home to the white-tailed deer, the bald eagle, sandhill cranes, turkeys, and bobcats), wildlife photography, hiking (more than 13 miles of hiking trails), camping, and picnicking.

Facilities include 30 modern, full-service campsites, complete with water and electric hookups, restrooms, hot showers, picnic tables and grills; youth and primitive camping; more than 13 miles of nature and hiking trails, boat launching facilities, an interpretive center, picnic tables, and concessions.

In pioneer days, southern central Florida was cattle country. The interpretive center offers a living history demonstration of what life must have been like for the "cow hunters" in 1876.

NEARBY ATTRACTIONS: Lake Apopka, Walt Disney World in Orlando, Wikiwa Springs State Park, Fort Mellon Historic Site, Ben White Raceway in Orlando, Black Hills Passion Play at Lake Wells, Bok Tower Gardens, Cypress Gardens, Prairie Lakes State Preserve, Lake Arbuckle State Forest, Paynes Creek State Historic Site, Highlands Hammock State Park, Sebring Race Track, Lake Istokpoga, Lake Placid, the Baseball City Stadium at Baseball City, and Orlando.

INFORMATION: Lake Kissimmee State Park, 14248 Camp Mack Road, Lake Wales, FL 33853. Telephone 813-696-1112. The park is located of SR 60, 15 miles east of Lake Wales.

Lower Wekiva River
State Reserve

The 4,636-acre Lower Wekiva River State Reserve on St. Johns Creek, Blackwater Creek, and Wekiva River, maintains a wide variety of plant and wildlife communities. It's a place where lovers of nature and the great outdoors can go to find all sorts of rare and interesting species not readily found elsewhere. The unique feature of the reserve is the system of backwater creeks, streams, and wetlands which provide habitats for alligators, otters, wood storks, sandhill cranes, and even black bears.

ACTIVITIES: Horseback riding, hiking, canoeing, primitive camping, nature study, bird watching, and wildlife photography.

Facilities at the reserve are limited and, with the exception of some backpack camping, it is a day-use-only area.

NEARBY ATTRACTIONS: Hontoon Island State Park, Lake Louisa State Recreation Area, Mead Botanical Gardens in Orlando, Lake Griffin, Lake Harris, Lake Eustis, Lake Apopka, Walt Disney World in Orlando, Wikiwa Springs State Park, Rock Springs Run State Reserve, Dade Battlefield State Historic Site, Lake Griffin State Recreation Area, Fort Mellon Historic Site, Ben White Raceway at Orlando, Clearwater Lake, Ocala National Forest, the Early American Museum in Silver Springs, the Reptile Institute also in Silver Springs, Silver Springs Wildwater, and Orlando.

INFORMATION: Lower Wekiva River State Reserve, 8300 West SR 46, Sanford, FL 32771. Telephone 407-330-6725. The reserve is located nine miles west of Sanford on SR 46.

Paynes Creek State Historic Site

The Paynes Creek State Historic Site covers an area that, after the second Seminole Indian War, was important to the settlements of Central Florida, and over a period of many years saw a great deal of conflict.

Needing to establish a permanent presence and a communications center in the area, as well as encourage the Indians to stay away from white settlements, the US authorities built a trading post for the Indians. Consequently the Kennedy/Darling store was established in 1849 at the place now known as Paynes Creek on the northern boundary of the Indian reservation. In July of that year five Indians opened fire on the store killing two of the clerks, Dempsey Widdon and George S. Payne.

Plans were made to campaign against the Indians and Federal troops were sent to Florida to eradicate them from the area. Part of the plan involved erecting a chain of forts, 10 miles apart, that would stretch from Manatee River to Indian River. Work began on the construction of the first fort, Chokonikla, on October 26th 1849, just one half-mile north of the trading post.

Exhibits at the visitor center interpret the Seminole Indians, the trading post, and Fort Chokonikla, and events that occurred in the area during those turbulent times. The park offers picnic shelters and tables, fishing on the Peace River, and facilities for the handicapped.

NEARBY ATTRACTIONS: Lake Kissimmee State Park, Lake Apopka, Walt Disney World in Orlando, Wikiwa Springs State Park, Fort Mellon Historic Site, Ben White Raceway in Orlando, Black Hills Passion Play at Lake Wells, Bok Tower Gardens, Cypress gardens, Prairie Lakes State Preserve, Lake Arbuckle State Forest, Highlands Hammock State Park, Sebring Race Track, Lake Istokpoga, Lake Placid, the Baseball City Stadium at Baseball City, and Orlando.

INFORMATION: Paynes Creek State Historic Site, PO Box 547, Bowling Green FL 33834. Telephone 813-375-4717. The site is one mile east of Bowling Green on SR 664A.

Rock Springs Run State Reserve

More than 12 miles of river frontage, sand pine scrub, pine flatwoods, bayheads, and swamps on the Rock Springs Run State Reserve and Wekiva River provide a varied and diverse range of natural habitats and plant communities. The preserve is strictly managed to ensure the flow of visitors does nothing to endanger the fragile ecosystem.

ACTIVITIES: Primitive camping, youth camping, horseback riding, hiking, canoeing, and backpacking. Optimum capacities for each use have been established to avoid degradation of the environment. A permit is required for primitive camping.

From time to time, special deer hunts are organized by the Florida Game and Freshwater Fish Commission. For more information, contact the Park Service (tel. 904-383-3311).

NEARBY ATTRACTIONS: Lake Griffin, Lake Harris, Lake Eustis, Lake Apopka, Walt Disney World in Orlando, Wikiwa Springs State Park, Lake Griffin State Recreation Area, Dade Battlefield State Historic Site, Fort Mellon Historic Site, Ben White Raceway in Orlando, Lake Louisa State Recreation Area, Mead Botanical Gardens in Orlando, Clearwater Lake, Ocala National Forest, the Early American Museum in Silver Springs, the Reptile Institute, also in Silver Springs, Silver Springs Wildwater, Hontoon Island State Park, and Orlando.

INFORMATION: Rock Springs Runs State Reserve, Route 1, Box 365D, Sorrento, FL 32776. Telephone 904-383-3311. The reserve is in Sorrento, off SR 46 via SR 433.

Tenoroc State Recreation Area

Set in the midst of an extensive system of lakes northeast of Lakeland, Tenoroc State Recreation Area once was the site of a large and, many say, destructive phosphate mining operation. The site has since been reclaimed, repaired, and transformed into what is arguably one of Florida's finest outdoor recreation areas. The fishing is as good as can be found anywhere, with an abundance of bass, bluegill, and crappie.

ACTIVITIES: Primitive camping, horseback riding, nature study and bird watching, picnicking and hiking.

Facilities at the park include hiking and horseback riding trails, boat ramps, and a large picnic pavilion. Due to special boating regulations, it's best to check with the Park Service before launching your boat. The types of boat permitted on the water vary from lake to lake.

NEARBY ATTRACTIONS: Lake Kissimmee State Park, Lake Apopka, Walt Disney World in Orlando, Wikiwa Springs State Park, Fort Mellon Historic Site, Ben White Raceway in Orlando, Black Hills Passion Play at Lake Wells, Bok Tower Gardens, Cypress Gardens, Prairie Lakes State Preserve, Lake Arbuckle State Forest, Paynes Creek State Historic Site, Highlands Hammock

State Park, Sebring Race Track, Lake Istokpoga, Lake Placid, the Baseball City Stadium at Baseball City, and Orlando.

INFORMATION: Tenoroc State Recreation Area, 3829 Tenoroc Mine Road, Lakeland FL 33805. Telephone 813-499-2421. Tenoroc State Recreation Area is northeast of Lakeland on SR 659.

Tosohatchee State Reserve

The 28,000-acre Tosohatchee State Reserve is the result of thousands of years of natural cyclical action – winds, floods, and fire. The reserve is home to several dozen varied and unique plant communities, marshes, swamps, flatwoods, and hammocks. These provide habitats for the teeming wildlife, including many rare and endangered species.

The reserve borders some 19 miles of St. Johns River in east Orange County. The land was purchased in 1977 under the Environmentally Endangered Lands Program, in an effort to preserve the great natural beauty of the area and the extensive wetlands. The name, Tosohatchee, translates roughly from a Native American language as "fowl creek," the name for the creek which flows through the northern portion of the reserve.

The Tosohatchee marshes are a popular feeding ground for many species of wading shore birds and, during the winter months, a refuge for vast numbers of migrating waterfowl. The heavily forested uplands are home to a wide variety of wildlife, including the bobcat, gray fox, wild turkey, assorted hawks and owls, white-tailed deer, and many different species of songbirds. Of the endangered species that live within the reserve, the eastern indigo snake, Florida panther, gopher tortoise, and bald eagle are just a few.

ACTIVITIES: Hiking, primitive camping, horseback riding (sorry, there are no overnight facilities for horses), bicycling, fishing, nature study and bird watching, wildlife photography, and limited hunting by special permit from the Florida Game and Fresh Water Fish Commission.

NEARBY ATTRACTIONS: Lake Griffin State Recreation Area, Lake Griffin, Lake Harris, Merritt Island, Lake Eustis, Lake Apopka, Walt Disney World in Orlando, Wikiwa Springs State Park, Rock Springs Run State Reserve, Dade Battlefield State Historic Site, Fort Mellon Historic Site, Ben White Raceway in Orlando, Lake Louisa State Recreation Area, Mead Botanical Gardens in Orlando, Clearwater Lake, Ocala National Forest, the Early American Museum in Silver Springs, the Reptile Institute also in Silver Springs, Silver Springs Wildwater, Hontoon Island State Park, and Orlando.

INFORMATION: Tosohatchee State Reserve, 3365 Taylor Creek Road, Christmas, FL 32708. Telephone 407-568-5893. The reserve is on Taylor Creek Road in Christmas about 25 miles east of Orlando, off SR 50.

Wekiwa Springs State Park

Wakiwa Springs State Park is an area of wild and scenic beauty that, even today, resembles the central Florida that was home to the Timucuan Indians of long ago.

Wekiwa Springs is the headwater of Wekiwa River in an area full of lush, green vegetation: upland hammocks, wetlands, and longleaf pine forests. It's a place where you can observe nature in all its natural splendor. From the wet forests that border the creeks, to the dry, sandy pinelands, the area literally teems with plant and animal life.

The Wekiwa River flows eastward for a short distance where it is joined by Rock Springs Run. Together they flow 15 miles to meet St. Johns River to the northeast. The spring is formed by the rushing waters of underground streams flowing through limestone caverns beneath Florida's central ridge.

ACTIVITIES: Fishing for largemouth bass, bluegill, and redbreast sunfish (both in Wekiwa River and Rock Springs Run); canoeing (rental canoes are available); hiking, nature study and bird watching; wildlife photography; and picnicking.

The park offers modern, full-service campsites, complete with water and electric hookups, restrooms, hot showers, picnic tables and grills; facilities for youth camping and primitive camping, including cabins, a meeting hall, and a central dining facility. There are more than 13 miles of nature and hiking trails, and an eight-mile day-use horseback riding trail with facilities for trailer parking; picnic facilities, and concessions.

NEARBY ATTRACTIONS: Lake Griffin, Lake Harris, Lake Eustis, Lake Apopka, Walt Disney World in Orlando, Lake Griffin State Recreation Area, Rock Springs Run State Reserve, Dade Battlefield State Historic Site, Fort Mellon Historic Site, Ben White Raceway in Orlando, Lake Louisa State Recreation Area, Mead Botanical Gardens in Orlando, Clearwater Lake, Ocala National Forest, the Early American Museum in Silver Springs, the Reptile Institute also in Silver Springs, Silver Springs Wildwater, Hontoon Island State Park, and Orlando.

INFORMATION: Wekiwa Springs State Park, 1800 Wekiwa Circle, Apopka, FL 32712. Telephone 407-884-2009. The park is on Wekiwa Springs Road, off SR 434 or SR 436, near Apopka.

The Southeast

Fort Pierce Inlet State Recreation Area

The 340-acre recreation area is set on the north shore of Fort Pierce Inlet. It's an area that offers some of the best Atlantic beaches, with rolling sand dunes and coastal hammocks where you can spend lazy afternoons in the hot Florida sunshine. Fort Pierce is also one of those hard-to-find romantic spots where one can share quiet moments with someone special, or simply spend some time alone and contemplate the wonders of creation. At dawn the sun breaks over the horizon in a blaze of golden glory, turning the sea and sand into a glittering wonderland.

ACTIVITIES: Hiking and bicycling along the miles of beaches, fishing the surf, surfing, swimming, and picnicking.

The park offers youth camping and, for nature lovers, the nearby Jack Island on the Intracoastal Waterway is a bird watcher's heaven.

NEARBY ATTRACTIONS: Port St. Lucie, Stuart, Hobe Sound, Jupiter Lighthouse, John D. MacArthur Beach State Park, St. Lucie Lock and Dam, Vero Beach, Lake Okeechobee, St. Lucie Inlet State Preserve, the Elliott Museum, Hobe Sound National Wildlife Refuge, Blowing Rocks Reserve, Jonathan Dickinson State Park, and the Flagler Museum in Palm Beach.

INFORMATION: Fort Pierce Inlet State Recreation Area, 905 Shorewinds Drive, Fort Pierce, FL 34949. Telephone 407-468-3985. The recreation area is four miles east of Fort Pierce, via North Causeway.

Hugh Taylor Birch State Recreation Area

This 180-acre recreation area lies between the Atlantic Ocean and the Intracoastal Waterway, within the confines of bustling Ft. Lauderdale. It's a tropical wonderland with four distinct biological communities where live an abundance of wildlife indigenous to southern Florida. A 'Gem' of the Florida park system.

The park runs group and youth camping and can accommodate up to 72 people.

ACTIVITIES: Fishing, hiking, jogging along the 1.7-mile course that rims the park, swimming, picnicking, and canoeing (rental canoes are available).

NEARBY ATTRACTIONS: John U. Lloyd Beach State Recreation Area, Gulfstream Park, Singing Pines Museum, Arthur R. Marshall-Loxahatchee National Wildlife Refuge, Pompano Beach, Boca Raton, Royal Palm Beach, Boynton Beach, Lighthouse Point,

Ft. Lauderdale and its beaches, Miami, and the Florida Everglades.

INFORMATION: Hugh Taylor Birch State Recreation Area, 3109 East Sunrise Blvd., Ft. Lauderdale, FL 33304. Telephone 305-564-4521. The recreation area is on East Sunrise Boulevard in Ft. Lauderdale, off A1A.

John D. MacArthur Beach State Park

John D. MacArthur, probably one of Florida's finest state-owned recreation areas, is a barrier island in northern Palm Beach County, a tiny oasis of natural beauty on the great vacation strip. It's a small area set aside to preserve the natural heritage of the sub-tropical coastal habitat that once covered southeast Florida. It offers a tiny refuge far away from the over-crowded, over-commercialized vacation hot-spots.

The park encompasses some 225 acres of uplands, a unique mixture of maritime hammock and mangroves that surround Lake Worth Cove, and another 535 acres of submerged terrain. John D. MacArthur is one of the finest examples of a sub-tropical habitat to be found anywhere in the South. The park is home to a wide variety of plant and animal life, including herons, ibis, roseate spoonbills, osprey, fiddler crabs, pelicans, tern, and sandpipers. Plant life indigenous to the park includes sea lavender, cabbage palms, mastic trees, gumbo limbos, strangler figs, and beach star. MacArthur Beach is also a prime nesting area for sea turtles, and, especially during the months between May and August, one can see large num-

Hoping for a bite, John D. MacArthur

bers of loggerhead, green, and leatherback turtles. Interested visitors should inquire about ranger-led turtle-watching walks, usually offered in June and July. A nature center contains exhibits, displays, and a video interpreting the barrier island habitat, its rare and varied plant life, and its animal communities.

A 1,600-foot boardwalk spans Lake Worth Cove from the nature center to the Atlantic beaches, where the sea is almost always warm and the sand is soft and inviting.

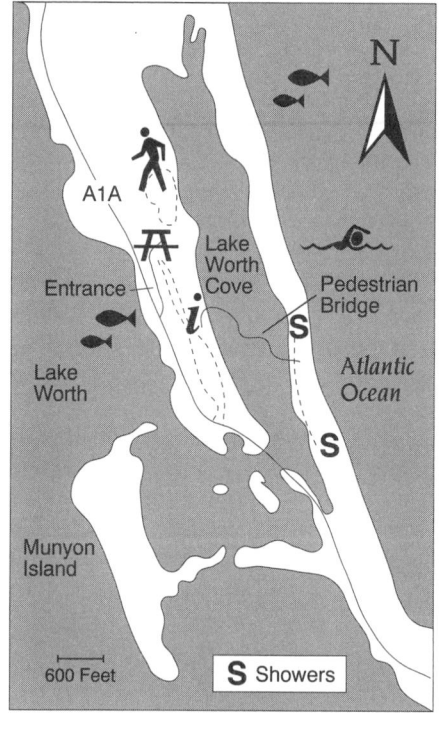

ACTIVITIES: Nature study and bird watching, wildlife photography, hiking along the beaches, surf fishing, swimming, picnicking, shell collecting, and snorkeling.

NEARBY ATTRACTIONS: Fort Pierce Inlet State Recreation Area, Port St. Lucie, Stuart, Hobe Sound, Jupiter Lighthouse, St. Lucie Lock and Dam, Vero Beach, Lake Okeechobee, St. Lucie Inlet State Preserve, the Elliott Museum, Hobe Sound National Wildlife Refuge, Blowing Rocks Reserve, Jonathan Dickinson State Park, and the Flagler Museum in Palm Beach.

The William T. Kirby Nature Center at John D. MacArthur Beach offers programs for adult and school groups as well as the general public on a wide variety of natural history subjects. The nature center is open from 9 AM until 5 PM Wednesday through Sunday.

INFORMATION: John D. MacArthur Beach State Park, 10900 SR 703 (A1A), North Palm Beach, FL 33408. Telephone 407-624-6950.

The park is about three miles south of the intersection of US 1 and PGA Boulevard on A1A.

John U. Lloyd Beach
State Recreation Area

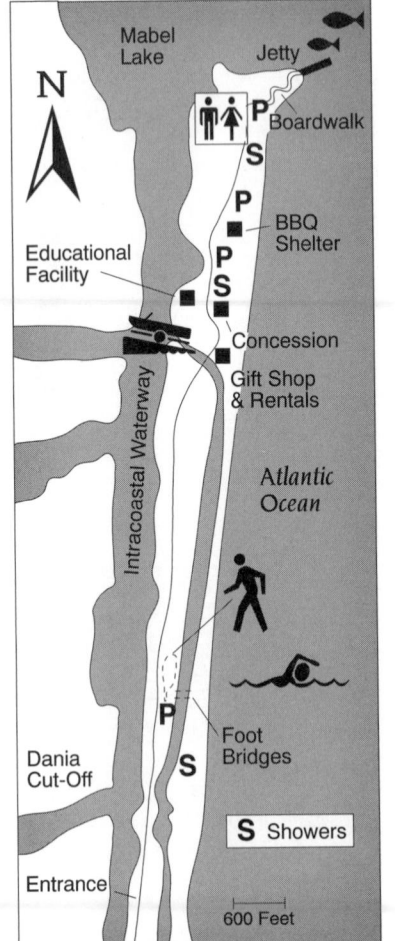

John U. Lloyd State Recreation Area is a 250-acre beachfront park on yet another of southern Florida's barrier islands off the Intracoastal Waterway. The park is a haven of natural habitats and vanishing resources. The Florida Park Service is waging a never-ending battle, not only to preserve what's left from previous use, but to restore the damaged areas to their once pristine condition. Lloyd Beach is one Broward County's most important sea turtle nesting areas. More than 10,000 hatchlings are produced on the beach each year, and there's an ongoing protection program to ensure that as many babies as possible survive.

On the west side of the park, along the Intracoastal Waterway, a manmade wetland is slowly, but surely, bringing back the red mangroves that were lost during the port expansion of 1989. These wetlands provide a natural nursery for all sorts of fish and other marine life. Another interesting area, a long strip of tidal waterway known as the New River Sound, is protected for the endangered manatee and other marine and animal life. The mangrove-lined sound is a place of wild and scenic beauty where you can take to the waters in a canoe and observe the surrounding wonders.

ACTIVITIES: Hiking, sunning on the beach, swimming, nature study and bird watching, wildlife photography and canoeing on the New River Sound, fishing either from the jetty or the beach.

Facilities at the park are extensive, but provide only for day-use activities. There is a paved, lighted jetty at the north end of the park which affords excellent fishing opportunities and is the perfect spot to watch the ships entering and departing Port Everglades. The park's broad sandy beaches provide hikers and joggers with opportunities for long and exhilarating walks. There are shaded picnic areas and a limited supply of picnic foods and supplies is available at the park concession stand, or at Coco's Cafe. The park also offers boat launching, fresh water showers at two locations on the beach, and rental canoes.

NEARBY ATTRACTIONS: Hugh Taylor Birch State Recreation Area, Gulfstream Park, Singing Pines Museum, Arthur R. Marshall-Loxahatchee National Wildlife Refuge, Pompano Beach, Boca Raton, Royal Palm Beach, Boynton Beach, Lighthouse Point, Ft. Lauderdale and its beaches, Miami, and the Everglades.

INFORMATION: John U. Lloyd Beach State Recreation Area, 6503 North Ocean Drive, Dania, FL 33004. Telephone 305-923-2833. The recreation area is in Dania, off A1A.

Jonathan Dickinson State Park

Covering more than 11,000 acres, Jonathan Dickinson is one of the largest parks in south Florida. It's a vast natural area with a great many distinct plant and wildlife communities. Almost 20% of the entire park is covered in coastal pine scrub, a biological community so rare it has been officially designated as "globally imperiled" by the state.

The Loxahatchee River, now one of the nation's "Wild and Scenic Rivers," winds its way through the park beneath a great green canopy of lush vegetation, offering a unique and truly remarkable natural world. The park's dunes, coastal hammock, mangroves, and the rich environment of the Loxahatchee riverbank, provide rare opportunities to observe endangered animals such as the gopher tortoise, bald eagle, scrub jay, and Florida sandhill crane.

ACTIVITIES: Fishing the Loxahatchee, canoeing, boating, hiking, horseback riding, nature study and bird watching, wildlife photography, bicycling, and picnicking.

Facilities at the park are extensive and include modern, full-service campsites, complete with water and electric hookups, restrooms, hot showers, picnic tables and grills, and facilities for primitive camping. There are many miles of nature and hiking trails, and day-use horseback riding trails with facilities for trailer parking. Several hiking trails through the endangered scrublands are accessible either from the parking lot at the entrance station, or from Hobe Mountain. There's an interpretive center, where visitors can join one of the ranger-led tours of the park, or a boat ride along the Loxahatchee River onboard the *Loxahatchee Queen*. There are two main campsites, boat launching facilities, picnic areas, and rental cabins available at the concession facility. Canoe and row boat rentals are also offered.

NEARBY ATTRACTIONS: Port St. Lucie, Stuart, Hobe Sound, Jupiter Lighthouse, John D. MacArthur Beach State Park, St. Lucie Lock and Dam, Vero Beach, Lake Okeechobee, St. Lucie Inlet State Preserve, the Elliott Museum, Hobe Sound National Wildlife Refuge, Blowing Rocks Reserve, Fort Pierce Inlet State Recreation Area, and the Flagler Museum in Palm Beach.

INFORMATION: Jonathan Dickinson State Park, 16450 S.E. Federal Highway, Hobe Sound, FL 33455. Telephone 407-546-2771. The park is located 12 miles south of Stuart on US 1.

Sebastian Inlet State Recreation Area

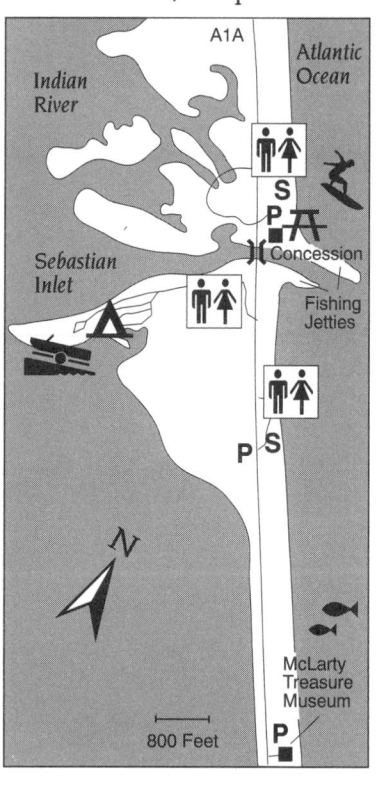

If you are a saltwater angler, then you'll find no finer location for your sport than the Sebastian Inlet State Recreation Area. But, more than that, the park is a veritable time machine waiting to transport you back to the days when Spanish treasure fleets turned eastward toward Europe and their home port of Cadiz. It was close to the Sebastian Inlet, in 1715, that a hurricane caused the wreck of an entire fleet of galleons returning to Spain from Mexico and Peru. The survivors of the catastrophe swam ashore and made camp some 1.5 miles south of the inlet. Today, on the site of the survivors' camp, the McLarty Treasure Museum houses a wealth of exhibits that tell the story of the shipwreck, the early attempts to salvage the treasure, and many artifacts and valuable objects recovered during later expeditions. The museum also features a slide show presenting the natural and cultural history of the area in great detail.

The park itself is on one of the many barrier islands that protect Florida's southeastern shoreline from the ravages of nature. It's a complex world of sandy beaches, dunes, coastal hammocks, bordered mangroves and forests that provides, not only important habitats for the wildlife community, but one of Florida's finest recreational facilities.

The Sebastian Inlet itself and the surrounding Atlantic waters provide some of the finest saltwater fishing, shrimping, and clamming in the state. There are two Atlantic jetties, catwalks under the Inlet bridge, more than three miles of beaches, and the Indian River giving access to an abundance of snook, redfish, bluefish, and Spanish mackerel.

ACTIVITIES: Swimming, snorkeling and scuba diving, hiking the miles of sandy beaches, sunning, bird watching and nature study (the park offers a rare opportunity to observe the osprey, many species of shore and wading birds, sea turtles, and, at times, the manatee), camping, and boating. The Sebastian Inlet is regarded as one of the finest surfing sites on the entire Atlantic coast, hosting several national surfing tournaments each year. Of special interest, during the months of June and July, are the night-time, ranger-led expeditions in search of nesting loggerhead turtles. If you want to join such an excursion you will need to contact the ranger station and make a reservation.

Facilities at the park include 51 modern, full-service campsites, complete with water and electric hookups, and restrooms. There's a boat ramp and dock, a picnic area, several sites with public restrooms and fresh water showers, plus parking facilities. A concession facility offers breakfast and lunch daily along with a variety of camping and fishing supplies, beach chairs, and rental fishing equipment.

NEARBY ATTRACTIONS: Lake Griffin State Recreation Area, Lake Griffin, Lake Harris, Merritt Island, Lake Eustis, Lake Apopka, Walt Disney World in Orlando, Wikiwa Springs State Park, Rock Springs Run State Reserve, Dade Battlefield State Historic Site, Fort Mellon Historic Site, Ben White Raceway in Orlando, Lake Louisa State Recreation Area, Mead Botanical Gardens in Orlando, Clearwater Lake, Ocala National Forest, the Early American Museum in Silver Springs, the Reptile Institute, also in Silver Springs, Silver Springs Wildwater, Hontoon Island State Park, Port St. Lucie, Stuart, Hobe Sound, Jupiter Lighthouse, John D. MacArther Beach State Park, St. Lucie Lock and Dam, Vero Beach, Lake Okeechobee, St. Lucie Inlet State Preserve, the Elliott Museum, Hobe Sound National Wildlife Refuge, and the Blowing Rocks Reserve. The entire area surrounding Sebastian

Inlet offers unlimited adventures. To name them all would be impossible, but the above list will give you with lots of ideas.

INFORMATION: Sebastian Inlet State Recreation Area, 9700 South A1A, Melbourne, FL 32951. Telephone 407-984-4852. The recreation area is on A1A in Melbourn Beach.

St. Lucie Inlet State Preserve

St. Lucie Inlet State Preserve is on yet another of southwest Florida's protective barrier islands; an island that provides an idyllic setting for one of those once-in-a-lifetime outdoor experiences so unique to the Sunshine State. Although the island is accessible only by private watercraft, a fact that makes the preserve a somewhat isolated and exclusive get-away, the park is well worth a visit.

St. Lucie Inlet is an important nature preserve, providing habitats for a variety of plant and marine wildlife, including the loggerhead, green, and leatherback turtle. A 3,300-foot boardwalk takes you on an extended tour through mangrove forests, hammocks of live oaks, cabbage palms, paradise trees, wild limes, cocoa plums, and ferns, leading down to miles of secluded beach. The preserve's unique situation and abundance of wildlife make it a paradise for naturalists and wildlife photographers.

ACTIVITIES: Fishing for snook, redfish, bluefish, and Spanish mackerel. Because of its inaccessibility, the preserve is a popular place to spend a romantic afternoon with a picnic basket, walking the miles of quiet, secluded beach, swimming, sunning, or snorkeling and scuba diving.

Facilities at the park are limited to day-use only.

NEARBY ATTRACTIONS: Fort Pierce Inlet State Recreation Area, Port St. Lucie, Stuart, Hobe Sound, Jupiter Lighthouse, John D. MacArther Beach State Park, St. Lucie Lock and Dam, Vero Beach, Lake Okeechobee, the Elliott Museum, Hobe Sound National Wildlife Refuge, Blowing Rocks Reserve, Jonathan Dickinson State Park, and the Flagler Museum in Palm Beach.

INFORMATION: St. Lucie Inlet State Preserve, c/o Jonathan Dickinson State Park, 16450 S.E. Federal Highway, Hobe Sound, FL 33455. Telephone 407-744-7603. The preserve is in Port Salerno on the Intracoastal Waterway, two thirds of a mile south of the inlet.

The Southwest

Cayo Costa State Park

Cayo Costa State Park is on one of a chain of barrier islands just a few miles northwest of Cape Coral. The islands themselves are important in that they are the first line of defense against the storms that otherwise would batter Charlotte Harbor and Pine Island.

Mangrove shoreline at Cayo Costa State Park

Although the island is accessible only by private boat or passenger ferry, Cayo Costa, and all it has to offer, presents the visitor with a stunning mixture of nature preserve and vacation destination. The natural features of the island include pine forests, oak palm hammocks, mangrove swamps, and mile after mile of pristine beach. It's a romantic spot where one might enjoy an evening on the beach with a well-filled picnic basket, a little good company, and watch the setting sun turn the western sky and the deep green emerald sea into a spectacular symphony of gold and silver.

ACTIVITIES: Fishing, boating, swimming, sunning, nature study and bird watching, wildlife photography, camping, hiking the sandy beach, and, during the winter months, shelling.

Facilities at the park include rental cabins, a picnic area and primitive camping.

NEARBY ATTRACTIONS: Myakka River State Park, the Crowley Museum and Nature Center, Sarasota Jungle Gardens, Warm Springs, the National Police Museum in North Port, Ponce De Leon Historic Park and Shrine, Gasparilla Island at Boca Grande, Cape Haze Aquatic Preserve, Boca Grande Lighthouse, Fort Myers, Lover's Key State Recreation Area, Everglades Wonder Gardens in Bonita Springs, Sanibel Lighthouse on Sanibel Island, Port Charlotte Beach near Englewood, Delnor-Wiggins Pass State Recreation Area, the Circus Winter Quarters at Venice, Don Pedro Island State Recreation Area, Collier-Seminole State Park and Fakahatchee Strand State Preserve (both south of Naples), and the Thomas Edison Home at Fort Myers.

INFORMATION: Cayo Costa State Park, PO Box 1150, Boca Grande, FL 33921. Telephone 813-964-0375. The park is located directly south of Boca Grande, and is accessible only by private boat or passenger ferry.

Collier Seminole State Park

Located on the fringe of the Florida Everglades, Collier-Seminole State Park offers visitors a rare glimpse of how the region must have looked before the arrival of the first European explorers. The 6,400-acre park features a vast hinterland of vegetation and wildlife so typical of the Everglades.

It was during the early 1940s that Barron Collier, a wealthy entrepreneur and property developer, decided to give something back to the state. He purchased the land, designed the park, and, in 1947, turned it over to the State of Florida.

Most of the park is dominated by a dense system of swamplands: mangroves, salt marshes, and cypress swamps, along with pine flatwoods and the rare Florida royal palm. One rather special feature is a tropical hammock of trees characteristic of the Yucatán and the West Indies. As one might imagine, such a lush tropical environment is home to a plethora of wildlife, including several of the state's threatened and endangered species. The brown pelican calls the park home, as does the wood stork, the bald eagle, the red-cockaded woodpecker, the American crocodile, the Florida black bear, and the mangrove fox squirrel. Sometimes, with a great deal of patience, it's possible to observe two of Florida's official state species: the rare Florida panther, and the official state marine mammal – the West Indian manatee. Another gem waiting for you to discover it.

ACTIVITIES: Fishing, canoeing the Blackwater River and the Ten Thousand Islands of the Gulf of Mexico, hiking the 6.5-mile trail through pine flatwoods and cypress swamps, walking the nature trail and boardwalk system, nature study and bird watching, wildlife photography, picnicking, and camping.

NEARBY ATTRACTIONS: Cayo Costa State Park, Myakka River State Park, the Crowley Museum and Nature Center, Sarasota Jungle Gardens, Warm Springs, the National Police Museum in North Port, Ponce De Leon Historic Park and Shrine, Gasparilla Island at Boca Grande, Cape Haze Aquatic Preserve, Boca Grande Lighthouse, Fort Myers, Lover's Key State Recreation Area, Everglades Wonder Gardens at Bonita Springs, Sanibel Lighthouse, Port Charlotte Beach near Englewood, the Circus Winter Quarters in Venice, Fakahatchee Strand State Preserve south of Naples, the Thomas Edison Home in Fort Myers, Rookery Bay National Estuarine Sanctuary, the African Safari at Caribbean Gardens close to Naples, and Delnor-Wiggins Pass State Recreation Area near Bonita Springs.

Facilities at the park are extensive and include 19 tent camping sites and 111 modern, full-service campsites on two sites. The full-service sites are complete with water and electric hookups, and restrooms. There's an interpretive center, an observation platform overlooking the salt marsh, a campfire circle, a boat ramp and a dock, a picnic area, public restrooms, parking facilities, and a concession facility where one can purchase a variety of snacks, drinks, and camping and fishing supplies. Canoe rentals are available, too.

INFORMATION: Collier-Seminole State Park, Route 4, Box 848, Naples, FL 33961. Telephone 813-394-3397. The park is located 17 miles south of Naples on US 41.

Delnor-Wiggins Pass
State Recreation Area

Delnor-Wiggins Pass is one of Florida's most popular recreation areas. Located on a barrier, separated from the mainland by tidal creeks and mangrove swamps, the natural coastal area of the park provides habitats for marine and bird life, featuring sea oats, sea grapes, and cabbage palms. A pass at the north end of the island provides a natural outlet for the Cocohatchee River. The backwaters of the park, occupying more than 80% of its area, and covered with lush green vegetation, provide a well protected refuge and a major source of nutrition for the abundance of marine animals that begin life here before heading out into the deep green waters of the Gulf of Mexico.

Naturalists and visitors to the park find the natural coastal system of parkland area and the shallow waters of the Gulf provide a home to wading birds, small mammals and reptiles, and to countless forms of marine life: soft corals, mollusks, crustaceans, fish, sea turtles, and, during the winter months, even the endangered West Indian manatee.

ACTIVITIES: Fishing, swimming, shelling, sunning, nature study and bird watching, wildlife photography, and hiking along the golden beach.

Although Delnor-Wiggins Pass is a day-use park, the facilities provided by the Park Service are extensive, and include five parking lots with a system of boardwalks, each allowing easy access to the beaches; several picnic sites with tables, grills, bicycle racks, and public telephones; public bathhouses with changing stalls and fresh water showers; and an observation tower. There's also a boat ramp for those wishing to explore Cocohatchee River and the Gulf of Mexico.

NEARBY ATTRACTIONS: Cayo Costa State Park, Don Pedro Island State Recreation Area, Myakka River State Park, the Crowley Museum and Nature Center, Sarasota Jungle Gardens, Warm Springs, the National Police Museum in North Port, Ponce De Leon Historic Park and Shrine, Gasparilla Island at Boca Grande, Cape Haze Aquatic Preserve, Boca Grande Lighthouse, Fort Myers, Lover's Key State Recreation Area, Everglades Wonder Gardens in Bonita Springs, Sanibel Lighthouse, Port Charlotte Beach near Englewood, the Circus Winter Quarters in Venice, Collier-Seminole State Park and Fakahatchee Strand State Preserve (both south of Naples), and the Thomas Edison Home at Fort Myers.

INFORMATION: Delnor-Wiggins State Recreation Area, 11100 Gulf Shore Drive North, Naples, FL 33963. Telephone 813-597-6196. The recreation area is six miles south of Bonita Springs, off CR 901.

Don Pedro Island
State Recreation Area

Don Pedro Island State Recreation Area lies on one of an extensive chain of barrier islands off the Gulf coast between Knight Island and Little Gasparilla Island. The day-use-only park is accessible only by private boat or the ferry operating from nearby Placida. The natural features of the park include sand dunes covered with protected sea oats, mangroves on the bay side of the island, and a wide, white sandy beach.

ACTIVITIES: Sunbathing and shelling along the mile-long park beach, surf fishing in the Gulf of Mexico, and swimming. Although facilities are fairly sparse, there are restrooms, boat docks for use by visitors and for fishing, and a picnic pavilion with tables and grills.

NEARBY ATTRACTIONS: Cayo Costa State Park, Myakka River State Park, Crowley Museum and Nature Center, Sarasota Jungle Gardens, Warm Springs, the National Police Museum in North Port, Ponce De Leon Historic Park and Shrine, Gasparilla Island at Boca Grande, Cape Haze Aquatic Preserve, Boca Grande Lighthouse, Fort Myers, Lover's Key State Recreation Area, Everglades Wonder Gardens in Bonita Springs, Sanibel Lighthouse, Port Charlotte Beach near Englewood, Delnor-Wiggins Pass State Recreation Area, the Circus Winter Quarters in Venice, Collier-Seminole State Park and Fakahatchee Strand State Preserve (both south of Naples), and the Thomas Edison Home in Fort Myers.

INFORMATION: Don Pedro Island State Recreation Area, c/o Cayo Costa State Park, PO Box 1150, Boca Grande, FL 33921. Telephone 813-964-0375. The park is located south of Placida and is accessible only by boat.

Fakahatchee Strand
State Preserve

Fakahatchee Strand State Preserve lies at the western edge of the vast Big Cypress Swamp National Preserve. The Big Cypress is a seemingly boundless, gently sloping limestone plain where, during the rainy season (June through September), the water flows slowly over the plain, southward through the mangrove swamps to the Gulf of Mexico.

In many places the flow of water has cut channels into the soft limestone which, over the countless years, have gathered deep tracts of fertile organic soil. The channels, which form long, narrow, densely populated swamp forests of cypress and mangrove, are known locally as "strands."

One such strand is the Fakahatchee Strand State Preserve; more than 20 miles long and varying in width from three to five miles. It is the largest and most unusual of the strands, and the major drainage channel of the southwestern section of Big Cypress Swamp. Over the years Big Cypress has suffered from the ravages of human exploitation – logging and land drainage – but even so, has still managed to survive and even thrive. The great stands of bald cypress, royal palms and epiphytic orchids, along with many other species of rare and wonderful plants, make the Fakahatchee Strand State Preserve unique in the Florida Park System.

ACTIVITIES: Nature study, bird watching and wildlife photography. A 2,000-foot-long boardwalk which meanders through the virgin cypress swamps offers the visitor a unique opportunity to observe nature at its very best.

NEARBY ATTRACTIONS: Miccosukee Tribal Headquarters near Pinecrest, Collier-Seminole State Park, Rookery Bay Natural Estuarine Sanctuary near Belle Meade, the African Safari at Caribbean Gardens, Naples, and, of course, Everglades National Park (there's a visitor center at Everglades City, close to Fakahatchee Strand State Preserve).

INFORMATION: Fakahatchee Strand State Preserve, PO Box 548, Copeland, FL 33926. Telephone 813-695-4593. The preserve headquarters are on Janes Memorial Scenic Drive, just west of Copeland on SR 29.

Gamble Plantation
State Historic Site

The Gamble mansion was the home of Major Robert Gamble and the nucleus of an extensive sugar plantation covering more than 3,500 acres. The mansion is the only surviving plantation house in southern Florida.

The mansion and the Judah P. Benjamin Confederate Memorial are a testament to the southern way of life, the economic system, and to south-

The Gamble Mansion

ern Florida as it was before the Civil War. Judah P. Benjamin was the Confederate Secretary of State. He was forced to take refuge at the Gamble Plantation when the Confederacy collapsed, and it was there that he awaited safe passage to England.

In 1925 the mansion and 16 acres were saved by the United Daughters of the Confederacy and donated to the State of Florida. The mansion and gardens have been renovated, refurnished and returned to a semblance of the glory they once enjoyed in the mid-19th century. The site is open Monday through Thursday, from 9 AM until 5 PM.

NEARBY ATTRACTIONS: Anclote Key State Preserve, Caladesi Island State Park, Honeymoon Island State Recreation Area, St. Petersburg Beach, Treasure Island, Little Manatee River State Recreation Area, Braden Castle Ruins in Bradenton, Spongeorama Large Sponge Fisheries, Madeira Beach, Indian Rocks Beach and Captain Nemo's Pirate Cruise, The Marina and the Marine Science Center, all in Clearwater.

INFORMATION: Gamble Plantation State Historic Site, 3708 Patten Avenue, Ellenton, FL 34222. Telephone 813-723-4536. The Gamble Plantation State Historic Site is in Ellenton on US 301 E.

Gasparilla Island Recreation Area

Situated on one of the great chains of barrier islands on the Gulf Coast, Gasparilla Island is a romantic place where legends of pirate treasure and beautiful captives are rife. The island, according to those legends, was named after the infamous pirate Captain José Gaspar, who settled here in the 1700s with his band of roughnecks. For years the pirates used the island as a base for raids on the mainland until, after a concerted effort by the United States, they were driven from the waters of the Gulf of Mexico.

Today the park is a refuge, not for corsairs, but for the people with a will to escape to the quiet beaches and the deep green waters of the Gulf. It's a place for sunbathing, swimming, fishing, gathering shells, and generally taking things easy.

NEARBY ATTRACTIONS: Cayo Costa State Park, Myakka River State Park, Crowley Museum and Nature Center, Sarasota Jungle Gardens, Warm Springs, the National Police Museum at North Port, Ponce De Leon Historic Park and Shrine, Cape Haze Aquatic Preserve, Boca Grande Lighthouse, Fort Myers, Lover's Key State Recreation Area, the Everglades Wonder Gardens at Bonita Springs, Sanibel Lighthouse on Sanibel Island, Port Charlotte Beach near Englewood, Delnor-Wiggins Pass State Recreation Area, the Circus Winter Quarters in Venice, Don Pedro Island State Recreation Area, Collier-Seminole State Park south of Naples, Fakahatchee Strand State Preserve, also south of Naples, and the Thomas Edison Home in Fort Myers.

INFORMATION: Gasparilla Island State Recreation Area, c/o Barrier Islands GEOpark, PO Box 1150, Boca Grande, FL 33921. Telephone 813-964-0375. This recreation area is located south of Boca Grande. It is accessible via the Boca Grande Causeway (private toll) at CR 775 and Placida.

Koreshan State Historic Site

Koreshan preserves the remains of a somewhat bizarre settlement on the banks of Estero River. It was in 1869 that a New York-born doctor by the name of Cyrus Teed claimed to have received a "divine illumination," a vision of all spiritual life as revealed to Teed by a deity. Teed began to preach his new religion, Koresh, and eventually, with a group of dedicated followers, moved southward from Chicago to establish his "New Jerusalem" in Estero. For a while the new religion seemed to flourish but, after Teed died in 1908 at the age of 69, the membership of the group began to decline until, in 1961, the four remaining members of the group deeded the 305 acres of their land to the State of Florida in Teed's memory.

ACTIVITIES: There's a hiking trail, a campfire circle, a boat ramp, a picnic area, public restrooms, and parking facilities. Canoe rentals are available and the Park Service offers guided walks and a series of campfire programs according to seasonal demand. Facilities at the site are quite extensive, and include 60 modern, full-service campsites on a well-protected site, complete with water, electric hookups, and restrooms.

Popular activities at the park include fishing, canoeing, camping picnicking, hiking, boating, nature study and bird watching, and photography.

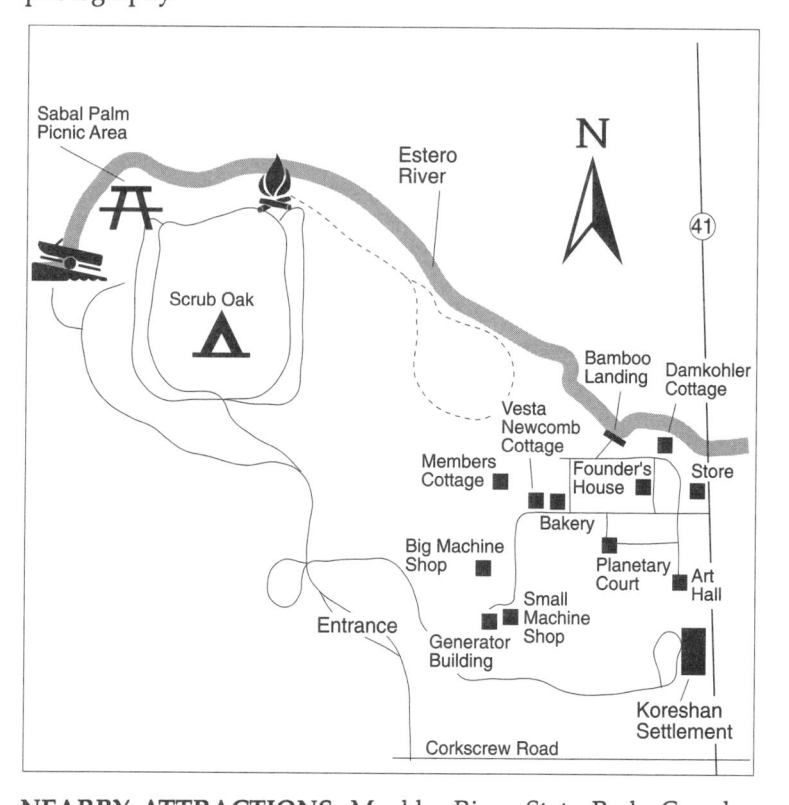

NEARBY ATTRACTIONS: Myakka River State Park, Crowley Museum and Nature Center, Sarasota Jungle Gardens, Warm Springs, the National Police Museum at North Port, Ponce De Leon Historic Park and Shrine, Gasparilla Island at Boca Grande, Cape Haze Aquatic Preserve, Boca Grande Lighthouse, Fort Myers, Lover's Key State Recreation Area, the Everglades Wonder Gardens in Bonita Springs, Sanibel Lighthouse on Sanibel Island, Port Charlotte Beach near Englewood, Delnor-Wiggins Pass State Recreation Area, the Circus Winter Quarters in Venice, Cayo Costa State Park, Don Pedro Island State Recreation Area, Collier-Seminole State Park and Fakahatchee Strand State Preserve (both south of Naples), and the Thomas Edison Home in Fort Myers.

INFORMATION: Koreshan State Historic Site, PO Box 7, Estero, FL 33928. Telephone 813-992-0311. The historic site is on US 41 at Corkscrew Road.

Lake Manatee
State Recreation Area

Lake Manatee is a 556-acre recreation area that extends for more than three miles along the south shore of Lake Manatee, a large reservoir providing water for Manatee and Sarasota counties. The park, a land of pine flatwoods, sand pine scrubs, marshes and hammock, provides a natural habitat for a variety of animal and plant life. It's a quiet area and somewhat remote. It's also a place to spend a few days in the great outdoors, camping, fishing, swimming, boating, canoeing, and picnicking. This area has earned the 'Gem' designation from the state of Florida.

ACTIVITIES: There's a hiking trail, a campfire circle, a boat ramp, a picnic area, public restrooms, and parking facilities. Private boats are permitted, but are limited to less than 20 horsepower. Water-skiing is not allowed. Facilities at the park include modern, full-service campsites on a well-protected site complete with water, electric hookups, and restrooms.

NEARBY ATTRACTIONS: Braden Castle Ruins in Bradenton, The Spongeorama Large Sponge Fisheries, Madeira Beach, Indian Rocks Beach, Gamble Plantation State Historic Site, Anclote Key State Preserve, Caladesi Island State Park, Honeymoon Island State Recreation Area, St. Petersburg Beach, Treasure Island, Little Manatee River State Recreation Area, and the Marine Science Center, Captain Nemo's Pirate Cruise and The Marina (all in Clearwater).

INFORMATION: Lake Manatee State Recreation Area, 20007 SR 64, Bradenton, FL 34202. Telephone 813-741-3028. The recreation area is located 15 miles east of Bradenton on SR 64.

Lovers Key
State Recreation Area

Lovers Key is a quiet, romantic backwater where it sometimes seems as if time stands still. The park comprises parts of Black Island, Lovers Key, and Inner Key. It's a 434-acre hinterland of canals and tidal lagoons, bordered by mangroves, which supports an almost infinite variety of fish and marine animals.

The remains of the maritime hammock on Black Island provides a home to several species of woodpeckers, owls, hawks, and songbirds. It's a popular nesting ground for the osprey, as well as a refuge for the wild marsh rabbit, the raccoon, and the squirrel. In the lagoons it's often possible to observe roseate spoonbills and reddish egrets feeding. Offshore, you can admire the visiting bottle-nosed dolphins playing in the sunshine, and perhaps the endangered West Indian manatee closer in, in the shallows.

ACTIVITIES: For recreation, Lovers Key is hard to beat. Some of the best onshore and offshore fishing grounds are on and around the park. Trout, redfish, snook, and tarpon are caught according to the season. Castnetting for mullet, too, is an activity unique to this somewhat out-of-the-way park. Other popular passtimes here include hiking, shelling and canoeing. Swimming, however, is not recommended because of the strong currents.

NEARBY ATTRACTIONS: Don Pedro Island State Recreation Area, Collier-Seminole State Park south of Naples, Fakahatchee Strand State Preserve, also south of Naples, Myakka River State Park, Crowley Museum and Nature Center, Sarasota Jungle Gardens, Warm Springs, the National Police Museum at North Port, Ponce De Leon Historic Park and Shrine, Gasparilla Island in Boca Grande, Cape Haze Aquatic Preserve, Boca Grande Lighthouse, Fort Myers, Cayo Costa State Park, the Everglades Wonder Gardens in Bonita Springs, Sanibel Lighthouse on Sanibel Island, Port Charlotte Beach near Englewood, the Delnor-Wiggins Pass State Recreation Area, the Circus Winter Quarters in Venice, and the Thomas Edison Home in Fort Myers.

INFORMATION: Lovers Key State Recreation Area, c/o Delnor-Wiggins Pass State Recreation Area, 11100 Gulf Shore Drive

North, Naples, FL 33963. Telephone 813-597-6196. Lovers Key
State Recreation Area is on CR 865 between Fort Myers Beach and
Bonita Beach in Lee County.

Myakka River State Park

Myakka River is one of the largest parks in the Florida system,
covering an area of 28,875 acres. It is a vast, diverse world of wild
and scenic beauty with an abundance of natural plant communities, lakes, river marshes, hammocks, and prairies.

The Myakka River flows for more than 12 miles through the park
on its journey to the Gulf of Mexico. The main road winds
through oak and palm hammocks, opening views across grassy
mashes, sloughs, and Upper Myakka Lake, where deer, raccoon,
and many species of wild birds can observed, either from the
park drive, or from the wooden bird walk.

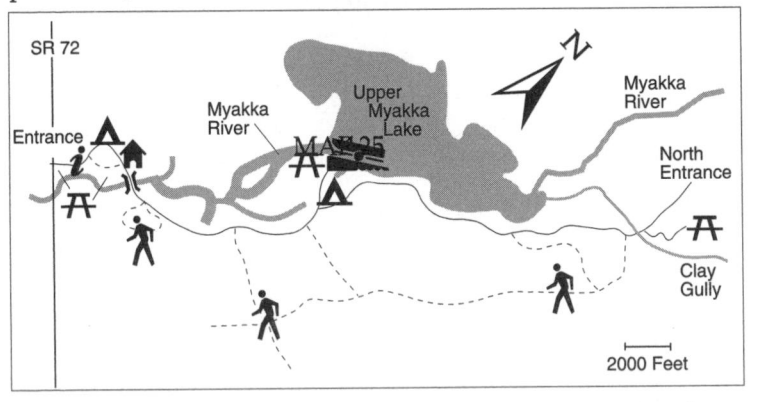

Beyond the paved drive, across the large, open expanses of pine
flatwoods, prairies, and wetlands, cottontails, red-shouldered
hawks, deer, and bobcats, can be seen at home in their natural
environment. The Myakka River, truly, is a naturalist's paradise.

For the vacationer, the facilities are varied and extensive, ranging
from full-service campsites and tenting campsites, to rustic rental
cabins furnished with two beds and a sofa-bed. There's a boat
basin and dock on Upper Myakka Lake where rental canoes and

boat launching facilities are offered. There's also a concession facility on the lake where one can rent boats and bicycles, or purchase camping, picnicking, and fishing supplies, along with snacks, soft drinks, and souvenirs.

ACTIVITIES: Backpacking the many miles of trail through the hammock, prairies, and pine flatwoods; horseback riding along 15 miles of bridleways available to visitors with their own horses; fishing the Myakka River and Upper Myakka Lake for bass, bream, and catfish; canoeing; and nature study, bird watching, and wildlife photography.

NEARBY ATTRACTIONS: Crowley Museum and Nature Center, Cayo Costa State Park, Sarasota Jungle Gardens, Warm Springs, the National Police Museum at North Port, Ponce De Leon Historic Park and Shrine, Gasparilla Island at Boca Grande, Cape Haze Aquatic Preserve, Boca Grande Lighthouse, Fort Myers, Lover's Key State Recreation Area, the Everglades Wonder Gardens at Bonita Springs, Sanibel Lighthouse on Sanibel Island, Port Charlotte Beach near Englewood, Delnor-Wiggins Pass State Recreation Area, the Circus Winter Quarters in Venice, Don Pedro Island State Recreation Area, Collier-Seminole State Park and Fakahatchee Strand State Preserve (both south of Naples), and the Thomas Edison Home in Fort Myers.

INFORMATION: Myakka River State Park, 13207 SR 72, Sarasota, FL 34241. Telephone 813-361-6511. This state park is located 12 miles east of Sarasota on SR 72.

Oscar Scherer State Recreation Area

Oscar Scherer State Recreation Area is an extensive tract of scrubby and pine flatwoods. The scrubby flatwoods are vital to Florida's diminishing population of rare and endangered birds and animals, offering a natural and protected habitat for several of the state's most endangered species, including the Florida scrub jay, the gopher tortoise, the gopher frog, and the indigo snake. Bald eagles, bobcats, river otters, and alligators also can often be seen in the park during the winter months. Another 'Gem' in the Florida park system.

The pine flatwoods, the second major plant community in the park, offers a home to a wide variety of songbirds and wood-peckers, as well as the gopher tortoise.

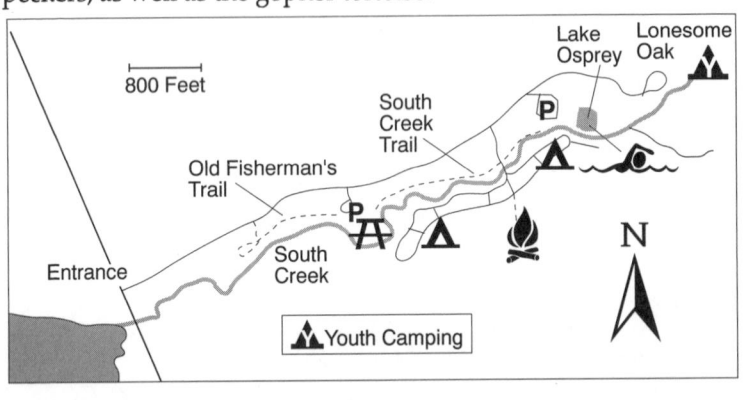

ACTIVITIES: While the park is an important destination for naturalists, bird watchers, and wildlife photographers, it also offers many other recreational activities. Camping is a popular pastime at Oscar Scherer, as are canoeing, swimming, and fishing. Anglers will find the combination of freshwater fishing above the dam, and saltwater fishing below it, a rare and unusual treat, while the small, freshwater Lake Osprey provides a perfect spot for swimming and relaxation.

Facilities at the park include a well-developed camping area with all the usual facilities, and a primitive camping area for those who really want to get close to nature. There's also a campfire circle, and canoes may be rented by the hour or by the day at the ranger station.

NEARBY ATTRACTIONS: Myakka River State Park, Crowley Museum and Nature Center, Cayo Costa State Park, Sarasota Jungle Gardens, Warm Springs, the National Police Museum at North Port, Ponce De Leon Historic Park and Shrine, Gasparilla Island at Boca Grande, Cape Haze Aquatic Preserve, Boca Grande Lighthouse, Fort Myers, Lover's Key State Recreation Area, the Everglades Wonder Gardens at Bonita Springs, Sanibel Lighthouse on Sanibel Island, Port Charlotte Beach near Englewood, Delnor-Wiggins Pass State Recreation Area, the Circus Winter Quarters at Venice, Don Pedro Island State Recreation Area, Collier-Seminole State Park south of Naples, the Fakahatchee Strand

State Preserve, also south of Naples, and the Thomas Edison Home in Fort Myers.

INFORMATION: Oscar Scherer State Recreation Area, 1843 South Tamiami Trail, Osprey, FL 34229. Telephone 813-483-5956. The recreation area is on US 41, two miles south of Osprey.

The South

Bahia Honda State Park

Bahia Honda, in the Florida Keys, is an area that features extensive sandy beaches and deep waters close enough offshore to provide exceptional swimming and snorkeling. But, more than that, the benevolent, sub-tropical climate of the keys has created a natural environment found nowhere else in the United States. That being so, it's no wonder that the park has an assortment of rare plants, including the yellow satinwood, the gumbo limbo, the silver palm, and the gravely endangered small-flowering lily thorn. A specimen of the yellow satinwood, and one of the silver palm, have been named as national champion trees. All of these wonders can be viewed along the nature trail that follows the shore of a tidal lagoon at the far end of Sandspur Beach.

Bahia Honda's geological base is the Key Largo limestone produced by a build-up of ancient coral formations similar to those found on living coral reefs to the south. Due to a drop in the sea level several thousands of years ago, the reef emerged from the sea, forming islands of which Bahia Honda is the southernmost exposed point.

Because of its unique swimming and snorkeling opportunities, the facilities at Bahia Honda are extensive. They include three modern campsites with extensive utilities, hookups, laundry facilities, restrooms and showers. There are three duplex cabins offering accommodations for up to eight people per unit, linen service, and utensils. The park's concession facility offers a limited range of groceries and camping and fishing supplies; diving equipment may be rented at the dive shop in the concession building. Other facilities include a campfire circle, freshwater showers on the beach, a marina with overnight docking and two boat launching ramps, as well as two picnic areas with shaded tables and barbecue grills.

ACTIVITIES: Hiking and guided walks along the park's nature trail, swimming and snorkeling, boating, sunning, beach fishing, and deep water charter boat fishing for tarpon (said to be the best in the state).

NEARBY ATTRACTIONS: Key Largo, Indian Key State Historic Site, Lignumvitae Key State Botanical Site, John Pennekamp Coral Reef State Park, Marathon, Long Key State Recreation Area, San Pedro State Archaeological Site, Fort Zachary Taylor State Historic Site in Key West, Key West National Wildlife Refuge, and many interesting attractions in Key West, including Key West Aquarium, Audubon House, and the Conch Tour Train.

INFORMATION: Bahia Honda State Park, Route 1, Box 782, Big Pine Key, FL 33043. Telephone 305-872-2353. The park is located 12 miles south of Marathon.

The Barnacle State Historic Site

The focus of The Barnacle State Historic Site is the home of Commodore Ralph Munroe at Coconut Grove. Coconut Grove is the product of a friendship between Charles and Isabella Peacock and Munroe. It was here in 1882, under the encouragement of Commodore Munroe, that the Peacocks established the first hotel on the southern Florida mainland. The hotel and the community that grew up around it flourished and became one of the most active and diversified in south Florida.

Today the spirit of the early lifestyles of the Peacocks and Commodore Munroe has been preserved in Munroe's home, The Barnacle. Visitors to the park enter by way of a footpath to Coconut Grove and find themselves transported back to the 1880s. It's an interesting and thought-provoking experience.

The Barnacle is open to the public Thursday through Monday, and tours of the house are conducted at 10 AM, 11:30 AM, 1 PM, and 2:30 PM.

INFORMATION: The Barnacle State Historic Site, PO Box 330995, Coconut Grove, FL 33233. Telephone 305-448-9445. The site is in Coconut Grove at 3485 Main Highway.

Cape Florida State Recreation Area

Bill Baggs Cape Florida State Recreation Area is on the southern tip of Key Biscayne. Back in the exploration days of Florida, the sandbars and uncharted reefs caused hundreds of shipwrecks and great loss of life aboard the great wooden sailing ships that plied the seas between the Americas and Europe.

For a long time things did not improve. Finally, to mitigate the hazards of the reef-strewn Florida coastline, the federal government planned a network of lighthouses along the eastern seaboard of Florida. As a result, Cape Florida Lighthouse was completed in 1825, and it still stands today. Ranger tours are conducted daily (except Tuesday) at 10:30 AM, 1 PM, 2:30 PM, and 3:30 PM.

The Park offers youth camping facilities, a hiking trail, a picnic area, a concession facility, and, of course, miles of broad, white, sandy beach.

ACTIVITIES: Swimming, sunning, fishing, hiking, picnicking, and just spending time relaxing in the ever-present Florida sunshine.

NEARBY ATTRACTIONS: Miami offers the Metro Zoo, Parrot Jungle, Fairchild Tropical Garden, the Orange Bowl Stadium, the Art Deco National Historical District and much more within the city itself. Also in the area are Biscayne National Park, Key Largo,

John Pennekamp Coral Reef State Park and the Serpentarium in Howard.

INFORMATION: Cape Florida State Recreation Area, 1200 S. Crandon Blvd., Key Biscayne, FL 33149. Telephone 305-361-5811. The recreation area is on the southern end of Key Biscayne, off the Rickenbacker Causeway (US 1), south of downtown Miami.

Fort Zachary Taylor
State Historic Site

As far back as 1836, before Florida had achieved statehood, the United States knew that the protection of Florida's coastline was of paramount importance. It was decided that a chain of forts should be established along the eastern seaboard. One of these would be built at Key West to protect the harbor.

Construction of the fort began in 1845, shortly after Florida achieved statehood. Five years later, in 1850, the fort was named Zachary Taylor, after the president who had died in office earlier that year. Construction was slow and, by the time the Civil War had broken out, the project was still incomplete. Construction was slowed by outbreaks of yellow fever, shortages of men and materials, hurricanes, and by the very remoteness of the location. The three-story fort was finally finished in 1866, some 21 years after construction had begun.

Today the fort has become landlocked. Dredging operations have surrounded it with acres of mud and fill. Through the efforts of volunteers, however, excavations of the fort's armaments began in 1968, and to date a number of cannons and ammunition dating from Civil War times have been recovered. Fort Zachary Taylor is well worth a visit.

ACTIVITIES: Picnicking, swimming, and fishing. Fresh water showers are available, as well as a picnic area, and a concession facility where visitors can buy snacks, soft drinks, and picnic and fishing supplies.

NEARBY ATTRACTIONS: Bahia Honda State Park, Key Largo, Indian Key State Historic Site, Lignumvitae Key State Botanical Site, John Pennekamp Coral Reef State Park, Marathon, Long Key State Recreation Area, San Pedro State Archaeological Site, Key West National Wildlife Refuge, and many interesting attractions in Key West, including Key West Aquarium, Audubon House, and the Conch Train Tour.

INFORMATION: Fort Zachary Taylor State Historic Site, PO Box 289, Key West, FL 33041. Telephone 305-292-6713. The site is located at Southard Street on Truman Annex.

Indian Key State Historic Site

Though you might not at first think it, Indian Key has a colorful history, and has passed through some very turbulent times. Ar-

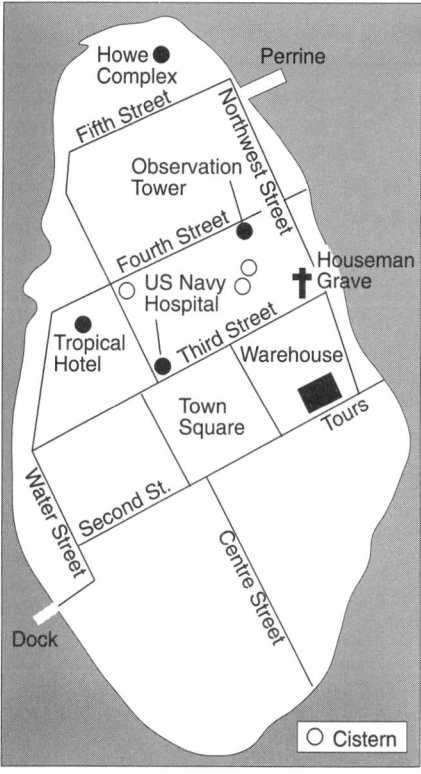

chaeological excavations have proven that the site was occupied by Indians for several thousands of years before the arrival of the Spanish conquistadors.

The key sits mid-way along the chain, some three-fourths of a mile southeast of the north shore of Lower Matecumbe Key. The tiny key is little more than 10 acres and is separated from the Overseas Highway by open water.

Exciting times at Indian Key really began when the wrecking and salvage industry came to the keys in the late 1700s as commercial ships began using the Gulf Stream and the Bahama Channel, which lie perilously close to the great coral reefs. In 1831 a Jacob Houseman bought the tiny island and made it headquarters for his wrecking business. During the years that followed Houseman and the island prospered. Soon there was a hotel, warehouses, wharves, and a permanent population fluctuating between 60 and 70 persons; life was good on Indian Key.

Then, on August 7, 1840, everything abruptly changed when the community was burned to the ground by Seminole Indians during the Second Seminole Indian War. The community never recovered from the catastrophe. Today the site has become something of a vacation spot for visitors to the Florida Keys and well worth a visit, if only for a picnic and a few minutes rest from a long journey southward.

Facilities at the site include modern, full-service campsites, a picnic area, and a boat ramp.

ACTIVITIES: Fishing, snorkeling, swimming, canoeing, boating, and picnicking.

NEARBY ATTRACTIONS: Key West National Wildlife Refuge, and many interesting attractions in Key West, including Key West Aquarium, Audubon House and the Conch Tour Train. Ther's also Bahia Honda State Park, Key Largo, Lignumvitae Key State Botanical Site, John Pennekamp Coral Reef State Park, Marathon, Long Key State Recreation Area, San Pedro State Archaeological Site, and Fort Zachary Taylor State Historic Site.

INFORMATION: Indian Key State Historic Site, c/o Lignumvitae Key State Botanical Site, PO Box 1052, Islamorada, FL 33036. Telephone 305-664-4815. Indian Key is on the ocean side of US 1 at Mile Marker 78.5. It is accessible only by private boat or charter boats from nearby marinas. Three-hour boat tours to the key depart Indian Key Fill on US 1 at 8:30 AM Thursday through Monday.

John Pennekamp Coral Reef State Park

John Pennekamp was the first underwater state park in the United States. The park covers some 70 nautical square miles of coral reefs, seagrass beds, and mangrove swamps. The park is an important one, in that it was designated to preserve a portion of the only living coral reef in the continental United States.

Coral reefs are many thousands of years in the making, formed from the skeletal remains of living corals and other plants and animals, all cemented together by limestone secretions and calcareous algae. The coral reef is an extremely fragile world, easily damaged by the interference of humans, and by chemical pollution, which kills the coral. The Florida Park Service is determined to see that such a catastrophe never happens at John Pennekamp.

The park encompasses 53,660 acres of submerged land and about 2,350 acres of uplands. The uplands make up a varied and natural habitat for many rare and endangered plants and marine animals.

Scuba diving at John Pennekamp

ACTIVITIES: Snorkeling, swimming, picnicking, boating, sailing, windsurfing, fishing, nature study, bird watching, photography, and camping.

Facilities at the park include modern, full-service camping sites with electrical and fresh water hookups. There are boat launching facilities, picnic areas, and a concession facility where you can take a glass-bottom boat ride out over the reef, partake in a snorkeling tour of the underwater park, try a few scuba diving lessons, or rent canoes, motor boats, and sail boats.

NEARBY ATTRACTIONS: Cape Florida State Recreation Area, North Shore State Recreation Area, Key Largo, the Serpentarium at Howard, and Biscayne National Park. Miami offers the Fairchild Tropical Garden, the Orange Bowl Stadium, the Art Deco National Historical District, Parrott Jungle (S. Miami), the Metro Zoo, plus many intown attractions.

INFORMATION: John Pennekamp Coral Reef State Park, PO Box 487, Key Largo, FL 33037. Telephone 305-451-1202. John Pennekamp Coral Reef State Park is on US 1 at Mile Marker 102.5, north of Key Largo.

Lignumvitae Key
State Botanical Site

The 280-acre Lignumvitae Key was acquired in 1919 by William J. Matheson, a wealthy chemist from Miami. It's a serene and somewhat remote island, supporting many rare and endangered plants. Trees indigenous to tropical forests, including the gumbo limbo, the mastic, the Jamaica dogwood, the poisonwood, the strangler fig, and the lignumvitae (for which the island is named), are all found here.

ACTIVITIES: Boating, fishing, swimming, and nature study. Guided one-hour nature walks are given 10:30 AM, and at 2:30 PM, Thursday through Monday. Visitors also can take a three-hour round-trip boat ride to Lignumvitae Key departing daily at 1:30 PM, from the Indian Key Fill on US 1. The park is closed on Tuesday and Wednesday.

NEARBY ATTRACTIONS: Indian Key State Historic Site, Key West National Wildlife Refuge, and many interesting attractions in Key West, including Key West Aquarium, Audubon House and the Conch Train Tour. There's also Bahia Honda State Park, Key Largo, John Pennekamp Coral Reef State Park, Marathon, Long Key State Recreation Area, San Pedro State Archaeological Site, and Fort Zachary Taylor State Historic Site in Key West.

INFORMATION: Lignumvitae Key State Botanical Site, PO Box 1052, Islamrada, FL 33036. Telephone 305-451-7617. This is one mile west of US 1 at Mile Marker 78.5, and is accessible only by private boat or by charter boats from nearby marinas.

Long Key State Recreation Area

Before Long Key was acquired by the Florida Park Service between 1961 and 1973, the sub-tropical climate and clear waters attracted explorers to the area. It was home to the Calusa Indians, then to Spanish settlers until, by 1912, with the establishment of the Key West expansion of the Florida East Coast Railroad, it was not such a remote and inaccessible area for travel. Long Key became an important depot for the railroad and when its owner, Henry Flagler, established Long Key Fishing Club, it became popular with some of the world's greatest saltwater fishermen. Unfortunately, Long Key's era of prosperity came to a violent end when a hurricane destroyed the railroad depot and fishing club in 1935.

With the acquisition of the key and eventual opening of it to the public in 1969, the area took on new life as one of Florida's premier state recreation and natural areas, with a good selection of vacation and recreational opportunities. These now include modern, full-service camping sites, with all the usual utilities, a campfire circle, three nature trails, a canoe trail, an observation tower offering spectacular views over most of the island, and a beachside picnic area.

ACTIVITIES: Hiking the nature trails, snorkeling, bird watching, nature study, photography, canoeing, and fishing in some of the most productive waters in the entire United States.

NEARBY ATTRACTIONS: Bahia Honda State Park, Key Largo, John Pennekamp Coral Reef State Park, Marathon, Lignumvitae Key State Botanical Site, Indian Key State Historic Site, Key West National Wildlife Refuge, and many interesting attractions in Key West, including Key West Aquarium, Audubon House, the Conch Tour Train, and Fort Zachary Taylor State Historic Site.

INFORMATION: Long Key State Recreation Area, PO Box 76, Long Key, FL 33001. Telephone 305-664-4815. The recreation area is located at Mile Marker 67.5 on the Overseas Highway.

North Shore State Recreation Area

North Shore is an oasis of lush, green tropical vegetation, deep blue sea, and wide sandy beaches, surrounded on three sides by the urban sprawl of Miami Beach. The 40-acre park was originally built in 1972 as the North Shore Open Space, but was taken over by Florida's State Park Service in 1987.

Today the park offers the opportunity for a few quiet hours of sunshine, sand, and sea, beyond the confines of the concrete jungle that is Florida's largest city, but close enough to stay in touch. North Shore is a day-use only park, a popular lunchtime getaway for the business population of the city.

ACTIVITIES: Swimming, sunning, walking, and bicycling.

NEARBY ATTRACTIONS: John Pennekamp Coral Reef State Park, Cape Florida State Recreation Area, the Serpentarium at Howard, Key Largo, and Biscayne National Park. Miami offers the Metro Zoo, Parrot Jungle (S. Miami), Fairchild Tropical Garden, the Orange Bowl Stadium, the Art Deco National Historical District, plus in-town amusements.

INFORMATION: North Shore State Recreation Area, c/o Oleta/North Shore GEOpark, 3400 NE 163rd Street, N. Miami Beach, FL 33160. Telephone 305-940-7439. The North Shore Recreation Area is east of Collins Avenue, between 79th and 87th Streets.

Oleta River State Recreation Area

Located on the banks of the scenic Oleta River and the Intracoastal Waterway, the park provides some of the finest recreational opportunities in the North Miami area. A parkland of mangrove forests, tidal backwaters, and hermetic marine environments, it offers an opportunity to observe a variety of bird life and mammals. The park is often visited by porpoises and the endangered Florida manatee. Oleta River is another 'Gem' awaiting discovery.

ACTIVITIES: Primitive tent camping, youth camping, canoeing the scenic Oleta River, bicycling, hiking, boating, fishing and swimming. There's a boat ramp, a picnic area, freshwater showers for public use, a 1,200-foot sandy beach for sunbathing, swimming, and saltwater fishing, and a 1.5-mile hiking trail.

NEARBY ATTRACTIONS: North Shore State Recreation Area, John Pennekamp Coral Reef State Park, Cape Florida State Recreation Area, Biscayne National Park, Key Largo, and the Serpentarium at Howard. Miami offers Parrot Jungle near S. Miami, Fairchild Tropical Garden, the Metro Zoo, the Orange Bowl Stadium, and the Art Deco National Historical District.

INFORMATION: Oleta River State Recreation Area, c/o Oleta/North Shore GEOpark, 3400 NE 163rd Street, N. Miami Beach, FL 33160. Telephone 305-947-6357. Oleta River State Recreation Area is located at 3400 N.E. 163rd Street in North Miami.

San Pedro Underwater Archaeological Preserve

San Pedro was a 280-ton Dutch-built ship which sailed as part of the fleet of New Spain in 1733. In 1960 the remains of the ship were discovered in the Hawk Channel, close to Indian Key, in 18 feet of water. During the years that followed the exciting discovery, several massive salvage expeditions stripped the carcass of the once-proud ship of all but a large pile of ballast stones. The wreck site covers an area some 90 feet long by 30 feet wide.

The underwater site has been enhanced by the addition of several replica cannons, an anchor, and a plaque offering wreck-site information. The site is accessible only by private boat, and to prevent anchor damage to the wreck, visitors are asked to tie up to the mooring buoys.

NEARBY ATTRACTIONS: Lignumvitae Key State Botanical Site, Bahia Honda State Park, Key Largo, John Pennekamp Coral Reef State Park, Marathon, Indian Key State Historic Site, Key West National Wildlife Refuge, and many interesting attractions

in Key West, including Key West Aquarium, Audubon House, the
Conch Tour Train and Fort Zachary Taylor State Historic Site.

INFORMATION: Long Key State Recreation Area, PO Box 776,
Long Key, FL 33001. Telephone 305-664-4815. San Pedro is in 18
feet of water approximately 1.25 nautical miles south from Indian
Key at LORAN coordinates 14082.1 and 43320.6.

General Information

PARK INFORMATION: Florida's state parks are open from 8 AM until sunset every day. Many of the state's museums and historic sites, however, are closed two days a week, and open hours may vary from site to site.

Fees are charged to help offset the ever-rising costs of providing protection, maintenance, and visitor services. Entrance fees vary throughout the state and are subject to change. Camping fees also vary according to the season, location, the number of persons using a particular site, extra vehicles, and the usage of electricity.

Annual Entrance Passes may be purchased by individuals and families. An individual pass costs $30 per year (subject to change). Family passes are good for up to eight persons and cost $50 per year (subject to change). Entrance passes are honored at all state parks (except Homosassa Springs State Wildlife Park where they are valid for a 33% discount). Passes can be purchased through park offices and by direct mail.

Pets are welcome in designated areas if they are kept on a six-foot, hand-held leash and are well behaved at all times. Pets are not permitted in camping areas, on beaches, or in the concession facilities. They also may be restricted in certain other areas of some parks.

Overnight Accommodations

CAMPING:

- **FULL FACILITIES CAMPING** offers water and electric hookups (in individual campsites) for both tent and RV campers. Restrooms and hot showers are conveniently accessible to all registered campers in these areas.

- **GROUP CAMPING** or **YOUTH CAMPING** is offered in designated areas for youth organizations, groups of families, or gatherings of friends. Facilities in group camping areas vary throughout the park system, from full-service group cabins to limited accommodations.

- **PRIMITIVE CAMPING** is offered in a variety of natural communities. Overnight backpacking and canoeing into these areas is strictly for the experienced and self-sufficient outdoor enthusiast.

- **BOAT CAMPING** is offered at some locations and usually includes mooring buoys and the use of the park's campground facilities: restrooms/showers/bathhouses. While some parks do feature marinas, overnight camping at the slips is limited, so it's best that you check with the park staff for availability.

CABINS are for the camper who likes a roof overhead. Florida's parks offer a variety of cabins in eight locations identified in the individual park listings. Some of the cabins feature the rustic appeal of the original Civilian Conservation Corps construction, while other contemporary cabins feature modern amenities.

- **VACATION CABINS** provide all the comforts of home, including private baths and kitchens. The facilities in these cabins vary from park to park, but typically sleep six, and may offer fireplaces and/or air conditioning.

- **PRIVATE CABINS** offer private sleeping quarters that are sometimes convenient to other park facilities.

- **GROUP CABINS** offer groups of cabins, or large sleeping quarters. These group camps feature fully-equipped kitchens, dining rooms, and/or meeting spaces.

RESORT LODGING is offered only at Wakulla Springs State Park.

Reservations for cabin rentals will be accepted no more than one year in advance and a deposit equal to a two-night stay is required for a confirmed reservation. Calls for reservations should be made between 8 AM and 5 PM Monday through Friday.

Like camping fees, cabin rental fees vary from park to park according to season and the type of facilities offered, and they are subject to change. Personal checks, Visa and MasterCard are accepted.

Activities

FISHING: Florida saltwater and freshwater fishing licenses are required for all persons aged 16 and older. Some exceptions are provided by Florida law. The fees collected have been designated specifically for improving and restoring fish habitats, building artificial reefs, researching marine life, tightening enforcement, and educating the public.

The Department of Natural Resources provides a pamphlet with exemption information and one with size and species limit information. To get your copies of "Go Fish," and "Know Your Limits," contact the Department of Natural Resources, Office of Fisheries Management & Assistance Services, Mail Station #240, 3900 Commonwealth Blvd., Tallahassee, FL 32399-3000, or telephone 904-922-4340.

To purchase a freshwater or saltwater fishing license, contact a county tax collector or visit a local bait or tackle shop. It's also a good idea to check with the park for any specific regulations that may be in effect at the time of your next fishing visit.

CANOE TRAILS: In addition to the waterways found in many of the state parks, Florida Park Service also administers some 36 canoe trails for the more serious canoeist within the Florida Recreational Trails System. While portions of this system do link with some of the state parks, most are publicly owned waterways that extend throughout the entire state, into National and State Forests, as well as county and city parks. The Florida Park Service offers a Canoe Guide that describes all these trails, lists trail mileage, and gives a difficulty rating.

TRAILS-TO-RAILS: The Florida Trails-to-Rails Program was established in 1987 as a means of buying and developing abandoned railroad corridors to provide the public with enjoyment and appreciation of outdoor areas in Florida. The Tallahassee-St. Marks Historic Railroad State Trail travels 16 miles between Tallahassee and the small, Gulf-coast village of St. Marks. Nearly 200,000 cyclists, hikers, and horseback riders enjoy this trail each year. The newest railroad trail is the 18-mile Gainsville-Hawthorne Rail Trail which connects the small country town of Hawthorne to Gainsville.

BICYCLING TRAILS: Several state parks have bicycling trails or roads. Consult the individual park listings for details. The Florida Park Service is committed to expanding park-to-park bike routes throughout Florida and is developing three tours ranging from 101 miles to 327 miles in length.

EQUESTRIAN TRAILS: Fifteen of Florida's state parks provide equestrian trails through some of the most scenic portions of Florida. Several of these have staging areas or corrals and overnight camping for horses and riders. Please call the individual parks when planning your ride, especially when organizing a group event, to learn about trail conditions and any special regulations the park may have.

Note that proof of a recent negative Coggins test is required of all horses as they enter the park.

LIVING HISTORY PROGRAMS: Many of Florida's state parks offer living history programs where visitors can learn what life might have been like for the Civil War soldier or early pioneer.

Military reenactments are presented annually at Dade Battlefield State Historic Site, Olustee Battlefield State Historic Site, and Natural Bridge Battlefield State Historic Site. Park rangers and volunteers portray the roles of common men and women in several parks on a year-round basis.

FESTIVALS AND EVENTS: The Florida Department of Natural Resourses offers a bi-annual publication highlighting the festivals, events, interpretive and environmental, and volunteer opportunities offered throughout the state.

From turtle watching and a Camellia Christmas to battle reenactments and environmental education workshops, "Festivals and Events" features all of these special occasions. You can pick up a copy at your favorite park or call 904-488-9872.

For more information, contact the Department of Natural Resources Park Information, 3900 Commonwealth Blvd., Tallahassee, FL 32399-3000. Telephone 904-488-9872.

Georgia

From the Blue Ridge Mountains in the north to the Okefenokee Swamp in the south, and from Providence Canyon in the west to Fort McAllister in the east, Georgia's 58 state parks and historic sites offer a variety of attractions: areas of wild and scenic beauty, museums of living history, and many reasonably priced overnight facilities, from the most basic of campgrounds, to rustic cottages, to sophisticated lodges that rival even the finest of resort hotels.

The Highlands

Amicalola Falls State Park

In Cherokee Indian language, Amicalola means "Tumbling Waters." Nothing could describe the spectacular 729-foot-high falls, the highest in Georgia, better than that. An eight-mile trail meanders through this 1,020-acre park, leading from the falls and then on to Springer Mountain and the southern end of the 2,150-mile

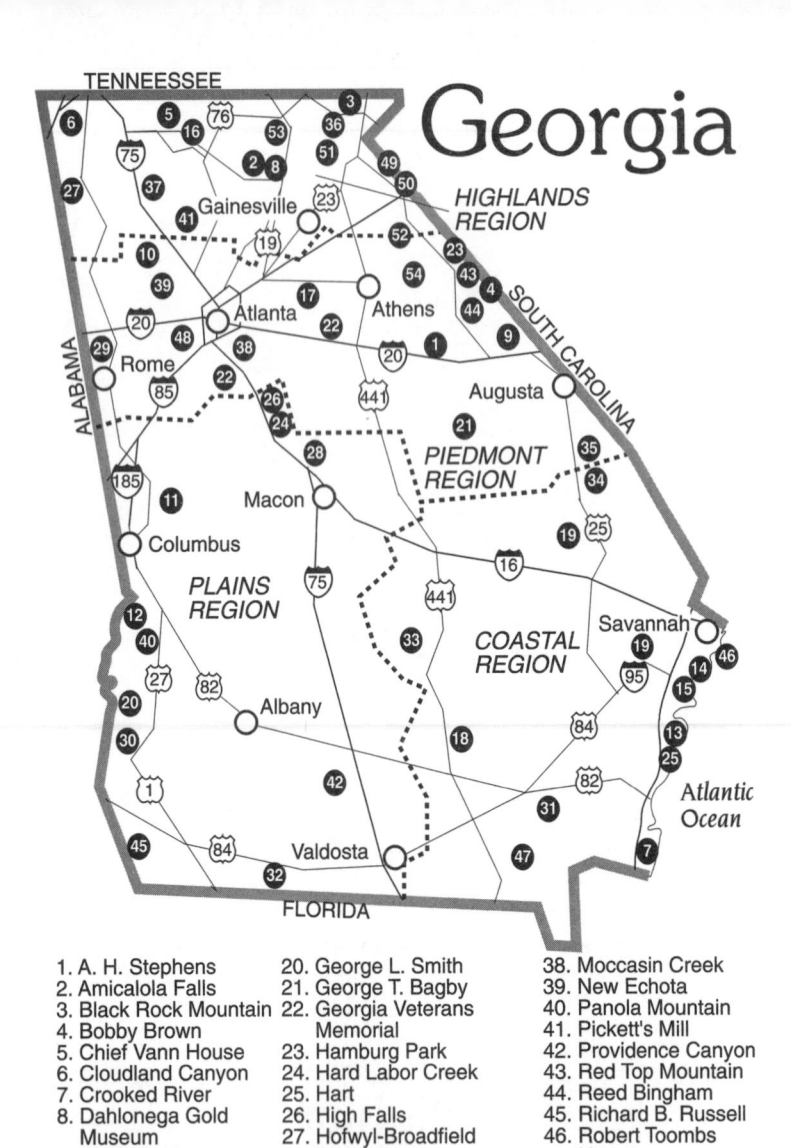

Georgia

TENNESSEE

ALABAMA

SOUTH CAROLINA

FLORIDA

HIGHLANDS REGION

PIEDMONT REGION

PLAINS REGION

COASTAL REGION

Atlantic Ocean

Gainesville

Atlanta

Athens

Augusta

Rome

Macon

Columbus

Savannah

Albany

Valdosta

1. A. H. Stephens
2. Amicalola Falls
3. Black Rock Mountain
4. Bobby Brown
5. Chief Vann House
6. Cloudland Canyon
7. Crooked River
8. Dahlonega Gold Museum
9. Elijah Clark
10. Etowah Indian Mounds
11. F. D. Roosevelt
12. Florence Marina
13. Fort King George
14. Fort McAllister
15. Fort Morris
16. Fort Mountain
17. Fort Yargo
18. General Coffee
19. Gordonia-Alatamaha

20. George L. Smith
21. George T. Bagby
22. Georgia Veterans Memorial
23. Hamburg Park
24. Hard Labor Creek
25. Hart
26. High Falls
27. Hofwyl-Broadfield Plantation
28. Indian Springs
29. James H. Floyd
30. Jarrell Plantation
31. John Tanner
32. Kolomoki Mounds
33. Laura S. Walker
34. Lapham-Patterson House
35. Little Ocmulgee
36. Magnolia Springs
37. Mistletoe

38. Moccasin Creek
39. New Echota
40. Panola Mountain
41. Pickett's Mill
42. Providence Canyon
43. Red Top Mountain
44. Reed Bingham
45. Richard B. Russell
46. Robert Toombs House
47. Seminole
48. Skidaway Island
49. Stephen C. Foster
50. Sweetwater Creek
51. Traveler's Rest
52. Tugaloo
53. Unicoi
54. Victoria Bryant
55. Vogel
56. Watson Mill Bridge

Appalachian Trail, which runs from Georgia to Maine. The trails within the park and along the Appalachian Trail offer the nature lover a treasure chest full of wildlife, and the opportunity to experience the great outdoors at its very best.

Facilities at the park include 17 tent and trailer sites, 14 rental cottages, three playgrounds, five picnic shelters, a rustic walk-in lodge, and a 57-room lodge with a restaurant and meeting facilities.

ACTIVITIES: Fishing, camping, hiking, nature study, bird watching, wildlife photography, and picnicking.

The park offers a full, year-round program of special events including Spring Wildflowers in April, Naturalist Programs, Summer's End Trading Days in August, an Overnight Backpacking Trip in October, and the Fall Leaf Displays, also in October.

NEARBY ATTRACTIONS: New Echota State Historic Site, the Appalachian Trail, Dahlonega Gold Museum, Historic Dahlonega, Vogel State Park, the alpine village of Helen, Unicoi State Park, the Chieftains Trail, Fort Mountain State Park, Chief Vann House State Historic Site, Ellijay Apple Country, and many local waterfalls.

INFORMATION: Amicalola Falls State Park and Lodge, Star Route, Box 215, Dawsonville, GA 30534. Telephone 706-265-8888. Park hours are from 7 AM to 10 PM and the park office hours are from 8 AM to 5 PM.

Amicalola Falls is 15 miles northwest of Dawsonville. Take Highway 53 west out of Dawsonville and then Highway 183 to Highway 52 east.

Black Rock Mountain State Park

Black Rock Mountain State Park is located high atop the Eastern Continental Divide close to the Georgia/North Carolina border. At an altitude of more than 3,600 feet, it is the highest state park in Georgia. The 1,500-acre park was named for its great granite cliffs and peaks, offering some of the most spectacular views of the southern Appalachian Mountains. On a clear day it's possible to see for more than 80 miles.

Major facilities at the park include 53 tent and trailer sites, 10 rental cottages, a visitor center, two picnic shelters, and a 17-acre lake.

ACTIVITIES: Mountain culture programs, camping (both pioneer and primitive camping is available), and hiking (including the Tennessee Rock Trail, the Ada-hi Falls Trail, and the James E. Edmonds Trail).

Annual special events are the Spring Wildflowers in May and Overnight Backpacking in the fall.

NEARBY ATTRACTIONS: Moccasin Creek State Park & Fish Rearing Station, Unicoi State Park & Lodge, Chattooga River for whitewater rafting, Sky Valley for snow skiing, and Tallulah Gorge.

INFORMATION: Rock Mountain State Park, Mountain City, Georgia, 30562. Telephone 706-746-2141. Park hours are from 7 AM to 10 PM and the park office is open from 8 AM to 5 PM.

The park is three miles north of Clayton, Georgia, via US 441.

Cloudland Canyon State Park

Cloudland is situated high on the western edge of Lookout Mountain. It is one of the most scenic parks in the state. An abundance of wildlife and wildflowers make it a mecca for the naturalist, especially in the spring and fall. The canyon itself, a great gash cut into the earth by Sitton Gulch Creek, varies in elevation from 1,800 feet at the highest point to 800 feet above sea level at the lowest point. Overlooks afford breathtaking views and a wooden walkway offers an exciting, though somewhat long and strenuous, climb down to the foot of the waterfall and the canyon floor.

Major facilities include 2,120 acres of rugged and scenic parkland, 75 tent and trailer sites, a 40-bed group camp, 16 rental cottages, a winterized group shelter, a swimming pool, tennis courts, and 30 walk-in campsites.

ACTIVITIES: Hiking (there are more than six miles of backcountry trails), picnicking (lots of tables and an open-air pavilion with grills), camping (comfort stations and pioneer camps), and photography.

The Park Service offers several annual special events including Crafts in the Clouds the third weekend in May (subject to change), a wildflower program, also during May, and an overnight backpacking trip in October.

NEARBY ATTRACTIONS: Chief Vann House State Historic Site, New Echota State Historic Site, James H. "Sloppy" Floyd State Park, Chickamauga National Battlefield, Lookout Mountain, and Chattanooga, Tennessee.

INFORMATION: Cloudland Canyon State Park, Route 2, Box 150, Rising Fawn, GA 30738. Telephone 706-657-4050. The park is open from 7 AM until 10 PM and the park office is open from 8 AM until 5 PM.

Cloudland Canyon State Park is about 10 miles south of Chattanooga on Georgia Route 136, 8 miles east of Trenton and I-59 and 18 miles west of Lafayette.

Chief Vann House State Historic Site

The Chief Vann House is a classic, two-story brick mansion that was built in 1804. Called the "Showplace of the Cherokee Nation," it was built by Chief James Vann. It is decorated with magnificent carvings, all done by hand and painted in natural colors of blue, red, green and yellow. Of the house's many features and antiques perhaps the most outstanding is a fine example of a cantilevered stairway.

Chief Vann is remembered for his contribution to the education of the Cherokee. He was responsible for bringing Moravian missionaries to teach children the Christian way of life. But Vann was still a Cherokee Indian and a polygamist. He had three wives and five children. He came to a violent end in 1809 for killing his brother-in-law in a duel and the house, along with Vann's other possessions and business interests, was passed on to his son, Joseph. In 1834 the government seized the house when "Rich Joe" Vann unknowingly violated state law by employing a white man. The house passed into the hands of white owners by way of a land lottery.

NEARBY ATTRACTIONS: Fort Mountain State Park, Cohutta Wilderness Area, New Echota State Historic Site, and Chieftains' Trail.

INFORMATION: Chief Vann House State Historic Site, Route 7, Box 7655, Chatsworth, GA 30705. Telephone 706-695-2598.

The house is open year-round on Tuesday through Saturday from 9 AM until 5 PM, and on Sunday from 2 PM until 5:30 PM, and is closed Mondays (except for some legal holidays), Thanksgiving and Christmas Day. There's a small admission fee. Group rates are offered with advance notice and bus parking is available.

Dahlonega Gold Museum And Historic Site

For more than 30 years the gold towns of Dahlonega and Auraria in north Georgia thrived as a river of yellow metal flowed in from the mountains. Gold was discovered in the region in 1828, 20 years before the great finds in California. From all points of the compass thousands of hopeful prospectors headed for the diggings located deep in the heart of the Cherokee Nation. It was the beginning of the gold rush era. A US Branch Mint was established in Dahlonega and from 1838 to 1861, the plant turned out more than $6 million in gold coins. Today the old Lumpkin County Courthouse is a museum dedicated to the "good old days" of the nation's first major gold rush. A wide range of exhibits, including a gold nugget that weighs in at more than five ounces, a 30-minute film show entitled "Gold Fever," and a series of special events, gives a unique look into the lives and times of pioneering families that lived, toiled and fought for their very existence in northern Georgia's gold fields.

Special events include Dahlonega Gold Rush Days in October, the July 4th Celebration, and an Old Fashioned Christmas.

NEARBY ATTRACTIONS: Gold Panning, The Smith House, Babyland General Hospital (home of the Adoption Doll), the alpine village of Helen, Amicalola State Park and Lodge, and Unicoi State Park and Lodge.

INFORMATION: Dahlonega Gold Museum State Historic Site, Public Square, Box 2042, Dahlonega, GA 30533. Telephone 706-864-2257. The museum is open year-round Monday through Saturday from 9 AM to 5 PM and on Sunday from 10 AM until 5 PM. It is closed on Thanksgiving and Christmas Day. There is a small admission fee and group rates are available with advance notice. Dahlonega Museum sits on the Public Square in Dahlonega, five miles west of Georgia 400.

Fort Mountain State Park

High on top of the mountain is an ancient, 855-foot-long stone wall, from which the park gets its name. No one knows for sure how the wall came to be there. It is thought that perhaps it was built in prehistoric times by local Indians as a means of fortification against other more hostile tribes. Some think it might have been built as a place to carry out ancient tribal ceremonies. We'll probably never know for sure. But that makes no difference. The mountain park, with its abundance of wildlife and the surrounding Chattahoochee National Forest, is a place of outstanding beauty, and well worth a visit.

The park offers over 1,900 acres of land, 70 tent and trailer sites, 15 cottages, more than 12 miles of mountain hiking trails, a swimming beach and bathhouse, and a miniature golf course.

ACTIVITIES: Hiking, boating (pedal boats for rent, but no private boats), and picnicking (there are seven shelters and 117 tables).

Annual events include Spring Wildflowers, Fort Mountain Mysteries in August, and overnight backcountry trips in October and November.

NEARBY ATTRACTIONS: Amicalola State Park and Lodge, New Echota State Historic Site, Chieftains' Trail, Chief Vann House State Historic Site, Cohutta Lodge and Restaurant, and Cohutta Wilderness Area.

INFORMATION: Fort Mountain State Park, Route 7, Box 7008, Chatsworth, GA 30705. Telephone 706-695-2621. The park is open from 7 AM until 10 PM daily and the park office hours are from 8 AM until 5 PM. Fort Mountain is seven miles east of Chatsworth on Georgia Highway 52. Take Exit 136 off I-75.

Hart State Park

Sitting on the banks of Lake Hartwell, Hart State Park offers some of the finest fishing in all of northeast Georgia. Largemouth bass, black crappie, bream, rainbow trout, and wall-eye abound in the sparkling waters of this great reservoir. The boat ramps and docks at the park offer easy access to the 56,000-acre lake. So, if it's watersports, boating, waterskiing, or swimming that you like, you will find no better place to do it than on Lake Hartwell.

Major facilities at the park include the 146 acres of parkland, 65 campsites, two cottages, a beach, and three picnic shelters.

ACTIVITIES: Fishing and most other watersports, as well as music programs in the Cricket Theater.

Annual events include the Labor Day Music Festival in September, Memorial Day Weekend Craft Show, and the Hot Rods of Hart Car Show on the first Sunday in November.

NEARBY ATTRACTIONS: Tugaloo State Park, Victoria Bryant State Park and nine-hole golf course, Elberton (Granite Capital of the World), two public golf courses within 20 miles, Georgia Guildstones, Blue Grass Concerts, marinas and boat rentals, and tennis at the Hart County Park.

INFORMATION: Hart State Park, 1515 Hart Park Road, Hartwell, GA 30643. Telephone 706-376-8756. Park hours are from 7 AM to 10 PM and the office is open from 8 AM until 5 PM.

The park is located east from Hartwell on US 29; turn left on ridge road and then go two miles to the park.

James H. Floyd State Park

This state park in northwest Georgia was named for James H. "Sloppy" Floyd, one of Georgia's most distinguished State Representatives. Sloppy Floyd served in the Georgia House of Representatives from 1953 until his death in 1974. The park is adjacent to the great Chattahoochee National Forest and offers fine fishing on two managed lakes.

Facilities include more than 260 acres of parkland, 25 tent and trailer sites, two lakes totaling about 51 acres (there are two boat ramps), a playground, pioneer camping, and picnicking; there are two shelters.

ACTIVITIES: Hiking, boating (electric motors only), fishing for crappie, bluegill, and catfish (there are two docks), and pedal boat rentals.

NEARBY ATTRACTIONS: Cloudland Canyon State Park, New Echota State Historic Site, Chickamauga and Chattanooga National Military Parks, Summerville Fish Hatchery, and Chieftains' Trail.

INFORMATION: James H. "Sloppy" Floyd State Park, Route 1, Box 291, Summerville, GA 30747. Telephone 706-857-5211. Park hours are from 7 AM to 10 PM and the park office is open from 8 AM until 5 PM.

The park is three miles southeast of Summerville on Marble Springs Road via US 27.

Moccasin Creek State Park

Nestled in the Blue Ridge Mountains, Moccasin Creek State Park is known as the place where spring spends summer. Here, on the shores of magnificent Lake Burton, among the hills and valleys of northeast Georgia, one finds the unspoiled countryside literally covered by a blanket of greenery and wildflowers, threaded through with tiny trout streams and back country trails. It's the perfect starting point for high country exploration or just to enjoy the peace and quiet of the mountains. If you're tired of the hustle and bustle of the big city, it's a place you can go to forget your worries and relax.

The park offers 32 acres of land, 53 tent and trailer sites, a boat dock and ramp, a playground, a wheelchair-accessible fishing pier, and a pavilion.

ACTIVITIES: Hiking the Moccasin Trail and, of course, the nearby Appalachian Trail. There's a fishing stream for senior citizens and children, and you can visit the trout rearing station adjacent to the park.

Annual events include the Georgia Mountain Trout Program and Contest in June, and the Lake Burton Arts & Crafts Festival in July.

NEARBY ATTRACTIONS: the alpine village of Helen, Unicoi State Park, LaPrade's Fishing Camp, Black Rock Mountain State Park, the Appalachian Trail, Tallulah Gorge, and Chattooga River.

INFORMATION: Moccasin Creek State Park, Route 1, Box 1634, Clarksville, GA 30523. Telephone 706-3194. The park is open from 7 AM until 10 PM and the park office hours are from 8 AM until 5 PM.

Moccasin Creek is 20 miles north of Clarksville on Georgia Highway 197.

New Echota State Historic Site

The Cherokee Nation once covered almost all of northern Georgia, western North Carolina, eastern Tennessee and northern Alabama. In 1821 the Cherokees made a remarkable step forward with the invention of a written form of their language. In 1825 they established their capital, New Echota, in northwest Georgia. It soon became a thriving community and government headquarters for the independent Indian nation, complete with a tavern and a bi-lingual newspaper, the *Cherokee Phoenix*, printed on a Washington hand press; all this by 1828. But this new-found prosperity was not to last. The Indians, who had tried to model their government and lifestyles after those of the white man, were gathered together in 1838 and herded westward along the Trail of Tears to reservations in Oklahoma. Today, New Echota is designated an Historic Site, where visitors can tour the reconstructed buildings: the Print Shop, the Supreme Courthouse, Vann's Tavern, and the original home of missionary Samuel A. Worcester.

Log cabins at New Echota State Historic Site

Annual events here include the Cherokee Festival, a New England Christmas, Artifacts Identification Day, and Gold Panning.

NEARBY ATTRACTIONS: Vann House State Historic Site, Fort Mountain State Park, and Chieftains' Trail.

INFORMATION: New Echota State Historic Site, 1211 Chatsworth Highway NE, Calhoun, GA 30701. Telephone 706-629-8151. The site is open year-round from Tuesday to Saturday from 9 AM until 5 PM and on Sunday from 2 PM until 5:30 PM. The site is closed on Thanksgiving and Christmas Day as well as Mondays (except legal holidays).

New Echota is one mile east of I-75, Exit 131, on Highway 225.

Traveler's Rest State Historic Site

Traveler's Rest was the center of Devereaux Jarrett's once thriving plantation. Jarrett was, at that time, the richest man in Tugaloo Valley and, in order to accommodate the growing numbers of travelers to northwest Georgia, he expanded the structure and opened it as an inn. It was a popular watering hole and the hotel register boasts many a famous name, including John C. Calhoun and Joseph E. Brown, the Civil War Governor of Georgia. The Traveler's Rest today is furnished much as it was back in Jarrett's day. Many of the antiques you will see in the old house were made by local craftsmen. In 1866 the house, with its 90-foot-long porch, hand-numbered rafters, and 20-inch-wide panelling, was recognized as a National Historic landmark, and is now open to the public.

A very special attraction at the Traveler's Rest is the Old-fashioned Christmas held on the second Sunday in December.

NEARBY ATTRACTIONS: Tallulah Gorge, Toccoa Falls, and Tugaloo State Park.

INFORMATION: Traveler's Rest State Historic Site, Route 3, Toccoa, GA 30577. Telephone 706-886-2256. The site is open year-round, Tuesday through Saturday, from 9 AM until 5 PM and on Sunday from 2 PM until 5:30 PM. In addition to legal holidays, it is closed on Mondays, Thanksgiving and Christmas Day.

The Traveler's Rest is located six miles east of Toccoa on US 123.

Tugaloo State Park

Tugaloo is an old Indian name for the river that once flowed freely through the open countryside here. The river is now covered by Hartwell Reservoir. The 390-acre Tugaloo State Park, which occupies a rugged peninsula jutting out into the Hartwell Reservoir, offers spectacular views and some of the finest year-round lake fishing in Georgia.

The park has 120 tent and trailer sites, 20 cottages, tennis courts, nature trails, a swimming beach and bathhouse, miniature golf, and two boat ramps.

ACTIVITIES: Volleyball and horseshoes, plus all sorts of watersports, including waterskiing and fishing (private boats are allowed on the lake). Entertainment at the park includes frequent Mountain Music programs. Of special interest is the annual Harvest Festival held in October.

NEARBY ATTRACTIONS: Victoria Bryant State Park and Golf Course, the Traveler's Rest Historic Site, the Ty Cobb Museum, Toccoa Falls, Hartwell Dam, and the alpine village of Helen.

INFORMATION: Tugaloo State Park, Route 1, Box 1766, Lavonia, GA 30553. Telephone 706-356-4362. The park is open from 7 AM until 10 PM and the office is open from 8 AM until 5 PM.

Tugaloo is just a couple of miles northeast of Lavonia, close to the South Carolina border. Take I-85 Exit 58 and go north on Georgia 17; follow the park signs to the right onto County Road 385, then head 1.5 miles to Georgia 328 and turn left. Proceed 3.3 miles to the park entrance on the right.

Unicoi State Park

Unicoi State Park is in the mountains of north Georgia only a couple of miles from the alpine village of Helen. Spectacular views of the rugged terrain, fine fishing for bass, crappie, bluegill, and catfish, an assortment of watersports, and a year-round program of activities make the park one of those unique spots on the face of the earth that you really can't afford to miss. It offers more than 1,000 acres of unspoiled parkland and lake, a magnificent 100-room lodge, cottages, and campsites.

The park has 84 tent and trailer sites, 30 cottages, a swimming beach, four lighted tennis courts, a 100-room lodge and conference center, a buffet-style restaurant, and a craft shop.

Events at the park include monthly special programs of activities, and Friday night and Saturday programs year-round.

NEARBY ATTRACTIONS: The alpine village of Helen, Dahlonega Gold Museum, Georgia Mountains Fair, Brasstown Bald (the highest point in Georgia), Babyland General Hospital (home of the Adoption Doll), Anna Ruby Falls, Moccasin Creek State Park, and Vogel State Park.

INFORMATION: Unicoi State Park and Lodge, PO Box 849, Helen, GA 30545. Call 706-878-2201 (office & group reservations) or 706-878-2824 (individual reservations). The park is open from 7 AM until 10 PM and the office hours are 8 AM until 5 PM.

Unicoi is two miles northeast of Helen via Georgia Highway 356.

Victoria Bryant State Park

Situated among the hills and valleys of Georgia's northern highlands, Victoria Bryant State Park offers a wonderful outdoor experience. If you're a hiking enthusiast you can enjoy more than five miles of nature trails that wind their way through the woodlands and surrounding area. Or, if you simply want to get away from it all, you will enjoy the picnicking, swimming, golf, and camping. There's even a well-stocked fish pond for the enthusiastic angler.

Facilities at the park include 25 tent and trailer sites, three playgrounds, a nine-hole golf course, a swimming pool, five picnic shelters, and two pioneer campsites.

ACTIVITIES: Hiking, golf (including a clubhouse and driving range), and pond-fishing (no boats allowed).

Annual events include the Jr.-Sr. Catfish Rodeo in April or May, the Independence Day Bluegrass Festival held over July 4th weekend, and Pioneer Skills Day the first weekend in November.

NEARBY ATTRACTIONS: Hart State Park, Lake Hartwell, the Traveler's Rest State Historic Site, and Tugaloo State Park.

INFORMATION: Victoria Bryant State Park, Route 1, Box 1767, Royston, GA 30662. Telephone 706-245-6270 (office) or 706-245-

6770 (golf course). The park is open from 7 AM until 10 PM and its office hours are 8 AM until 5 PM.

The park is located two miles north of Franklin Springs on Georgia Highway 327.

Vogel State Park

Vogel is one of Georgia's oldest state parks. Located in the Blue Ridge Mountains in the northeast and within the confines of the Chattahoochee National Forest, the park is steeped in local folklore; stories of Indian battles and buried gold that tickle the imagination. Vogel, with its 280 acres of parkland and forests, is arguably one of Georgia's most beautiful state parks.

The park has more than 17 miles of hiking trails, 110 tent and trailer sites, 36 rental cottages, a 20-acre lake, a miniature golf course, a swimming beach with bathhouse, four picnic shelters, pioneer camping, pedal boats, and a family group shelter.

ACTIVITIES: Hiking, nature study, bird watching, wildlife photography, picnicking, and boating (pedal boats only).

Annual events here include a Wildflower Program in April, Old Timer's day in August, and several seasonal festivals.

NEARBY ATTRACTIONS: Unicoi State Park, Dahlonega Gold Museum, October Foliage Display, Moccasin Creek State Park, Amicalola Falls State Park and Lodge, and the Walasi-yi Center.

INFORMATION: Vogel State Park, Route 1, Box 1230, Blairsville, GA 30512. Telephone 706-745-2628. Park hours are from 7 AM until 10 PM and the office is open from 8 AM until 5 PM.

The park is located 11 miles south of Blairsville on US 19/129.

The Piedmont Region

A. H. Stephens State Historic Park

This park, close to Crawfordville in northeast Georgia, was named after the Vice President of the Confederacy and one-time Governor of Georgia, A. H. Stephens. The park offers visitors both natural and historic attractions. Liberty Hall was the home Stephens built for himself around 1875. The house and the Confederate museum, which houses one of the most extensive collections of Confederate artifacts and memorabilia to be found anywhere in Georgia, and the beautiful gardens and outdoor facilities, make the park a natural choice, not only for the history buff, but for nature lovers as well.

The park itself features 1,189 acres, camping facilities for 25 tent or trailer sites, a nature trail, two picnic areas, and a fishing lake. Fishing is available throughout the year. Private fishing boats are allowed (electric motors only) and rental boats are available if needed. The museum offers an educational program and an audio-visual show. Special events include the Stephens' Homecoming in April and Gaslight Tours in the fall.

NEARBY ATTRACTIONS: Hamburg State Park, Robert Toombs House State Historic Site, Mistletoe State Park, Hard Labor Creek State Park & Golf Course, and Lake Oconee.

INFORMATION: A. H. Stephens State Historic Park, PO Box 235, Crawfordville, GA 30631, 706-456-2602. Park hours are from 7 AM to 10 PM. The office is open from 8 AM to 5 PM (subject to change).

To reach the park take Exit 55 from I-20 and go north on Highway 22 for two miles. Go east on US 278 for one mile to Crawfordville and follow the park service signs.

Bobby Brown State Park

Bobby Brown State Park is named for Lt. Robert T. Brown, who gave his life while serving in the US Navy in World War II. The park itself is situated on the site of the old town of Petersburg, where the Broad and Savannah rivers flow into Clark Hill Reservoir. Petersburg was once a thriving community in the late 1700s. Now it is just a small part of Georgia's colorful history. The area where great southern plantations flourished is now a 665-acre park open for all to enjoy.

Major facilities at the park include 61 tent and trailer sites, a boat ramp and dock, three picnic shelters, a swimming pool, concessions and, of course, the 78,000-acre lake.

ACTIVITIES: Fishing for bass, crappie, bluegill, and catfish, boating, waterskiing, swimming, hiking, and camping (there are two pioneer camping sites and one group shelter). A special event at the park is the annual Fall Camper Reunion.

NEARBY ATTRACTIONS: Elijah Clark State Park, Watson Mill Bridge State Park, Robert Toombs House Historic Site, Lake R. B. Russell State Park, and Pioneer Nancy Hart's Cabin.

INFORMATION: Bobby Brown State Park, Route 4, Box 232, Elberton, GA 30635. Telephone 706-213-2046. The park is open from 7 AM to 10 PM and its office is open from 8 AM until 5 PM.

The park is 21 miles southeast of Elberton off Georgia Highway 72, on Bobby Brown Park Road.

Elijah Clark State Park

This 447-acre park is named for one of Georgia's most famous frontiersman and a leader of pioneers during the Revolutionary War. It is situated on the western shore of Clark Hill Lake and features reconstructed cabins, and a museum with a variety of exhibits, including everyday work tools and utensils used in the late 18th century. Visitors to the park will enjoy a unique educational experience as they tour the cabins and see the grave of Clark and his wife Hannah.

Facilities here include 165 tent and trailer sites, a white sandy beach and boathouse, six picnic shelters, 20 lakefront cottages, and a miniature golf course and playground.

ACTIVITIES: Camping, hiking, fishing for bass, crappie, bluegill, and catfish, nature study, bird watching, wildlife photography, golf and picnicking.

Annual events at the park include a Pioneer Rendezvous in October, and a Log Cabin Christmas in December.

NEARBY ATTRACTIONS: Mistletoe State Park, Historic Washington, Clarks Hill Dam, Bobby Brown State Park, and Robert Toombs State Historic Site.

INFORMATION: Elijah Clark State Park, Box 293, Route 4, Lincolnton, GA 30817. Telephone 706-359-3458. The park is open from 7 AM to 10 PM and the office is open from 8 AM until 5 PM.

It is located six miles north of Lincolnton on US 378.

Etowah Indian Mounds State Historic Site

These flat-topped mounds – the largest standing over 60 feet high and covering more than three acres – were the nucleus of an important religious center and home to several thousand Indians. The mounds were, in fact, platforms for the temple, the High-Priest's home, and the burial grounds of the Etowah Indians from around 1000 to 1500 A.D. Artifacts found at the site and now on display in the museum help us to understand the lives and culture of the people who once inhabited this area. Exhibits in the museum include tools and ceremonial objects made of stone, wood, shell, and copper.

Annual events here include Indian Skills Day in spring, Artifacts Identification Day in April and November, and several Astronomy Programs.

NEARBY ATTRACTIONS: Chieftains' Trail, Lake Allatoona, Weinman Mineral Museum, and Red Top Mountain State Park and Lodge.

INFORMATION: Etowah Indian Mounds State Historic Site, 813 Indian Mounds Rd. SW, Cartersville, GA 30120. Telephone 404-387-3747. The site is open all year from Tuesday to Saturday from 9 AM until 5 PM and on Sunday from 2 PM until 5:30 PM and is closed on Mondays (except legal holidays). The site is also closed on Thanksgiving and Christmas Day.

The site is five miles southwest of I-75 Exit 124.

Fort Yargo State Park

Fort Yargo State Park features a unique log fort built in the late 1700s as protection for the settlers in the area against local Cherokee and Creek Indians. The 1,800-acre park now offers some of the best camping and fishing in all of Georgia, including a Will-A-Way Recreation Area, designed for use by special groups. The facility includes cottages, a group camp, food service facilities, and picnicking and fishing areas.

Amenities at the park include 47 tent and trailer sites, a 250-capacity camp for groups, a 260-acre lake with beach, two tennis courts and a miniature golf course.

ACTIVITIES: Hiking the nature trail, fishing for bass, crappie, bluegill, and catfish, boating (canoe, jon boat, and pedal boat rentals), nature study, bird watching, wildlife photography, and picnicking – there are five shelters with 116 tables, and two group shelters.

NEARBY ATTRACTIONS: Gordonia-Alatamaha State Park, and Magnolia Springs State Park.

INFORMATION: Fort Yargo State Park, PO Box 764, Winder, Georgia, 30680. Telephone 404-867-3489 or 404-867-5313 (Will-A-Way). The park is open from 7 AM to 10 PM. The park office is open from 8 AM until 5 PM.

Fort Yargo is one mile south of Winder on Georgia Highway 81.

Hamburg State Park

The old water-powered grist mill at Hamburg State Park is still operating today much as it did when it was built more than 70 years ago. There's a country store where one can buy a bag of stone-ground corn meal and an assortment of recipe books to go with it. The museum is packed with exhibits: the tools and the agricultural implements that were part of everyday life in a bygone age. In addition, the park and its 225-acre lake offers a wonderful outdoor experience. Fishing here is claimed to be the best anywhere.

The park offers 30 tent and trailer sites, one group and two picnic shelters, pioneer camping, a museum, the grist mill, and a country store.

ACTIVITIES: Fishing the well-stocked lake for catfish, bass, bluegill, and crappie, boat rentals (pedal boats, canoes, and fishing boats), and educational programs at the museum.

Annual events include Canoe the Ogeechee in March and April, and the Fall Harvest Festival held the third weekend in September.

NEARBY ATTRACTIONS: Lake Oconee, Millidgeville, the Old Aaron Burr Jail, A. H. Stephens State Historic Park, and Lake Sinclair.

INFORMATION: Hamburg State Park, Route 1, Box 233, Mitchell, GA 30820. Telephone 912-552-2393. The park is open from 7 AM to 10 PM, and the park office is open from 8 AM until 5 PM.

The park is located six miles to the northeast of Warthen via Hamburg Road off Georgia Highway 102.

Hard Labor Creek State Park

Hard Labor Creek, so folklore has it, was named either by the slaves who worked the fields nearby, or by the local Indians who found the creek difficult to ford. We'll never know for sure. Either way, the 5,800-acre park has became a mecca for lovers of the great outdoors. There's something here for just about everyone, from horseback riding, to fishing, to hiking, to golfing. The park can rightfully boast about owning one of the finest and most challenging, public, full-service, 18-hole golf courses in the entire southeastern United States.

Facilities here include 49 tent and trailer sites, two lakes, two group shelters, horse stables and bridleways, 20 rental cottages, a swimming beach and bathhouse, four picnic shelters and a BBQ.

ACTIVITIES: Golfing (there's a pro shop, a grill restaurant, rental carts, and a driving range), boat rentals (pedal boats, fishing boats and canoes), horseback riding (there are 15 miles of trails; sorry, no horse rentals, bring your own), hiking (2.5 miles of trails), nature study, bird watching, wildlife photography, and picnicking.

Annual events include the Civilian Conservation Corps Reunion in spring, and the Christmas Golf Tournament in December.

NEARBY ATTRACTIONS: Oconee National Forest, Stone Mountain Park, Lake Oconee, Historic Madison, and Panola Mountain State Conservation Park.

INFORMATION: Hard Labor Creek State Park, PO Box 247, Rutledge, GA 30663. Telephone 706-557-3001 or 706-557-3006 (golf course). The park is open from 7 AM to 10 PM and the park office is open from 8 AM until 5 PM.

Take I-20 Exit 49 into Rutledge and then proceed two miles on Fairplay Road into the park.

John Tanner State Park

Some of the best recreational facilities anywhere in Georgia's State Park System are found at John Tanner. You can enjoy a simple day out in the park, a "get-away" weekend, or even a couple of weeks of outdoor vacationing. There's great fishing, boating, and swimming on two lakes, hiking backcountry trails, and the largest sandy beach found in any of Georgia's state parks. If it's nightlife you're looking for, Atlanta is only a half-hour or so away along I-20.

The park has 78 tent and trailer sites, a group lodge, a six-unit motor lodge and a miniature golf course.

ACTIVITIES: Hiking the exercise and nature trails, and boating; boat rentals are available by the hour, the half-day, or the full-day (private boats are permitted but only those powered by electric motors).

Annual events include an Arts & Crafts Show in the fall, a Triathlon in the summer, and Christmas in Georgia, held in mid-December.

NEARBY ATTRACTIONS: Sweetwater Creek State Park, Atlanta, and the Six Flags Over Georgia Theme Park.

INFORMATION: John Tanner State Park, 354 Tanner's Beach Road, Carrolton, GA 30117. Telephone 404-830-2222. The park is open from 7 AM to 10 PM and its administrative office is open from 8 AM until 5 PM.

John Tanner Park is six miles west of Carrolton off Georgia Highway 16.

Mistletoe State Park

Mistletoe State Park, nestled on the shores of Clark Hill Lake, takes its name from Mistletoe Junction. In times gone by the local people would meet in the area where the park now stands to gather mistletoe for the holiday season. Today the 1,900-acre park with its 76,000-acre lake is more famous as one of the best bass fishing spots in the United States.

It offers 107 tent and trailer sites, 10 cottages, three boat ramps, four walk-in campsites, a pioneer camp, four picnic shelters, one group shelter, and a swimming beach.

ACTIVITIES: Hiking the more than six miles of trails, nature study, bird watching, wildlife photography, picnicking, and, of course, fishing for largemouth and smallmouth bass, bluegill, catfish, and crappie.

NEARBY ATTRACTIONS: Robert Toombs State Historic Site, Elijah Clark State Park, A. H. Stephens State Historic Park, Augusta, Clarks Hill Dam, and Historic Washington.

INFORMATION: Mistletoe State Park, Route 1, Box 335, Appling, GA 30802. Telephone 706-541-0321. The park is open from 7 AM to 10 PM and the park office is open from 8 AM until 5 PM.

The park is located off Georgia Highway 150, 12 miles north of I-20, Exit 60.

Panola Mountain
State Conservation Park

Panola Mountain is, in fact, a single 100-acre granite rock very similar in many ways to its northern neighbor, Stone Mountain. Unlike Stone Mountain, however, Panola still wears its mantle of vegetation and is home to a variety of wildlife. The mountain is designated a National Natural Landmark. The Park Service offers an assortment of nature programs, guided hikes, and special activities throughout the year.

The park has an interpretive center, a picnic area and four shelters, and a number of hiking and nature trails.

ACTIVITIES: Nature study, bird watching, wildlife photography, picnicking, hiking the more than six miles of trails (these include two miles of self-guided nature trails, and a 3.5-mile nature walk and fitness trail), guided mountain hikes every Saturday and Sunday, educational programs on the ecology of the mountain and the forest floor, and many interesting and informative interpretive exhibits.

Annual special events include Spring Wildflower Walks in April, Fall Wildflower Walks in September, and an Environmental Discovery Program for children aged 5 to 13 during June, July and August.

NEARBY ATTRACTIONS: Hard Labor Creek State Park and Golf Course, Indian Springs State Park, Atlanta, Sweetwater Creek State Park, and High Falls State Park.

INFORMATION: Panola Mountain State Park, 2600 Highway 155 SW, Stockbridge, GA 30281. Telephone 404-389-7801. Park hours

Hiking trail on Panola Mountain   are from 7 AM until 6 PM (or dark) from September 15th to April 14th, and from 7 AM until 9 PM April 15th to September 14th. The interpretive center hours are from 7 AM until 5 PM Tuesday through Friday, and 12 noon until 5 PM on Saturday and Sunday.

The park is 18 miles southeast of Atlanta on Georgia Highway 155 via I-20 Exit 36.

Pickett's Mill
State Historic Site

Pickett's Mill is claimed to be "one of the best preserved Civil War battlefields in the nation." It was on this site that a full corps of General Sherman's Union Army, under the command of General Oliver O. Howard, suffered a major defeat on its march toward Atlanta. On May 27, 1864, after having been stopped two days earlier at the Battle of New Hope, Sherman ordered Howard to take his corps, more than 14,000 men, and outflank the Confederate forces, some 10,000 men under the command of General Patrick Cleburne. After a march of more than five hours, Howard arrived at Pickett's Mill, only to find Cleburne ready and waiting for him. There ensued a bloody battle that lasted into the night. Again and again Howard's divisions attacked the Confederate positions, only to be repulsed. By morning the Federals withdrew from the field, leaving more than 1,600 dead and wounded behind them. The Confederate losses were only 500.

Today the battlefield looks much the same as it did in 1864. The Confederate earthworks are still there and visitors can wander the old roads and walk through the ravine that became the final resting place for hundreds of Union soldiers. The Park Service offers a variety of living history demonstrations in which authentically uniformed personnel act out the everyday lives of soldiers in the Civil War era.

Annual events here include the Battle of Pickett's Mill Commemoration.

NEARBY ATTRACTIONS: Etowah Indian Mounds, Red Top Mountain State Park and Lodge, Sweetwater Creek State Conservation Park, and Kennesaw Mountain National Military Park.

INFORMATION: Pickett's Mill State Historic Site, 2640 Mt. Tabor Road, Dallas, GA 30132. Telephone 404-443-7850. The site is open year-round Tuesday through Saturday from 9 AM until 5 PM and on Sundays from 2 PM until 5:30 PM. It is closed on Mondays (except for legal holidays) and on Thanksgiving and Christmas Day.

Pickett's Mill is just five miles northeast of Dallas off Georgia Highway 381.

Red Top Mountain
State Park

Red Top Mountain is named for the color of its earth. The region is rich in iron ore and once was an important mining district. The 1,950-acre park is on a peninsula of Lake Allatoona and is an extremely popular center for outdoor activities. Fishing is probably the main attraction, but the wildlife and chances to explore make the park a popular place for families and businessmen alike.

Facilities here include 125 tent and trailer sites, 18 rental cottages, a 33-room lodge with restaurant, tennis courts, and a swimming beach.

ACTIVITIES: Hiking the more than seven miles of nature trails, nature study, bird watching, wildlife photography, picnicking, boating (there's a marina, two boat ramps and five docks), and fishing for largemouth and smallmouth bass, crappie, bluegill, and catfish. Waterskiing also is popular and private boats are permitted on the lake with no restrictions.

The lake at Red Top Mountain

NEARBY ATTRACTIONS: Etowah Indian Mounds State Historic Site, Kennesaw Mountain National Military Park, Atlanta, Weinman Mineral Museum, Chieftains' Trail, and Lake Allatoona.

INFORMATION: Red Top Mountain State Park & Lodge, 653 Red Top Mountain Rd., SE, Cartersville, GA 30120. Telephone 404-975-0055. The park is open daily 7 AM to 10 PM and the park's office hours are 8 AM to 5 PM.

The park is near Cartersville, two miles east of I-75 via Exit 123.

Richard B. Russell State Park

Richard B. Russell is situated on a site that was home to the Paleo Indians more than 10,000 years ago. Located on the edge of 26,500-acre Russell Lake, it is one of Georgia's newest state recreational areas. The lake offers the finest fishing and the best boating. All of the park's facilities are wheelchair-accessible.

Major facilities at the park include a swimming beach and concessions, a boat ramp and dock, and three picnic shelters.

ACTIVITIES: Hiking, fishing, boating, waterskiing, swimming, nature study, bird watching, wildlife photography, and picnicking.

NEARBY ATTRACTIONS: Bobby Brown State Park, Watson Mill Bridge State Park, Victoria Bryant State Park, Hart State Park, Richard B. Russell Dam & Lake, the Georgia Guide Stones, and the Granite Museum.

INFORMATION: Richard B. Russell State Park, Route 2, Box 118, Elberton, Georgia, 30635. Telephone 706-213-2045. The park is open from 7 AM until dark, and the park office is open from 8 AM until 5 PM.

The park is located nine miles northeast of Elberton off Georgia Highway 77 on Ruckersville Road.

Robert Toombs House
State Historic Site

Robert Toombs was a controversial, though successful southerner. A one-time admired planter, lawyer, state legislator, US congressman, and senator, he had ambitions to become president of the Confederacy. He was to be disappointed, however, and upon the election of Jefferson Davis he accepted a commission in the Army of Northern Virginia. His career in the army was all but a disaster and eventually he resigned to spend the war years at home in Washington, Georgia, brooding and complaining. When General Sherman, at the head of his invading Union Army, sent soldiers to arrest him, Toombs managed to escape and flee the country. He spent the next two years in exile and, upon his return to the United States, refused to accept a pardon, stating, "I am not loyal to the existing government of the United States and do not wish to be suspected of loyalty."

The Toombs House has been restored to its Civil War era condition and is full of antiques, exhibits, and artifacts of the times. Visitors can view a dramatic film that portrays Toombs in his later life telling his story to a young reporter.

NEARBY ATTRACTIONS: Historic Washington, the Washington-Wilkes Museum, Mistletoe State Park, and A. H. Stephens State Historic Park.

INFORMATION: Robert Toombs State Historic Site, PO Box 605, Washington, Georgia, 30673. Telephone 706-678-2226. The house is open year-round Tuesday through Saturday from 9 AM until 5 PM and Sundays from 2 PM until 5:30 PM. It is closed on Mondays, legal holidays, and on Thanksgiving and Christmas Day.

Robert Toombs House is located at 216 East Robert Toombs Avenue in Washington, GA.

Sweetwater Creek
State Conservation Park

It's difficult to believe that Sweetwater Creek is only minutes from downtown Atlanta. Almost 2,000 acres of wilderness parkland here features a diversity of natural resources including more than five miles of trails and meandering streams, the ruins of a Civil War era textile mill, and George Parks Reservoir.

Facilities at the park include a group shelter and BBQ pit, 11 picnic shelters, two fishing docks, a bait and tackle shop, playgrounds, and several educational programs.

ACTIVITIES: Hiking the five-mile nature trail, nature study, bird watching, wildlife photography, picnicking, lake and stream fishing for bass, crappie, bluegill, and catfish, and boating (electric motors only; small boats, canoes and fishing boats, are available for rent).

Annual events include an Arts & Crafts Show (call for dates), and year-round naturalist programs.

NEARBY ATTRACTIONS: John Tanner State Park, Lithia Pure Water Springs, Atlanta, and the Six Flags Over Atlanta Theme Park.

INFORMATION: Sweetwater Creek State Conservation Park, PO Box 816, Lithia Springs, Georgia, 30057. Telephone 404-944-1700. The park is open from 7 AM until dark, and the park office is open from 8 AM until 5 PM.

To reach the park take I-20 west from Atlanta to Exit 12 at Thornton Road, turn left and go 1/4-mile. Turn right onto Blairs Bridge Road, then turn left onto Mount Vernon Road and proceed to the park.

Watson Mill Bridge State Park

Watson Mill Bridge is, without doubt, one of the most picturesque state parks in Georgia. At 229 feet, the 100-year-old bridge, supported by a lattice truss system and held together by wooden pins, is the longest covered bridge standing on an original site in Georgia. Even though the fine old bridge is the park's main attraction, there's much more to enjoy. It's an ideal spot for an afternoon of picnicking, walking in the forest or along the riverbank, bird watching, or even an overnight stay in the campground.

Facilities here include 21 tent and trailer sites, a five-acre mill pond, pioneer camping, group shelters, three picnic shelters, and canoe and boat rentals.

ACTIVITIES: Hiking and picnicking, and learning all about the old grist mill.

Annual special events include day and overnight canoe trips, a Civil War Encampment, Georgia Awareness Weekend in August, and an assortment of outdoor concerts held throughout the summer and at Christmas.

NEARBY ATTRACTIONS: Victoria Bryant State Park, Robert Toombs State Historic Site, Bobby Brown State Park, the Granite Capital of the World, and the University of Georgia in Athens.

INFORMATION: Watson Mill Bridge State Park, Route 1, Box 190, Comer, Georgia, 30629. Telephone 706-783-5349. The park is open from 7 AM until dark, and the park office is open from 8 AM until 5 PM.

Watson Milll Bridge State Park is three miles south of Comer off Georgia Highway 22.

The Coastal Region

Crooked River State Park

Crooked River State Park is set on the banks of the river from which it takes its name. The freshwater fishing is good all the year-round, though private boats are limited to 10 HP. There are more than seven miles of canoe trails to explore, as well as the 400-acre lake. Of special interest are the ruins of the old McIntosh Sugar Works. The mill was built around 1825 and was used during the Civil War years to produce starch. For those who love being active outdoors there's swimming, hiking, camping, fishing, and miniature golf to enjoy. All of which make Crooked River an exciting and unusual outdoor experience.

Crooked River offers 21 tent and trailer sites, a winterized group shelter, four picnic shelters, as well as canoe and fishing boat rentals.

Annual special events include a Saltwater Fishing Clinic in February, Wildflower Day in March, and an Arts & Crafts Show in September.

NEARBY ATTRACTIONS: Cumberland Island, Jekyll Island, and Okefenokee National Wildlife Refuge.

INFORMATION: Crooked River State Park, 3092 Spur 40, St. Mary's, Georgia, 31558. Telephone 912-882-5256. The park is open from 7 AM until dark, and the park office is open from 8 AM until 5 PM.

The park is located 10 miles north of St. Mary's on Georgia Spur 40, or east of Kingsland, 12 miles off US 17, and eight miles from Interstate 95.

Fort King George
State Historic Site

For more than 10 years, from 1721 to 1732, Fort King George marked the southernmost limits of the British Empire on the North American Continent. The original fort is long gone, but the one that stands today is a faithful reconstruction of the one that was garrisoned by His Majesty's 41st Independent Company. During the years following the building of the fort a settlement of frontiersmen and women grew up around it. That settlement, Darien, was to become, over the next two hundred years, one of the largest timber exporters in the world. The ruins of three of the old sawmills can still be seen today. The museum at the fort houses a fine collection of exhibits, and visitors can watch a slide show that tells the story of the area from the Spanish occupation, through British rule, and then Darien's heyday.

Special events at the fort include Historical Reenactments in the spring and fall, the Coastal Ranger on July 4th, Native Americans in September, and the Fort King George Christmas in December.

NEARBY ATTRACTIONS: Holwyl-Broadfield Plantation, Sapelo Island, Lewis Island Natural Area, Harris Neck National Wildlife Refuge, Georgia's Golden Islands, Historic Jekyll Island, Fort Frederica, and many coastal museums and beaches.

INFORMATION: The fort is open year-round Tuesday through Saturday from 9 AM until 5 PM and on Sunday from 2 PM until

5:30 PM. It is closed on Mondays, except for legal holidays, and on Thanksgiving and Christmas Day. There is a small admission fee and group rates can be negotiated with advance notice. Picnic tables and bus parking are available.

The fort is in Darien, three miles east of I-95, Exit 10.

Fort McAllister
State Historic Park

Fort McAllister is probably the most complete and best preserved Confederate earthwork fortification in the entire country. The fort was built to defend the Confederate blockade runners in the approaches to the Great Ogeechee River. The wreck of one such blockade runner, *Rattlesnake*, lies in shallow water just a couple of hundred yards from the Northwest Angle. The fort fell to General Sherman on December 13th, 1864.

The massive walls of Fort McAllister were built by hand. Once the site had been chosen, it was cleared of trees and the walls were laid out as a wooden framework. Earth was then piled against the wooden support and allowed to settle. The framework was then removed and the entire structure was covered in sod to retain the loose earth.

Canon at Fort McAllister

Visitors here will have no difficulty traveling back in time to the days when it was bustling with soldiers of the Confederate garrison. The complex has been so well preserved it could be re-garrisoned and defended again in a very short time. Of course, modern technology would destroy it in a matter of seconds, but you get the idea! A self-guided tour of the fort takes in 15 stops, including one at an old parade ground. Other stops on the tour show The Hot Shot Gun (a 32-pounder that fired red-hot solid shot), the Hot Furnace, the Center Bombproof, the Left Angle, the eight-inch Colombiad (a huge coastal gun), the Reconstructed Magazine (the storage for shot, shell, and powder), the Rifled Gun Position, the Mortar Battery and the Northwest Angle. There's also a museum packed with Civil War artifacts and bits and pieces recovered from the Confederate blockade runner, *Rattlesnake.*

The park has 1,700 acres of coastal parkland, 65 tent and trailer sites, hiking trails, boat ramps and a dock, two picnic shelters, one group shelter, and a museum.

ACTIVITIES: Picnicking, audio-visual shows, and educational programs and tours.

Annual events here include a 4th of July Barbecue Picnic & Craft Show, year-round tours of the fort, and Labor Day and winter Musters.

NEARBY ATTRACTIONS: Wormsloe State Historic Site, Ski-daway Island State Park, Fort Pulaski National Monument, Fort Jackson, Sunbury Historic Site, and Historic Savannah.

INFORMATION: Fort McAllister State Historic Park, Box 394-A, Fort McAllister Road, Richmond Hill, Georgia, 31324. Telephone 912-727-2339. The park is open from 7 AM until 10 PM, and the office from 8 AM until 5 PM. The fort itself is open all year Tuesday through Saturday from 9 AM until 5 PM and on Sunday from 2 PM until 5:30 PM. It is closed on Mondays except for legal holidays, and on Thanksgiving and Christmas Day.

The park is 10 miles east of I-95 on Georgia Spur 144; take Exit 15 off I-95.

Fort Morris State Historic Site

Fort Morris on the Medway River was the site of several attacks by British forces during the Revolutionary War. Twice the American defenders were able to withstand combined land and sea attacks by the Redcoats. Then, on January 9th, 1779, the fort fell to a superior British force and remained under British control until they finally evacuated Georgia in 1882. During the occupation several of the prominent local people were imprisoned at the fort, including George Walton, one of the signers of the Declaration of Independence. When the British moved out they left the fort and the once-bustling seaport of Sunbury was left in ruins.

Today you can tour the remains of the earthworks and enjoy the scenic beauty of Saint Catherine's Sound. There's also a museum and many exhibits that describe life and times much as they must have been in the colonial seaport of Sunbury.

Annual events at the site include a Revolutionary War Battle Reenactment in February; Sunbury – A Town and Its People, in April; and Indigo – A Colonial Export in October.

NEARBY ATTRACTIONS: Historic Midway, Fort Stewart Museum, Fort McAllister State Historic Park, Wormsloe State Historic Site, Skidaway Island State Park, and historic Savannah.

INFORMATION: Fort Morris State Historic Site, Route 1, Box 236, Midway, Georgia, 31320. Telephone 912-884-5999. The site is open year-round Tuesday through Saturday from 9 AM until 5 PM and on Sunday from 2 PM until 5:30 PM. It is closed on Mondays, except for legal holidays, and on Thanksgiving and Christmas Day. There is a small admission fee and group rates are offered with advance notice. Picnic tables and bus parking are available.

The site is seven miles east of I-95 Exit 13 on Georgia 38.

General Coffee State Park

The land for the park, which is named for General John Coffee, a famous local planter, US Congressman, and Indian Fighter, was donated to the state by a group of Coffee County citizens in 1970. It is a mecca for wildlife enthusiasts. On both sides of the Seventeen-Mile River that winds its way through 1,500 acres of parkland, creating four small lakes along the way, the park is home to a wide variety of birds, snakes, turtles, mammals, and wildflowers, including several endangered species – among them the indigo snake and the gopher turtle. Once again Georgia offers its visitors a unique and unforgettable outdoor experience.

The park offers 25 tent and trailer sites, a four-acre lake, a winterized group shelter, a swimming pool and bathhouse, six picnic shelters, and a log cabin donated to the park by the Douglas Exchange Club after it was used in the city's 1976 bicentennial celebration.

ACTIVITIES: Hiking nature trails, fishing, nature study, bird watching, wildlife photography, and picnicking.

Annual events here are a Fishing Rodeo in June, Pioneer Skills in June, and an Archery Demonstration in August.

NEARBY ATTRACTIONS: Little Ocmulgee State Park, Okefenokee Swamp, and Georgia Agrirama Agricultural Museum.

INFORMATION: General Coffee State Park, Route 2, Box 83, Nicholls, Georgia, 31554. Telephone 912-384-7082. The park is open from 7 AM until 10 PM, and the park office is open from 8 AM until 5 PM.

The park is six miles east of Douglas on Georgia Highway 32.

George L. Smith State Park

George L. Smith is one of Georgia's favorite recreational parks. The surrounding natural beauty, combined with Watson Mill, the dam, the mill pond with its cypress trees, the covered bridge, the wildlife and the fine fishing, make the 1,350-acre park one of those unique outdoor experiences never to be forgotten.

Facilities here include 21 tent and trailer sites, a 400-acre lake, a winterized group shelter, fishing boat and canoe rentals, and four picnic shelters.

ACTIVITIES: Freshwater fishing throughout the year for bass, crappie, bluegill, and catfish, boating (private boats are permitted but are limited to motors of 10 HP or less), canoeing (there are more than seven miles of canoe trails to explore), nature study, bird watching, wildlife photography, and picnicking.

Annual events include a fishing tournament in May and an Arts & Crafts Festival in October.

NEARBY ATTRACTIONS: Gordonia-Alatamaha State Park and Magnolia Springs State Park.

INFORMATION: George L. Smith State Park, PO Box 57, Twin City, GA 30471. Telephone 912-763-2579. The park is open from 7 AM until 10 PM, and the park office from 8 AM until 5 PM.

George L. Smith State Park is four miles southeast of Twin City, off Georgia Highway 23.

Gordonia-Alatamaha State Park

This is a place that, for more than 20 million years, time forgot. Then, about a million years ago, the area emerged from the oceans, the climate tempered, and life spread from the mainland into this new coastal region. Today it's become something of an outdoor resort. There's a nine-hole golf course, a 12-acre fishing lake, and a host of other great facilities to enjoy.

Major facilities at the park include 23 tent and trailer sites, a nine-hole golf course, a tennis court, a swimming pool, four picnic shelters, a winterized group shelter, and a miniature golf course.

ACTIVITIES: Nature study, bird watching, wildlife photography, picnicking, golfing, exploring, hiking, and lake fishing (no private boats are permitted).

Annual events here include Wildflower Day in April, and July 4th Fireworks.

NEARBY ATTRACTIONS: George L. Smith State Park, Little Ocmulgee State Park and Golf Course, Fort Stewart Military Reservation, and historic Savannah.

INFORMATION: Gordonia-Alatamaha State Park, PO Box 1047, Reidsville, GA 30453. Telephone 912-557-6444 or 912-557-6445 (golf course). The park is open from 7 AM until 10 PM, and the office from 8 AM until 5 PM.

The park is in Reidsville off US 280.

Hofwyl-Broadfield Plantation State Historic Site

This old plantation has its roots set deep into what once was the Old South. In 1807, William Brailsford of Charleston established a rice plantation here among the swamps along the Alatamaha River. When the rice industry here reached its zenith, the plantation had grown to more than 7,300 acres and employed more than 350 slaves. The Civil War brought about the beginning of the end for Hofwyl-Broadfield. At the war's end the slaves were freed and labor to plant rice became scarce. Rice was last planted at Hofwyl-Broadfield in 1915. Then Brailsford's descendants converted the plantation into a dairy. The dairy closed in 1943. Eventually, in 1973, the family willed the plantation to the state and it was turned into the State Historic Site it is today; a window onto Georgia's turbulent past.

Visitors can wander among magnolias and camellias, stroll beneath oak trees, and visit the fine ante-bellum home. The house is filled with antiques and bric-a-brac of times gone by. The museum houses a model of a working rice plantation, many other exhibits, as well as a slide show depicting the lives and times of the plantation's slaves and their owners.

Annual events held here include a Plantation Christmas, and Black History (in February).

NEARBY ATTRACTIONS: Fort King George Historic Site, Historic Jekyll Island, St. Simons Island, Fort Frederica, and Georgia's beaches.

INFORMATION: Hofwyl-Broadfield Plantation State Historic Site, Route 10, Box 83, Brunswick, Georgia, 31520. Telephone 912-

264-9263. The site is open year-round Tuesday through Saturday from 9 AM until 5 PM, and on Sunday from 2 PM until 5:30 PM. It's closed on Mondays, except for legal holidays, and on Thanksgiving and Christmas Day. There is a small admission fee and group rates are offered with advance notice. Bus parking is available.

The plantation is located between Brunswick and Darien on US 17, one mile east of I-95, Exit 9.

Laura S. Walker State Park

Laura Walker was a Georgia naturalist, teacher, writer, and civic leader. She was a great lover of nature and the outdoors, especially the trees. She was also a dedicated worker for the preservation of Georgia's natural beauty. The park is located close to the Okefenokee Swamp and is famous for its wildlife: birds, animals, and wildflowers.

This 300-acre park offers 44 tent and trailer sites, a 120-acre lake and pool, nine picnic shelters, four group shelters, a nature trail, a group camp, and a dock and boat ramp.

ACTIVITIES: Fishing for bluegill, crappie, bass, and catfish (private boats are permitted), boating (rentals are available), waterskiing, hiking, nature study, bird watching, wildlife photography, and picnicking.

Annual special events include the Okefenokee 10K race held in March and an Easter Egg Hunt in April.

NEARBY ATTRACTIONS: Okefenokee Swamp and Wildlife Refuge, Okefenokee Swamp Park, and Hofwyl-Broadfield Plantation State Historic Site.

INFORMATION: Laura S. Walker State Park, 5653 Laura Walker Road, Waycross, GA, 31501. Telephone 912-287-4900. The park is open from 7 AM until 10 PM, and the park office is open from 8 AM until 5 PM.

Laura S. Walker is located nine miles southeast of Waycross on Route 177.

Little Ocmulgee State Park

Little Ocmulgee is one of Georgia's premier state park resorts. In 1935 local landowners along the Little Ocmulgee River began donating the land to the state and, with the help of the Civilian Conservation Corps and the National Parks Service, a dam was built, roads were installed, and facilities were added until, in 1940, the park was opened to the public. Today the park is a full-service state resort offering every amenity the discerning vacationer could ever want, including a magnificent public golf course.

Facilities in this 1,400-acre park include 58 tent and trailer sites, a 30-room lodge and restaurant, 10 rental cottages, a swimming pool, a 260-acre lake, six picnic shelters, one group shelter, two tennis courts, a group camp, pioneer camping, and an 18-hole golf course.

ACTIVITIES: Fishing (rental boats are available), boating and waterskiing (private boats are permitted), hiking (there's a trail and a boardwalk), nature study, bird watching, wildlife photography, picnicking, and golfing on the full-service facility (there's a golf pro and a miniature golf course).

Events held here annually include an Arts & Crafts Festival on the first weekend in April, the Civilian Conservation Corps Reunion on the first Saturday in April, and a Christmas Decorations Workshop on the first Saturday in December.

NEARBY ATTRACTIONS: Georgia Veterans State Park, General Coffee State Park, and Gordonia-Alatamaha State Park.

INFORMATION: Little Ocmulgee State Park and Lodge, PO Box 149, McRae, Georgia, 31055. Telephone 912-868-7474 or 912-868-6651 (golf course). The park is open from 7 AM until 10 PM, and the park office is open from 8 AM until 5 PM.

The park is located two miles north of McRae via US 319 and 441.

Magnolia Springs State Park

During the Civil War this beautiful southern recreation area was the site of Camp Lawton, a Confederate prisoner of war camp. Today not much is left of the prison, just a few rotting timbers that do little to conjure up the image of the camp and its turbulent past. The natural spring from which the park takes its name pumps into the lake some nine million gallons of sparkling water every day. The 948-acre park with its abundance of wildlife offers plenty to see and do throughout the year.

Magnolia Springs has 26 tent and trailer sites, a swimming pool, group shelters, eight picnic shelters, an 85-capacity group camp, five cottages, a boat dock and three playgrounds.

ACTIVITIES: Hiking along the two well-laid-out nature trails, nature study, bird watching, wildlife photography, picnicking, and fishing and boating. Private boats are permitted and rental fishing boats and canoes are available.

Annual events held here are a fishing tournament in May, Canoe the Ogeechee in October, and a clogging and square dancing weekend in November.

NEARBY ATTRACTIONS: Millen National Fish Hatchery Aquarium, George L. Smith State Park, and Historic Savannah.

INFORMATION: Magnolia Springs State Park, Route 5, Box 488, Millen, GA 30442. Telephone 912-982-1660. The park is open from 7 AM until 10 PM and the park office hours are 8 AM until 5 PM.

The park is five miles north of Millen on US 25.

Stephen C. Foster State Park

This park, situated on Jones Island, is the western entrance to the wild and wonderful world of the great Okefenokee Swamp. Named after the songwriter, it's your introduction to an alien world set deep in the heart of southern Georgia. The lush vegetation of the cypress swamp and its waterways is inhabited by a population of more than 200 species of birds, 40 species of mammals, at least 50 different reptiles and some 60 different species of amphibians. At night, when the hot, southern sun has disappeared below the treetops to the west, this vast, sub-tropical world comes to life with sounds of the swamp. Visitors can enjoy the Okefenokee from the comfort of an elevated boardwalk, or get really close to nature by taking a guided boat tour through the maze of silent waterways. Everyone who has the time should make a point to visit Stephen C. Foster, for it really is the experience of a lifetime.

Major facilities offered are 66 tent and trailer sites, nine cottages, three picnic shelters, and an interpretive center.

ACTIVITIES: Hiking the 1/2-mile Trembling Earth Nature Trail, guided boat tours, boat rentals (canoes, motorboats, and jon boats), nature study, bird watching, wildlife photography, and exploring more than 25 miles of public-use waterways.

Annual events at the park include Man in the Swamp in November, Okefenokee Birding, and a variety of interpretive programs throughout the year.

NEARBY ATTRACTIONS: Okefenokee Swamp Park, Okefenokee National Wildlife Refuge, and Suwanee Canoe Recreation Area.

INFORMATION: Stephen C. Foster State Park, Route 1, Box 131, Fargo, GA 31631. Telephone 912-637-5274. The park is open from 7 AM until 7 PM September 15th to February 28th, and from 7 AM until 5 PM March 1st to September 14th. Park office hours are from 8 AM until 5 PM.

Stephen C. Foster Park is 18 miles northeast of Fargo via Georgia Highway 177.

Skidaway Island State Park

More than 500 acres of salt and freshwater marshes make this wild and beautiful park a nature lover's paradise. The Park Service on Skidaway Island offers a complete series of educational programs on the environment, the wild birds that inhabit the area, and the sea life. But visitors to the park will find much more to interest them as they hike the nature trails and explore the park's many historical and archaeological treasures.

The park has 88 tent and trailer sites, five picnic shelters, a playground, and a swimming pool.

ACTIVITIES: Hiking, nature study, bird watching, wildlife photography, picnicking, and outdoor games.

Annual events at the park include the Coastal Birds Program in April, Seafood Delights in the fall, and Wild Game Cooking in winter.

NEARBY ATTRACTIONS: Historic Savannah, Skidaway Marine Institute, Sunbury State Historic Site, Fort McAllister State Historic Park, and Wormesloe State Historic Site.

INFORMATION: Skidaway Island State Park, Savannah, GA 31406. Telephone 912-356-2523 or 356-2524. The park is open daily from 7 AM until 10 PM and office hours are from 8 AM until 5 PM.

This park is six miles southeast of Savannah on Diamond Causeway. Take I-16 to Savannah and Exit 34 at I-516, then turn right onto Waters Avenue and proceed to Diamond Causeway.

The Plains Region

F. D. Roosevelt State Park

The Franklin D. Roosevelt State Park is set on Pine Mountain and was a large part of the four-term president's life. It was here that Roosevelt sought treatment for polio that struck him down in 1921. The 10,000-acre park has something to offer just about everyone – fishing, boating and a wide variety of other outdoor activities.

The park has 140 tent and trailer sites, two lakes, a swimming pool, picnic areas, a family or group shelter, a nature lodge, and 21 cabins.

ACTIVITIES: Fishing, boating, plus hiking and backpacking along the 23 miles of nature trails.

Annual events include Orientation Meetings, a 46-mile Ultra Run, a series of environmental and educational activities, and the Civilian Conservation Corps Reunion held in September.

NEARBY ATTRACTIONS: Callaway Gardens, Warm Springs Village, the Roosevelt Institute, and West Point Lake.

INFORMATION: F. D. Roosevelt State Park, 2870 Georgia Highway 190, Pine Mountain, GA 31822. Telephone 706-663-4858. The park is open daily from 7 AM until 10 PM and the park's office hours are from 8 AM until 5 PM Saturday through Thursday and from 8 AM until 8 PM on Fridays.

The park is just off I-85 west of Warm Springs on Georgia Highway 190, or south of Line Mountain off US 27.

Florence Marina State Park

This park is located at the northern end of Lake Walter F. George on the Chattahoochee River. Situated as it is, the park is a mecca for those who love watersports. The area is rich in early American history and the Kirbo Interpretive Center offers visitors a peek into local history, from Paleolithic times through the early pioneer days to the present.

Major facilities at the park include 44 tent and trailer sites, a miniature golf course, 10 rental cottages, a clubhouse, an interpretive center, a marina with 66 boat slips, two tennis courts, a swimming pool, and a lighted fishing pier.

ACTIVITIES: Boating (there are six docks), camping, and fishing.

Annual events include a crappie fishing tournament in March, an Easter Egg Hunt, an Astronomy Evening in August, a Native American Day in September, and Haunted Halloween.

NEARBY ATTRACTIONS: Fort Benning Base and Museum, Providence Canyon State Park, Eufaula National Wildlife Refuge, Westville Historic Village, and the Confederate Navy Museum.

INFORMATION: Florence Marina State Park, Route 1, Box 36, Omaha, GA 31821. Telephone 912-838-6870. The park is open daily from 7 AM until 10 PM and the office hours are from 8 AM until 5 PM.

Florence Marina State Park is 16 miles west of Lumpkin at the end of Georgia Route 39C.

George T. Bagby State Park

George T. Bagby State Park is situated at the southern end of the 48,000-acre Lake Walter E. George. The park covers a total of 300 acres. If you're looking for a place to get away from it all, this great wild and scenic area of open water and big skies is it. If you're looking for comfort along with your outdoor experience, you will find that here, too. The modern lodge offers all the amenities of a large hotel and yet is able to maintain an atmosphere of isolation, serenity, and even adventure. If you love watersports, the boating and fishing is among the best found anywhere in Georgia.

The park has 50 tent and trailer sites, several picnic shelters (handicapped-accessible), five rental cottages, a swimming beach, a marina with a full-service dock and boat ramp, and a 30-room lodge complete with restaurant and gift shop.

ACTIVITIES: Hiking, picnicking, boating (private boats are permitted), and fishing.

The two annual special events at the park are a Crappie Fishing Tournament held in April, and a Halloween Hayride.

NEARBY ATTRACTIONS: Westville Historic Village, Kolomoki Mounds State Park, and Providence Canyon State Park.

INFORMATION: George T. Bagby State Park & Lodge, Route 1, Box 201, Fort Gaines, GA 31751. Telephone 912-768-2571. The park is open from 7 AM until 10 PM and the park office hours are 8 AM until 5 PM.

The park and lodge are three miles north of Fort Gains off Georgia Highway 39.

Georgia Veterans Memorial State Park

This park, more than 1,300 acres of gardens, groves, and woodland on the shores of Lake Blackshear, was established as a permanent memorial to all of the U.S veterans who served, fought, and died for freedom. It's a quiet area, a place where one can leave the hustle and bustle of city life far behind and spend a few hours, or even a few days, relaxing in the serenity of one of Georgia's most beautiful and sacred places. If it's outdoor activities that you're looking for, there's plenty for you to see and do: golf, swimming, boating, waterskiing, fishing, hiking, nature study, bird watching, wildlife photography, picnicking, and lots more.

Big Gun at Georgia Veterans Memorial

Facilities at the park include 83 tent and trailer sites, 10 rental cottages, an 18-hole golf course, pool and beach, and a winterized group shelter.

Annual events here are a Memorial Celebration, Veterans Day Ceremonies, a Catfish Festival in May, and Christmas on the Flint in December.

NEARBY ATTRACTIONS: Plains, Georgia (home of President Jimmy Carter), Historic Americus, Georgia Agrirama Agricultural Museum, Providence Canyon State Park, and Andersonville National Historic Site.

INFORMATION: Georgia Veterans Memorial State Park, 2459-A US 280W, Cordele, GA 31015. Telephone 912-276-2371 or 276-2377. The park is open 7 AM until 10 PM and the park office hours are 8 AM until 5 PM.

The veterans park is nine miles west of I-75, Exit 33, near Cordele on US 280.

High Falls State Park

The thriving little industrial town that once stood on the site of High Falls State Park is no more. It became a ghost town towards the end of the 19th century when it was bypassed by the railroad. Today the park is an oddly beautiful place that attracts visitors from around the state. The 650-acre lake offers fine fishing, and there are hiking trails, along with isolated areas of great natural beauty.

Facilities here include 142 tent and trailer sites, a screened-in group shelter, a swimming pool, and a miniature golf course.

ACTIVITIES: Canoeing, hiking along the two scenic trails and visiting the waterfalls.

Events held here annually are the Forsythia Festival and Crappie Tournament in March, the Fall

Thundering Falls at High Falls

Family Camp-Out Weekend, and the Christmas Tree Trimming Program.

NEARBY ATTRACTIONS: Oconee National Forest, Piedmont National Wildlife Refuge, Indian Springs State Park, and Jarrell Plantation State Historic Site.

INFORMATION: High Falls State Park, Route 5, Box 202-A, Jackson, GA 30233. Telephone 912-994-5080. The park is open from 7 AM until 10 PM and the office hours are 8 AM until 5 PM.

The park is two miles east of I-75, Exit 65 and High Falls Road.

Indian Springs State Park

Indian Springs is said to be the oldest state park in the United States. Its claim to fame is the sulpher spring, a former gathering and healing place for Creek Indians, from which it takes its name. The Creeks signed away their rights to the land in 1821 and the government disposed of all but 10 acres of what was then called

Indian Springs Reserve. Local residents of Butts County, however, purchased some 513 acres adjoining the reserve and donated it to the state.

Today the 523-acre park includes the original mineral spring, a 105-acre lake, and a museum.

The Spring House, Indian Springs State Park

It also offers 90 tent and trailer sites, 10 cottages, seven picnic shelters, and a miniature golf course.

ACTIVITIES: Hiking the nature trails, boating (private boats of 10 HP or less; rental boats are available), and picnicking.

Annual events include a week-long astronomy program in August, a Southeastern Indian Celebration in September, and a Christmas Decorations Workshop in December.

NEARBY ATTRACTIONS: Oconee National Forest, Piedmont National Wildlife Refuge, High Falls State Park, and Jarrell Plantation State Historic Site.

INFORMATION: Indian Springs State Park, Route 1, Box 439, Flovilla, GA 30216. Telephone 404-775-7241. The park is open from 7 AM until 10 PM and the office hours are 8 AM until 5 PM.

Indian Springs State Park is located south of Jackson on Georgia Highway 42.

Jarrell Plantation
State Historic Site

The Jarrell Plantation is an original southern plantation founded in the early 1840s by John Fitz Jarrell. The original house, along with some 20 other buildings, still stands. The buildings, original tools and machinery, and many family heirlooms and antiques, offer a look through the window of time into Georgia's past. Visitors can tour the old home, the three-story barn, the smokehouses, the cane furnace, the steam-powered grist mill, the saw mill, the shingle mill, the blacksmith shop, and the syrup mill.

Annual events include 100 Years of Jarrell Clothing, Sheep Shearing, Spinning and Weaving, a 4th of July Celebration, Labor Day on the Farm, Cane Grinding and Syrup Making, and Christmas Candlelight Tours.

NEARBY ATTRACTIONS: Lake Juliette, Piedmont National Wildlife Refuge, High Falls State Park, and Indian Springs State Park.

INFORMATION: Jarrell Plantation State Historic Site, Route 2, Box 220, Juliette, Georgia 31046. Telephone 912-986-5172. The site is open year-round Tuesday through Saturday from 9 AM until 5

PM and on Sundays from 2 PM until 5:30 PM. It is closed on Mondays, and on Thanksgiving and Christmas Day.

The Jarrell Plantation is located southeast of Juliette, and 18 miles from I-75 Exit 60.

Kolomoki Mounds
State Historic Park

The 1,300-acre Kolomoki State Park is not only a popular recreational area, it's an important archaeological site as well. The seven mounds from which the park takes its name were built by the Swift Creek and Weeden Island Indians during a period that encompassed most of the 12th and 13th centuries. They include Georgia's oldest temple mound, two burial mounds, and four ceremonial mounds. There's a museum and interpretive center with many informative exhibits depicting the Indians and their culture.

Major facilities at the park include 35 tent and trailer sites, a group camp, two lakes, a boat dock and ramp, rental boats, several hiking trails, two swimming pools, a miniature golf course and seven picnic shelters.

ACTIVITIES: Hiking, fishing, boating, and camping. Private boats are permitted on the lakes.

The annual events held here are a Biathlon in July, and Indian Artifacts Day in October.

NEARBY ATTRACTIONS: Lake Seminole, George T. Bagby State Park, Lake Walter F. George, and Seminole State Park.

INFORMATION: Kolomoki Mounds State Historic Park, Route 1, Box 114, Blakely, GA 31723. Telephone 912-723-5296. The park is open from 7 AM until 10 PM; the office from 8 AM until 5 PM.

The park is six miles to the north of Blakely off US 27.

Lapham-Patterson House
State Historic Site

Located in the heart of Thomasville, the Lapham-Patterson House is one of the most extraordinary examples of a Victorian Resort House in the nation. The house was built around 1885 as the winter home of Chicago shoe merchant, C.W. Lapham. The magnificent architecture includes fishscale shingles, oriental porch decorations, pine floors, a cantilevered balcony, and a fine example of a double-flue chimney and walk-through stairway. The Lapham-Patterson House was named a National Historic Landmark in 1975.

Events held here each year are a Victorian Christmas, a quilt show, a rose show in April, and various Victorian Culture Programs.

NEARBY ATTRACTIONS: Seminole State Park, the Hardy Bryan House, Thomas County Historical Society Museum, and Pebble Hill Plantation.

INFORMATION: Lapham-Patterson House State Historic Site, 626 N. Dawson Street, Thomasville, GA 31792. Telephone 912-225-4004. The house is open year-round Tuesday through Saturday from 9 AM until 5 PM and on Sundays from 2 PM until 5:30 PM. It is closed on Mondays, Thanksgiving, and Christmas Day.

Providence Canyon
State Conservation Park

Providence Canyon is unique in that, although it was formed by the action of water, there is no great river flowing along its bottom. In fact, the canyon was formed by intense rainfall over the last few hundred years. Folklore has it that the great canyon began to form when the run-off from one of Georgia's pioneer settler‚s plowed fields washed out a tiny gully. The next rainfall washed away even more, and subsequent downpours continued the erosion, thus creating a natural phenomenon that continues to grow proportionately to this day. It's been said that a single heavy storm can increase the depth of the canyon by a staggering eight inches.

Providence Canyon

Providence Canyon is a wild place. Canyon walls provide a splendid backdrop of natural colors for trees and the wildflowers growing in abundance throughout the area. Be sure to bring your camera.

The park offers two picnic shelters, a family group shelter, 10 miles of hiking and backcountry trails, pioneer camping, and an interpretive center. Each year the park holds Spring and Fall Wildflower Days, and the Kudzu Takeover Day in August.

NEARBY ATTRACTIONS: Westfield Historic Village, Kolomoki Mounds State Park, Bedingfield Inn, and Florence Marina State Park.

INFORMATION: Providence Canyon State Park, Route 1, Box 158, Lumpkin, GA 31815. Telephone 912-838-6202. The park is open from 7 AM until 6 PM from September 15th through April 14th, and from 7 AM until 9 PM from April 15th through September 14th. The park office is open from 8 AM until 5 PM.

Providence Canyon is seven miles west of Lumpkin on Georgia Highway 39C.

Reed Bingham State Park

This 1,600-acre state park is one of the most popular centers for outdoor activities in southwest Georgia. The 375-acre lake offers fine fishing for crappie, bass, catfish and bream, as well as boating, canoeing, and waterskiing. For the land lubber there are almost four miles of hiking and nature trails to explore Georgia's great outdoors.

Facilities here include 85 tent and trailer sites, a beach, four boat ramps and three fishing docks, seven picnic shelters, four group shelters, and the Coastal Plains Nature Trail.

Annual gatherings at Reed Bingham include 4th of July Music and Fireworks, Old Fashioned Games on Memorial Day and Labor Day, and Buzzard Day the first Saturday in December.

NEARBY ATTRACTIONS: Paradise Public Fishing Area at Tifton, Banks Lake National Wildlife Refuge, and the Georgia Agrirama also in Tifton.

INFORMATION: Reed Bingham State Park, Route 2, Box 394B-1, Adel, GA 31620. Telephone 912-896-3551. The park is open from 7 AM until 10 PM; the park office is open from 8 AM until 5 PM.

The park is just six miles west of Adel on Georgia Highway 37.

Seminole State Park

The park is small (only 350 acres) compared to many of Georgia's great parks, but what it lacks in size it more than makes up for with its natural beauty and abundance of wildlife and wildflowers. Seminole is set on the banks of 37,500-acre Lake Seminole, which is famed for its sport fishing. It offers visitors a place where they can get away from it all, get close to nature, and find peace and quiet, leaving the crowded city streets far behind.

The park offers 50 tent and trailer sites, 10 rental cottages, a swimming beach, two fishing docks, three boat ramps, a nature trail, a miniature golf course, as well as family and group shelters.

ACTIVITIES: Boating (rental boats are available at the marina), fishing, waterskiing, swimming, and a program of summer nature programs.

NEARBY ATTRACTIONS: Kolomoki Mounds State Park, and Lapham-Patterson State Historic Site.

INFORMATION: Seminole State Park, Route 2, Donalsonville, GA 31745. Telephone 912-861-3137. The park is open from 7 AM until 10 PM and the park office is open from 8 AM until 5 PM.

The park is 16 miles south of Donalsonville via Georgia Highway 39, or 23 miles west of Bainbridge on Georgia Highway 253.

General Information

HOW THE PARKS ARE ORGANIZED: The 58 parks and historic sites, and the more than 60,000 acres included in this system are organized geographically into four regions: the Highlands in the north, the Piedmont Region at the center of the state, the Plains Region to the southwest, and the Coastal Region to the southeast. For the sake of ease and efficiency the parks are listed by region and in alphabetical order.

OPENING TIMES: While all 58 locations are open the year-round, most of the historic sites and all of the swimming and golf facilities are closed on Mondays, except on legal holidays. Although the hours may vary at some locations, park offices open daily from 8 AM to 5 PM, and the parks open daily at 7 AM and close at 10 PM with the exception of Providence Canyon, Panola Mountain, and Stephen C. Foster, which operate special seasonal schedules. The historic sites open daily at 9 AM to 5 PM Tuesday through Saturday; 2 PM to 5:30 Sunday; closed Mondays (except legal holidays), Thanksgiving, and Christmas. Hours vary at Little White House (9 AM to 5 PM daily; closed Thanksgiving and Christmas) and Dahlonega Gold Museum (9 AM to 5 PM Monday through Saturday; 10 AM to 5 PM Sunday; closed Thanksgiving and Christmas).

THE GEORGIA PARKPASS: A Georgia ParkPass is required for parked vehicles in all state parks. Visitors may pay a daily fee or purchase an annual parking pass for display in their vehicle. The ParkPass is valid at all state parks visited on the same day. Guests at the lodges, cottages, and campgrounds pay a single fee good for the duration of their visit. Organized school groups visiting in buses are exempt. Wednesdays are free days for the day-use visitor. An annual ParkPass may be purchased at all parks and historic sites. A senior citizen (62 years and older) annual ParkPass is also available. There is a small admission charge at historic sites; registered guests at lodges and cottages are admitted free or at discounted rates. All fees collected are used for park maintenance and repair.

SPECIAL PROGRAMS: In order to help the public better understand and experience the rich variety of Georgia's natural and historic wonders, a diversity of special programs is offered throughout the year at many of the state park locations: backpacking clinics, folk skills, hikes, canoe excursions, living history demonstrations, music festivals, and many special family-oriented holiday programs.

Facilities

CAMPING: Facilities are available at 39 of Georgia's state parks. These include tent or trailer camping sites, RV sites, walk-in camping, pioneer camping, and group camp facilities. Tent, trailer, and RV campsites feature electrical and water hookups, cooking grills, and picnic tables. All campgrounds have modern comfort stations and dump sites. Many offer laundry facilities and camping supplies. Most campsites are available on a first-come, first-served basis; however, each campground has a number of sites that can be reserved in advance.

- **TENT, RV, AND TRAILER CAMPING** campgrounds are open from 7 AM to 10 PM. Registration at the park office is required no later than 8 PM on the day of arrival and before setting up camp. Late arrivals must pay the camping fee the following morning. Mastercard and Visa are accepted. Check-out time is 1 PM. There is a 14-day maximum stay allowed at each campsite.

  Two-day reservations are accepted for a limited number of campsites. A non-refundable deposit of two night's camping fees must be paid within seven days of making the reservation. Reservations may be made in person or by telephone up to three months in advance.

  Campers under the age of 18 must be accompanied by an adult willing to accept responsibility. Organized groups may not occupy campsites in tent, RV, or trailer camping areas. Group and pioneer camping facilities are available elsewhere in the parks.

- **PIONEER CAMPSITES** with water and primitive sanitary facilities are available at many parks for organized groups. A small charge per person and advance reservations are required. Pioneer campsites do not accommodate RVs or trailers.

- **GROUP CAMPS AND LODGES** are available at several of Georgia's state parks for organized groups. Many group campgrounds include sleeping quarters, kitchens, dining rooms, assembly rooms, activity areas, and swimming facilities. Rental fees vary from park to park and reservations are required.

COTTAGES: Cottages are available at nearly all state parks and are fully equipped with stoves, refrigerators, kitchen and dining utensils, bed linens, blankets, and towels. All cottages are heated and most are air-conditioned. Many cottages have porches or decks and wood-burning fire-places or stoves (firewood is not provided).

- Reservations are taken by individual parks up to 11 months in advance. A one-night deposit is required within seven days of making a reservation. Reservations are not confirmed until the deposit is received. Deposits not received result in cancellation of the reservation. From June 1st to Labor Day, reservations for less than one week are not accepted unless they are made less than one month in advance and are for at least two days. From Labor Day until May 31st, there is a minimum two-day reservation rule, one-night occupancy is allowed, but there is an additional surcharge. Priority is given in the following order: 1st, in person; 2nd, by telephone; 3rd, by mail; and to the longest stay requested. Mastercard and Visa are accepted.

- Check-in time is 4 PM to 10 PM. The park must be notified if you intend to arrive late and registration is not allowed after 10 PM except in an emergency. Reservations are not held after 11 AM of the second day and deposits will be forfeited unless the park has been notified of your late arrival. Check-out time is 11 AM at all parks.

  Deposits may be refunded if a 72-hour notice is given to the park; a cancellation fee will be deducted from the deposit. Unused portions of a reservation period may be refunded when minimum occupancy requirements have been satisfied. A deposit receipt is required for a refund.

- Maximum occupancy of the cottages varies. Occupation of a cottage is limited to 14 nights. Cottages are not available for church or civic groups, fraternities, sororities, schools groups, family reunions, or youth groups. A responsible adult must accompany all guests under 18 years of age.

LODGE FACILITIES are available at Amicalola Falls, George T. Bagby, Little Ocmulgee, Red Top Mountain, and Unicoi state parks. The lodges offer a special and natural setting for an unforgettable "getaway" experience or an unusual group meeting in some of Georgia's most beautiful regions. Each lodge offers easy access either to mountains, rivers and lakes, golf courses, or hiking trails.

The number of guest rooms at the lodges varies from 30 to 100. The rooms vary too. Some offer special features such as sleeping lofts for children, suites with separate bedrooms, and some have private porches. Handicapped-equipped and non-smoking rooms are available at all lodges. Children under 12 years of age stay free when accompanied by an adult in the same room. Each room has a television, telephone, and individual climate control. A limited number of port-a-cribs is available. There are no rollaway beds or cots. Maximum occupancy is four in double rooms and six in loft rooms. Check-in time is 4 PM. Check-out time is 11 AM.

For group getaways, conferences and meetings, Georgia's lodges offer the convenience of ultra modern meeting facilities designed to enable groups to focus on their programs and activities, and at the same time enjoy the retreat-like atmosphere of the great outdoors. When the meetings are over there are fine golf courses, tennis, swimming, hiking, fishing and boating. Interpretive programs and special events are offered the year-round, along with access to some of Georgia's finest historical and natural attractions. All facilities are fully equipped and staffed to handle meeting and group functions for 150 to 400 persons. Complimentary audio-visual equipment is available upon request. Each lodge offers a full-service restaurant and catering facilities. Diners may choose à la carte or buffet-style breakfasts, lunches and dinners. On-site catering is available for banquets, receptions, and meeting breaks. Group reservations can be made up to five years in advance and the Lodge Conference Coordinators can be called upon to assist in the planning and organization of such events.

Individual lodge information is listed under each park location, or you can call the individual lodge directly. Lodge reservations are accepted up to 11 months in advance. Reservations are confirmed upon receipt of an advance deposit, which can be paid by check, cash, credit card, or a credit card guarantee. Cancellations are allowed up to 4 PM with no penalty. Guaranteed reservations are held unless cancelled before the cut-off time. However, reservations not cancelled and non-arrivals will be charged one night's lodging plus tax. Mastercard, Visa, American Express, and Diners Club are accepted.

Overnight Accommodation Rates

COTTAGES DAILY: One bedroom, Sunday through Thursday $40; Friday & Saturday, $50. Two bedroom: Sunday through Thursday, $59; Friday and Saturday, $60. Three bedroom: Sunday through Thursday, $60; Friday and Saturday, $70. Will-A-Way two bedroom: special groups Sunday through Thursday, $35; Friday and Saturday, $35. General: Sunday through Friday, $50; Friday and Saturday, $60. There is a $15 surcharge for one-night visits, and a $10 handling fee per unit for cancellations. There is $10 off Sunday through Thursdays, December 1st through March 31st for senior citizens (65 & over).

LODGES: Amicalola Falls Lodge: Double/King room December 1st through March 31st, $45; April 1st through November 30th, $55. Junior Suite/King Loft December 1st through March 31st, $65; April 1st through November 30th, $75. Executive Suite December 1st through March 31st, $90; April 1st through November 30th, $100.

Lake Walter F. George Lodge: Double Room, year-round, $35; Junior Suite, year-round, $70.

Pete Phillips Lodge: Double Room, year-round, $47; Junior Suite, year-round, $70.

Red Top Mountain Lodge: Double Room, December 1st through March 31st, $40; April 1st through November 30th, $45. Junior Suite, December 1st through March 31st, $65; April 1st through November 30th, $65.

Unicoi Lodge: Double Room/Loft Weekdays, December 1st through March 31st, $30; April 1st through November 30th, $50. Double Room/Loft Weekends, December 1st through March 31st, $40; April 1st through November 30th, $50.

Lodge rates are based upon single occupancy and while they are correct at the time of this writing they are subject to change without notice. Each additional adult is $6. Children under 12 years of age stay free when accompanied by an adult in the same room.

CAMPSITES: Tent, pop-up, RV campsites, $10; Senior citizens 65 and over, $8. Reservation fee, $5 (the rate applies only when the vehicle is registered to the senior citizen). Walk-in Campsites and Squirrel's Nest, $6. Pioneer Campsites per person, $1 (supervised groups only, $15 minimum). Primitive camping per person, $3.

Group camps $3 per person per day. Each camp has a minimum occupancy and a one-week minimum stay during June, July, and August. There is a $10 handling fee for cancellations and a cleanup/damage deposit is required. Camp facilities vary, but typically include dormitory sleeping quarters, restrooms/showers. kitchen, and a dining area. Call the individual park for details.

GROUP LODGES: John Tanner and Cloudland Canyon, June 1st through Labor Day, $100 daily; after Labor Day the rate drops to $80 daily.

Activities

HISTORIC SITES: There are 14 historic state parks in Georgia. They offer the visitor an insight into the state's rich cultural heritage and range in scope from the small courthouse museum through North American Indian sites, Civil War battlefields, Revolutionary and Confederate forts, to great southern plantations. Many of the sites offer interpretive museums, audio-visual presentations, living history demonstrations, and guided or self-guided tours. All charge a small admission fee and most offer special rates to tour groups and youth groups with advance notice.

SWIMMING: Most parks have swimming pools or beaches open from June 1st each year through Labor Day. Opening hours are, with a few exceptions, from 11 AM to 6 PM Wednesday through Sunday; they are closed on Mondays and Tuesdays, with the exception of legal holidays. At Red Top Mountain State Park, Ft. Yargo, Hard Labor Creek, John Tanner, Indian Springs, and High Falls, the facilities are open from 1 PM to 7 PM each day Tuesday through Sunday and closed on Mondays with the exception of legal holidays. Registered cottage and lodge guests swim free. Camping guests pay the regular fees.

PICNICKING: Almost all of Georgia's state parks and historic sites offer picnicking facilities in one form or another. There is no charge for the use of open tables but picnic shelters may be reserved for a small fee. Shelters not reserved are available at no charge on a first-come, first-served basis. Many of the parks offer group shelters, screened and winterized, with tables, chairs, grills, stoves and refrigerators. Restrooms are always nearby. Please contact the individual parks for availability, shelter capacities, fees and reservations.

HIKING AND NATURE TRAILS: Almost all of Georgia's state parks and historic sites feature a variety of designated hiking trails and backcountry walks varying in length from a few hundred yards to as much as seven miles. The walks feature the local plant and wildlife habitats, and offer the visitor a special look at some of the nation's most spectacular scenic and geological features.

BICYCLING: There's nothing quite like the get-away-from-it-all feeling of biking through a quiet stretch of glorious countryside. For sheer scenic beauty Georgia's parks are hard to beat. Cyclists can enjoy traveling the backcountry trails and roads at a pace reminiscent of the casual days of turn-of-the-century America, missing nothing of the natural sights and sounds of the countryside along the way. Park campsites allow enough room to park four bikes and pitch two two-man tents. Contact the Georgia Department of Industry, Trade and Tourism at PO Box 1776 Atlanta, GA 30301 to receive a handy book, "Georgia Bicycle Touring Guide."

FISHING AND BOATING: More than 27 of Georgia's state parks are on major lakes or rivers. The facilities usually offer boat ramps and docks. Several of the major locations have fully-equipped marinas offering everything from boating supplies and fuel to groceries. Waterskiing is permitted on the lakes and the campsites and cottages are always near the water. Most locations offer excellent fishing. Rental boats are available for hire, and private fishing boats, sailing boats, and canoes are permitted at some locations. There are some size and motor restrictions on the smaller parks (check the individual listings for details), but there are no fees for fishing the park lakes, rivers, or streams. A valid Georgia resident/non-resident fishing license is required for persons aged 16 or older, and trout stamps are required when fishing the trout streams.

GOLF: Some of the finest golf courses in the entire southeast are to be found in Georgia's state parks. For the most part, the courses remain uncrowded and feature magnificent scenery and superbly manicured greens and fairways. A special feature is the policy of unlimited golf on weekdays and the low-cost annual passes that are good for use at any of the five courses. Each location offers overnight accommodations and affordable green fees and cart rentals, with discounted rates for senior citizens.

SPECIAL SUMMER PROGRAMMING: During the summer months Georgia's state parks and historic sites are staffed with fully trained interpretive specialists offering a variety of special and exciting programs. These range from nature hikes through living history programs, hiking and backpacking, canoeing, outdoor recreational skills, and local crafts. Call the individual parks for more information and program schedules.

INFORMATION: To receive a complete information package, including accommodations, a map of park locations, and an annual guide to special events, you can call the nearest state park, historic site, or the Public Information Office, 404-656-3530. Alternatively, write to the Public Information Office, Georgia State Parks & Historic Sites, 1352 Floyd Tower East, 205 Butler Street, SE. Atlanta, GA 30334.

Kentucky

There are 46 state parks in the Kentucky system and three more in the planning stage. All of them have been designed to offer the visitor a total outdoor recreational and environmental experience. Since the days of Daniel Boone, visitors to Kentucky have been attracted by the legendary scenic beauty of its rolling grasslands, its many historic sites, tranquil lakes, thundering waterfalls, slow flowing rivers and majestic sandstone bluffs, its mysterious caves and lush mountain forests, all of which offer a perfect family adventure.

Each park in the Kentucky system has a distinct character all of its own and takes full advantage of the surrounding natural beauty. Fifteen of the parks, each uniquely designed to comple-ment the setting, claim resort status, with facilities that would rival many of the famous coastal resorts: executive retreats, ban-quets, meetings and conventions, and a variety of activities tai-lored to meet any and all group or individual needs. They offer a wide variety of accommodations designed to suit every individ-ual, family, or group need, including rustic, full-service family cottages, modern full-service camping sites, and primitive camp-

Kentucky

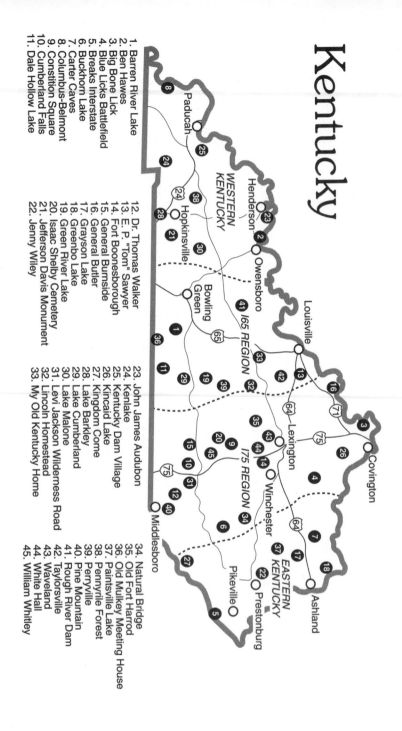

1. Barren River Lake
2. Ben Hawes
3. Big Bone Lick
4. Blue Licks Battlefield
5. Breaks Interstate
6. Buckhorn Lake
7. Carter Caves
8. Columbus-Belmont
9. Constition Square
10. Cumberland Falls
11. Dale Hollow Lake
12. Dr. Thomas Walker
13. E. P. "Tom" Sawyer
14. Fort Boonesborough
15. General Burnside
16. General Butler
17. Grayson Lake
18. Greenbo Lake
19. Green River Lake
20. Isaac Shelby Cemetery
21. Jefferson Davis Monument
22. Jenny Wiley
23. John James Audubon
24. Kenlake
25. Kentucky Dam Village
26. Kincaid Lake
27. Kingdom Come
28. Lake Barkley
29. Lake Cumberland
30. Lake Malone
31. Levi Jackson Wilderness Road
32. Lincoln Homestead
33. My Old Kentucky Home
34. Natural Bridge
35. Old Fort Harrod
36. Old Mulkey Meeting House
37. Paintsville Lake
38. Pennyrile Forest
39. Perryville
40. Pine Mountain
41. Rough River Dam
42. Taylorsville
43. Waveland
44. White Hall
45. William Whitley

ing sites which will appeal to the most dedicated outdoorsmen and women.

Many of Kentucky's state parks are dedicated to the colorful history of the state, and combine a variety of modern vacation facilities with a fascinating window on the past. Such attractions might feature museums, outdoor reenactments, living history demonstrations, craft shows, and guided tours. No other park system in the southeastern United States offers a more complete range of services and facilities.

The Kentucky State Park System is organized, for easy access from Kentucky's interstate highways, into four regions: The Reeling Waterways Region in Western Kentucky with 10 parks; The Cave Corridor Region centered around I-65 with 10 parks; The Wilderness Trail Region with I-75 running through the center of it has 20 parks; and The Mountain Gateway in the eastern section of the state has six parks.

Western Kentucky

The Reeling Waterways

Ben Hawes State Park

If you love golf, then Ben Hawes is the place for you. Located in Owensboro, Kentucky's third largest city, the park offers a fine 18-hole course, along with a challenging nine-hole par-3 course. Pros and beginners alike will find the golf at Ben Hawes exciting and worth the trip. There are no overnight facilities here, but there is a well stocked pro shop and an archery range for those who like to try something a little different. There are several tennis courts, a softball field, a hiking trail, a picnic shelter and a playground.

INFORMATION: Ben Hawes State Park, Box 761, Owensboro, KY 42302-0761. Telephone the park office 502-684-9808, or the pro shop 502-685-2011.

The park is just four miles west of Owensboro off US 60.

Columbus-Belmont State Park

Columbus-Belmont State Park, located high above the Mississippi River close to the Kentucky/Missouri border, is one of the state's smaller recreational facilities. The park has an important history. The Civil War Battle of Belmont in 1861 was a struggle to control the mighty commercial waterway and block access to the South by Union gunboats and troop transports. The remains of the massive chains that used to block the waterway can still be seen today.

The park's facilities, though not nearly as extensive as some of the others, make for a pleasant and not-to-be-missed outdoor experience. There are 38 camping sites, with all the usual utilities including utility hookups, dump site, central service station with restrooms, showers, grocery store, and laundry. There's a concession stand, gift shop, miniature golf course, museum, picnic shelters, playground, and 2.5 miles of hiking trails.

NEARBY ATTRACTIONS: Lake Barkley State Resort Park, Kentucky Dam Village State Resort Park, Kenlake State Resort Park, Jefferson Davis Monument State Historic Site, Pennyrile Forest State Resort Park, and Fort Donnelson National Battlefield Park in Dover, Tennessee.

INFORMATION: Columbus-Belmont State Park, PO Box 8, Columbus, KY 42032-0008. Telephone 502-677-2327.

The park is 36 miles southwest of Paducah on Kentucky Highway 80.

Jefferson Davis Monument State Historic Site

At just 19 acres, Jefferson Davis is one of the smallest of Kentucky's state parks. The park and monument are dedicated to the memory of the Confederacy's one and only President. The 351-

foot obelisk that marks his birthplace features an elevator that carries visitors to an observation deck where they can enjoy one of the finest panoramic views in the entire state.

Aside from the 19 acres of rolling parkland there is a museum, a gift shop, picnic shelters, and a playground for the children to enjoy.

INFORMATION: Jefferson Davis Monument State Historic Site, PO Box 10, Fairview, KY 42221-0010. Telephone 502-886-1765.

The park is located 10 miles east of Hopkinsville on US 68.

John James Audubon State Park

This fine park, set just south of the Ohio River, is dedicated to the famed naturalist who spent much of his time observing the subjects of his paintings while he lived in nearby Henderson. The peaceful woods have been preserved much as they were when John Audubon walked among them. The park museum contains several priceless original prints from the folio edition of Audubon's *The Birds of America*, published from 1826 to 1833.

Museum & Nature Center at John James Audubon

Facilities at the park include five family cottages available year-round, 71 campsites with all the usual utilities including hook-ups, a dump site, a central service station with restrooms, showers, a grocery store, and laundry. There's a beach, boating, fishing, tennis courts, a nine-hole golf course and pro shop, almost six miles of hiking trails, the Audubon Memorial Museum, and a nature preserve lake.

ACTIVITIES: Golfing, swimming, fishing, nature study and bird watching, wildlife photography, hiking, and a variety of planned recreation activities offered by a fully qualified staff of directors and naturalists. There's also a playground and several picnic shelters.

INFORMATION: John James Audubon State Park, PO Box 576, Henderson, KY 42420-0576. Telephone 502-826-2247.

The park is in Henderson on US 41 north.

Kentucky Dam Village State Resort Park

Kentucky Dam Village Resort is on a 40-mile-long peninsula bound by Lake Barkley and Kentucky Lake. Known internationally as the Land Between the Lakes, it is an extensive wildlife refuge and outdoor vacation area that reaches from the northern tip of Kentucky Lake across the state border into Tennessee.

The resort has a great deal to offer the discerning vacationer with a penchant for outdoor adventure. Facilities include 221 campsites available year-round, complete with utility hookups, dump stations, and central service stations with restrooms, showers, and laundry facilities. There are 72 secluded cottages, also offered throughout the year, ranging from small efficiency units to luxury three-bedroom executive cottages. Fresh linens are available at each cottage on a daily basis.

For a taste of luxury you might like to stay for a day or two at the imposing main lodge, where all rooms have private balconies or patios overlooking the lake. The facility and staff are fully qualified and aim to please every visitor's needs.

If you're looking for a unique golfing package, a few days at the Village Green Inn next to the 18th hole on the resort golf course might be just the ticket!

Other facilities at the resort include a large convention center, dining rooms, swimming pools, tennis courts, gift shop, grocery store, picnic shelters, planned recreation activities for those who like to have their vacations organized for them, a marina with 100 open slips and 225 covered slips, miniature golf course, 18-hole golf course, and a 4,000-foot lighted airstrip. Rental pedal boats, pontoons, rowboats, fishing boats, and ski boats are available at the marina, and there's a pro shop at the golf course.

ACTIVITIES: Hiking, boating, waterskiing, fishing, swimming, and golf.

NEARBY ATTRACTIONS: Paducah, Columbus-Belmont Battlefield State Park, Kenlake State Resort Park, Lake Barkley State Resort Park, Jefferson Davis Monument State Historic Site, Pennyrile Forest State Resort Park, and Fort Donnelson National Battlefield Park in Dover, Tennessee.

There are various vacation, weekend, and golf packages available throughout the year at both the main resort lodge, and at the Village Green Inn.

INFORMATION: Kentucky Dam Village State Resort Park, PO Box 69, Gilbertsville, KY 42044-0069. The lodge telephone number is 502-362-4271; the marina 502-362-8386. The toll-free reservation number is 800-325-0146.

The resort is situated 21 miles southeast of Paducah. From Paducah, take I-24 east to US 62, then go to US 641 east.

Kenlake State Resort Park

Kenlake is on the western shores of massive Kentucky Lake. The resort offers all the grandeur associated with great hotels of an age gone by, a gracious blend of southern hospitality and the panoramic beauty of the Land Between the Lakes. Visitors can choose between a vacation of quiet relaxation in the fresh air and sunshine, or an active outdoor experience that might include anything from high-speed watersports, to sailing on sparkling waters, golf on a challenging nine-hole course, tennis, or exploring the vast hinterland either on foot or in a variety of motorized vehicles.

The 1,800-acre resort offers a complete range of vacation and convention facilities, among them a 48-room lodge, 34 cottages, and 92 campsites with all the usual facilities, including utility hookups, a dump site, a central service station with restrooms, showers, a grocery store, and laundry facilities. There's a dining room and gift shop, meeting and convention facilities, swimming pool, full-service marina with 76 open slips and 130 covered slips, tennis center with four indoor courts and five outdoor courts, golf pro shop, hiking trail, planned recreation activities offered by a fully qualified staff of recreation directors and naturalists, and several picnic shelters. Rental boats, including fishing boats, pontoons, and ski boats, are available at the marina.

Vacation packages such as special weekends and golfing breaks are all available throughout the year.

NEARBY ATTRACTIONS: Columbus-Belmont Battlefield State Park, Kentucky Dam Village State Resort Park, Lake Barkley State Resort Park, Jefferson Davis Monument State Historic Site, Pennyrile Forest State Resort Park, and Fort Donnelson National Battlefield Park in Dover, Tennessee.

INFORMATION: Kenlake State Resort Park, Route 1, Box 522, Hardin, KY 42048-9737. Telephone the lodge at 502-474-2211; the marina at 502-474-2245; reservations at 800-325-0143.

Kenlake resort is 40 miles southeast of Paducah. Take I-24 to Purchase Parkway, then US 68E. From I-24 north, Exit US 68/Kentucky Highway 80W.

Lake Barkley State Resort Park

This wonderful resort park encompasses some 3,700 acres on the eastern shores of Barkley Lake, and is the third state resort park on the waters surrounding the Land Between the Lakes. Lake Barkley is one of the largest manmade lakes in the world, so it's no wonder that the focus of activity here is on the water and the natural wonderland that embraces it. It's a place to spend tranquil hours in the late afternoon watching the sun drop and turn the lake into a burnished mirror of golden metal, to wander the nature trails along the shoreline, or to simply sit in the shade and enjoy the sights and sounds of nature on a lazy afternoon.

This impressive lodge was designed by Edward Durrell Stone and has some 120 rooms and four luxury suites offering breathtaking views of the lake and surrounding countryside. A second facility, Little River Lodge, offers 10 more rooms and another luxury suite.

The Lodge offers spectacular views of Lake Barkley

The facilities at the resort are extensive. The main resort complex includes a convention center, dining room, coffee shop, and gift shop. There are also 13 family cottages available year-round, 78 campsites, all complete with utility hookups, dump site, central service station with restrooms, showers, grocery store, and laundry facilities. There's a convenient swimming pool, tennis courts, a trap shooting range for those who like to shoot but have a soft heart, plus more than nine miles of hiking and horseback riding trails through the surrounding woodlands. There's also a 4,800-foot lighted airstrip for easy access from the air.

A variety of planned activities is offered by a large and fully-qualified staff of recreation directors and naturalists, who can also help to coordinate and supervise daily summer activities and interpretive events. Their expertise will ensure that your family visit is the educational and fun-filled experience of a lifetime.

Of special interest to active vacationers and conventioners alike is the Executive Fitness Center, complete with Nautilus equipment, resident aerobics instructors, racquetball courts, tanning beds, a sauna, steamroom and whirlpool. Lake Barkley also boasts a challenging 18-hole golf course complete with pro shop and equipment rental.

The full-service marina offers 60 open slips and 112 covered slips, along with rental fishing boats, pontoons, canoes, rowing boats, and ski boats. As usual, the resort has a variety of vacation, weekend, and golf packages; all available throughout the year.

NEARBY ATTRACTIONS: Columbus-Belmont Battlefield State Park, Kentucky Dam Village State Resort Park, Kenlake State Resort Park, Jefferson Davis Monument State Historic Site, Pennyrile Forest State Resort Park, and Fort Donnelson National Battlefield Park in Dover, Tennessee.

INFORMATION: Lake Barkley State Resort Park, Box 790, Cadiz, KY 42211-0790. Telephone the lodge 502-924-1131; the marina 502-924-9954; reservations toll-free 800-325-1708.

Lake Malone State Park

Lake Malone is one of those small outdoor trips that packs a punch of monumental proportions. Everything here comes in small quantities, but offers vacation opportunities of the highest order. Cliffs of pale gold and steep sandstone bluffs rise dramatically from the waters of the lake. Spend quiet hours wandering among the pines on the cliff tops, or hiking the forest trails lined with mountain laurel, holly, and wildflowers. Enjoy lazy afternoons fishing, or simply drifting upon the tranquil waters of Lake Malone.

The 325-acre park offers limited facilities that include 20 campsites with all the usual utilities including hookups, a dump site, a central service station with restrooms, showers, a grocery store, and laundry facilities. There's also a boat dock with 40 open slips, and fishing boats, pontoons, canoes, and rowboats are available for rent. There's a picnic shelter and a playground as well.

INFORMATION: Lake Malone State Park, Dunmore, KY 42339-0093. Telephone 502-657-2111.

The park is located less than five miles from Dunmore. Take US 431 from Greenville south to Kentucky Highway 973.

Pennyrile Forest
State Resort Park

A tiny plant named Pennyroyal, used by pioneer settlers as a cooking additive, gave its name to this most perfect of back-to-nature hideaways that overlooks the beautiful Pennyrile Lake. Seclusion is the watchword at this off-the-beaten-path resort, where you can choose between a rather small, but nonetheless full-service, rustic lodge, or one of the charming log cottages across the lake. Each has its own private dock and picnic area. Whatever you choose, there is very little at Pennrile to disturb the peacefulness of the resort – only the hypnotic sounds of nature, the splash of fish rising to the surface of the lake, the chirping of the crickets on a hot summer's evening, or the trilling of the songbirds in the early morning.

Facilities at the park include The Lodge, which has 24 rooms, a dining room, gift shop, and meeting rooms. There are also 13 rustic cottages, 68 campsites with all the usual facilities, tennis courts, a swimming pool, picnic shelters and playgrounds, a swimming beach, a nine-hole golf course, a miniature golf course, more than seven miles of hiking trails, and a variety of activities planned and organized by a qualified staff of directors and naturalists.

The resort offers a variety of vacation, weekend, and golf packages; all available throughout the year.

NEARBY ATTRACTIONS: Columbus-Belmont Battlefield State Park, Kentucky Dam Village State Resort Park, Kenlake State Resort Park, Jefferson Davis Monument State Historic Site, Lake Barkley State Resort Park, and Fort Donnelson National Battlefield Park in Dover, Tennessee.

INFORMATION: Pennyrile Forest State Resort Park, 20781 Pennyrile Lodge Road, Dawson Springs, KY 42408-9212. Telephone 502-797-3421; reservations 800-325-1711.

The park resort is 20 miles northwest of Hopkinsville on Kentucky Highway 109N.

The Interstate 65 Region

The Cave Corridor

Barren River Lake State Resort Park

Barren River Lake Resort Park is less than an hour's drive south of Mammoth Cave National Park. After spending a day wandering the mysterious caverns you may feel like something a little less claustrophobic and you couldn't do much better than spending a few days on the shores of beautiful Barren River Lake. Here, the air is always fresh, the scenery spectacular, and the sunsets eye-popping.

The modern resort lodge with its 51 well-appointed rooms, full-service convention facilities, and dining room, is a fitting and natural companion for the 22 secluded executive cottages on the curving shoreline of the lake. It is no wonder, then, that this magnificent 2,187-acre resort has become one of the most popular vacation destinations in Kentucky.

In addition to the lodge and cottages, there are some 99 modern campsites, each with hookups, a dump site, a central service station with restrooms, showers, a grocery store, and laundry.

The full-service marina here offers a range of water-borne activities that will enable the visitor to make full use of the lake. There are rental fishing boats, houseboats, pontoons, and rowboats; 100 open slips, and 40 covered slips. There's also a formidable 18-hole golf course complete with pro shop and rental equipment, a miniature golf course, a swimming pool, a bike and fitness trail (bikes can be rented too), hiking trails, and tennis courts.

There are a variety of planned recreational programs offered by a full staff of qualified directors and naturalists. Weekend, vacation and golf packages are available throughout the year.

INFORMATION: Barren River Lake State Resort Park, 1149 State Park Road, Lucas, KY 42156-9709. Telephone the resort office 502-

646-2151, the marina 502-646-2357, or toll-free for reservations 800-325-0057.

The resort is 44 miles southwest of Bowling Green. Take I-65 to the Cumberland Parkway, then US 31E south.

Dale Hollow Lake State Park

Dale Hollow Lake is situated on the Kentucky/Tennessee border in the foothills of the Cumberland Plateau. The 28,000-acre expanse of water boasts the world's record catch for smallmouth bass at 11 lbs., 15 oz. The fish was caught less than a half-mile from the park marina.

At almost 3,400 acres, this is the second largest park in the Kentucky system. Surrounded by rolling grasslands and hardwood forests, it's an outdoor paradise with plenty to see and do for all. More than 14 hiking trails and bridleways, with 24 campsites featuring hitching posts, allow direct access to the thousands of acres, and miles of shoreline, beyond the park.

The 144 campsites come complete with hookups, a dump site, three central service stations with restrooms, showers, a grocery store, and laundry facilities.

The marina offers 36 open slips, a variety of rental boats, and "The Catch of the Day" restaurant which seats up to 48 people for breakfast, lunch and dinner.

Fishing on the lake is always excellent. Smallmouth, largemouth, white bass, crappie, muskie, bluegill, catfish, and rainbow trout abound in the deep, blue-green waters, and there's always the chance of a record-breaking catch.

Other facilities at the park include a swimming pool, picnic tables and grills, playgrounds, and a picnic shelter complete with restrooms.

ACTIVITIES: Educational programs are offered by a fully qualified staff of recreation directors and naturalists from Memorial Day through Labor Day. Annual special events include a Glogger's Weekend in May, a Quilt Show in June, and Singing by the Lake in September.

INFORMATION: Dale Hollow Lake State Park, 6371 State Park Road, Bow, KY 42714-9728. Telephone 502-433-7431.

From Cave City, take Kentucky Highway 90 east, then go south on Kentucky Highways 449, and 1206.

E. P. "Tom" Sawyer State Park

Claimed to be a "377-acre oasis on the outskirts of the Louisville metropolitan area," Tom Sawyer State Park is arguably the finest fitness and athletic complex in the entire state. The park features every sport imaginable, from gymnastics to model airplane flying, and from swimming to bicycle moto cross.

The heart of the facility is the Activities Center which houses a gymnasium which seats up to 600 spectators, indoor courts for basketball, volleyball, and badminton. There's locker and shower facilities, a game area, a meeting room, and administrative offices. Leagues and clinics are offered at various times of the year. Morning and evening exercise classes, including water aerobics in the summer, are offered for men and women. The weight room is open all year and membership is required for use of the facilities. Gymnastics and physical education is offered for boys and girls, ages preschool through adult.

The park has a fine Olympic-size swimming pool, open to the general public from noon until 6:30 PM. Admission is charged, but member discounts are available. Swimming lessons, swim team meets, water exercise classes, and water polo are scheduled in the morning and evening.

A one-mile fitness trail with 10 exercise stations offers the ultimate in structured training. Joggers may join the 100/500/1,000 Mile Club and receive an award by running or walking the designated distances on the park grounds.

The park has eight soccer fields and three lighted softball fields. Soccer and softball leagues, clinics, and lessons are available for all skill levels.

The 12 lighted tennis courts are open from 7 AM until 10 PM daily. Park sponsored leagues and lessons for various ages and levels of competition are offered during the summer months.

Other facilities at the park include a BMX bicycle track which is considered to be one of the best in the country. All riders must wear protective gear and comply with park and track rules. BMX races are held on weekends, spring through fall. There's also a model airplane flying field with a 400-foot lighted runway. The facility may be used by all pilots who are members of the Tom Sawyer Model Aircraft Association. Flying hours are 8 AM to 9 PM daily, except for dates reserved for approved flying contests.

There's a picnic area and a shelter with tables, grills, and a restroom. Concession facilities are located near the pool and the softball fields. An assortment of planned activities for both adults and children is offered by a fully qualified recreation director who oversees the various daily programs.

The park hosts many special events throughout the year, including an annual Mini-triathlon, the BMX Grand Nationals, radio-controlled air shows, and a full program of softball and soccer tournaments.

INFORMATION: E. P. "Tom" Sawyer State Park, 3000 Freys Hill Road, Louisville, KY 40241-2172. Telephone 502-426-8950.

In Louisville, take the Gene Snyder Freeway northeast to the westbound Westport Road exit.

Green River Lake State Park

All the fun of the lake is available at Green River Lake State Park. The 8,200-acre lake and 1,300-acre park feature an extensive beach, a marina with 200 covered slips, along with rental fishing boats, ski boats, pontoons, and house boats. The fishing is out of this world, with all the usual species including largemouth, smallmouth, and white bass, catfish, crappie, and bluegill.

Accommodations here include 156 campsites complete with hookups, a dump site, a central service station with restrooms, showers, a grocery store, laundry, and a gift shop. There's also a miniature golf course, picnic table and grills, a picnic shelter, a playground, and a fully paved model aircraft flying strip.

ACTIVITIES: An assortment of planned activities for both adults and children is offered by a fully qualified staff of recreation directors and naturalists.

INFORMATION: Green River Lake State Park, 179 Park Office Road, Campbellsville, KY 42718-9351. Telephone 502-465-8255.

The park is situated south of Campbellsville on Kentucky Highway 55.

Lake Cumberland State Resort Park

Because of its location on the shores of mighty Lake Cumberland the focus of the resort, as might be expected, is on the water and all related sports: boating, sailing, waterskiing, canoeing and, of course, fishing. The magnificent 50,000-acre lake boasts more than 1,200 miles of spectacular shoreline and some of the most breathtaking scenery in the Eastern United States. The fishing is "marvelous." Lake Cumberland is said to contain more bass, walleye, bluegill, and crappie than any other lake in America.

The lake is one of Kentucky's most romantic spots. It's a place where magnificent scenery, sparkling waters, and spectacular sunsets lend a unique atmosphere of seclusion to nature's beauty. Pick one of the many secluded lakeside spots and spend a quiet afternoon with a well-stocked picnic basket, a cool breeze blowing off the lake, some good company, and relax as the afternoon turns slowly into evening and the sun sets over the lake in a blaze of bronze, copper and gold.

The imposing Lure Lodge and convention center offers magnificent views of the lake, an indoor swimming facility complete with a glass-backed elevator, a plant-filled atrium, and an exercise room and hot tub.

To get away from the resort atmosphere of the lodge, you might wish to consider the quiet seclusion of cozy Pumpkin Creek Lodge, or any one of the resort's famous Wildwood Cottages, all nestled in secluded woodland settings.

There are some 147 campsites complete with hookups, a dump site, a central service station with restrooms, showers, a grocery store, and laundry. A full-service marina offers all the amenities one would expect to find at a major holiday resort: rental fishing boats, pontoons, ski boats, rowboats, and 147 open slips. There is a picnic shelter and playground for the kids to enjoy.

The resort also has an exercise room, a fine nine-hole, par-3 golf course and pro shop, a miniature golf course, horseback riding, more than four miles of hiking trails, a nature center, and several tennis courts.

As always, the resort offers a variety of vacation, weekend, and golf packages; all available throughout the year.

ACTIVITIES: Golfing, swimming, fishing, nature study and bird watching, wildlife photography, hiking, and a variety of planned recreational programs offered by a full staff of qualified directors and naturalists.

INFORMATION: Lake Cumberland State Resort Park, 5465 State Park Road, Jamestown, KY 42629-7801. Telephone the resort office 502-343-3111, the Marina 502-343-2525, or toll-free for reservations 800-325-1709.

From I-65, exit onto the Cumberland Parkway, then take US 127. From I-75, exit onto Kentucky Highway 80 west.

Lincoln Homestead State Park

The focus of this pleasant 120-acre, day-use-only park is the original cabin home that belonged to Abraham Lincoln's mother, and a replica of the 1782 cabin where his father grew up. The park's fine 18-hole golf course stands on the land where Captain Abraham Lincoln, the President's grandfather, built his first home on Kentucky soil. Visitors to the park are often overwhelmed by the strong sense of history that seems to pervade the cabins and parkland.

Amenities at the park include the golf course and pro shop, an interesting and informative museum, a picnic shelter with tables and grills, and a playground.

INFORMATION: Lincoln Homestead State Park, 5079 Lincoln Road, Springfield, KY 40069-9606. Telephone 606-336-7461.

Take the Bluegrass Parkway to US 150 east, or to Kentucky Highway 555.

My Old Kentucky Home
State Park

The magnificent mansion on Federal Hill, overlooking 235 acres of rolling parkland and formal gardens, is as appealing today as it was in 1852 when it inspired Stephen Foster to write his immortal ballad.

Costumed guides await the visitor, ready and able to transport them back to a time of chivalry, gentility, and southern hospitality.

On cool summer evenings from mid-June to Labor Day, the

Mansion and grounds of My Old Kentucky Home

"Stephen Foster Story" is played out in an outdoor amphitheater. In December, Christmas candlelight tours are the highlight of the holiday season.

My Old Kentucky Home offers 39 campsites, which include hookups, a dump site, a central service station with restrooms, showers, a grocery store, laundry facilities, and a gift shop. There's a fine 18-hole golf course, a pro shop and club rentals, a picnic shelter with tables and grills, and a playground for the children.

INFORMATION: My Old Kentucky Home State Park, PO Box 323 Bardstown, KY 40004-0323. Telephone 502-348-3502. For more details about the Stephen Foster Story, call toll-free 800-626-1563.

The park is in Bardstown on US 31E/150.

Old Mulkey Meeting House State Historic Site

The Old Mulkey Meeting House is the oldest log meeting house in the state. It was built in 1804 during a period of fervent religious revival. Several early pioneers are buried in the local churchyard, including Daniel Boone's sister. It's a small park intended for day use only, but offers some 60 acres of parkland, picnic facilities, and a playground.

INFORMATION: Old Mulkey Meeting House State Historic Site, 1819 Old Mulkey Road, Tomkinsville, KY 42167-8766. Telephone 502-487-8481.

From Bowling Green, off I-65, take US 231 south to Kentucky Highway 100 east.

Rough River Dam
State Resort Park

Rough River Dam is another of those parks where seclusion is more than just a concept. Hidden away in the hills of Western Kentucky, overlooking a magnificent 4,860-acre lake of deep, blue-green waters, the Rough River Dam State Resort offers a vacation, or perhaps just a day out in the countryside, with a difference. The resort lodge maintains 40 well-appointed, quiet rooms, each with a private lakeside balcony or patio. The resort's rustic cottages offer you a chance to get-away from the rigors of big business and enjoy the wonders of nature one-on-one.

The park has a variety of accommodation options. The lodge is equipped with meeting and convention facilities, a full-service dining room, and a gift shop. There are also 15 fully equipped rental cottages, and 66 modern campsites with hookups, a dump site, a central service station with restrooms, showers, a grocery store, and laundry.

A special feature of the park resort is the full-service marina, where you can rent fishing boats, pontoons, and rowboats. In addition, the park marina has 195 open slips, 30 open houseboat slips, and 48 covered slips. There's also a nine-hole, par-3 golf course and pro shop, a fitness trail and a hiking trail, several tennis courts and a range of planned recreational programs offered by a full staff of qualified directors and naturalists. A 2,800-foot lighted airstrip is within walking distance of the lodge.

Rough River Dam offers a variety of vacation, weekend, and golf packages; all are available throughout the year.

INFORMATION: Rough River Dam State Resort Park, Route 1, Box 1, Falls of Rough, KY 40119-9701. Telephone the resort office 502-257-2311, or toll-free for reservations 800-325-1713.

The resort is located off Kentucky Highway 79. Take the Western Kentucky Parkway north at Caneyville.

Taylorsville Lake State Park

This is another of Kentucky's day-use-only state parks, but what a park. "A Fisherman's Dream Come True?" It surely is. Taylorsville is said to be Kentucky's most heavily stocked lake. Record catches are commonplace here. The blue-green water literally teams with bass, crappie, and bluegill. A good day's sport is all but assured.

Facilities at the park include the 3,000-acre lake, more than 1,600 acres of parkland, hiking and horseback riding trails, and picnic facilities. For those who love the water, there is a full-service marina with 38 open slips and 144 covered slips, boat ramps, and refreshment facilities. An assortment of rental boats, including fishing boats, house boats, and pontoons are also available.

INFORMATION: Taylorsville Lake State Park, PO Box 509, Taylorsville, KY 40071-0509. Telephone the park office 502-477-8713, or the Marina 502-477-8766.

From Louisville take I-64 to the Gene Snyder Freeway south and Kentucky Highway 44. Go three miles to the park entrance.

The Interstate 75 Region

The Wilderness Trail

Big Bone Lick State Park

In prehistoric times, the warm salt springs that still bubble from the ground at Big Bone Lick attracted all sorts of great animals: mammoths, mastodons, and bison. Many became trapped in the swamps and died. The bones of those great beasts were left behind in the land and offer clues about the Kentucky of millions of years ago. Today, a buffalo herd grazes contentedly on the lush green parkland, seemingly oblivious to the thousands of people who visit the park each year.

The 525-acre park offers 62 campsites with hookups, a dump site, a central service station with restrooms and showers, a grocery store, laundry facilities, and a gift shop. There's also a picnic shelter with tables and grills, and a playground for the children,

ACTIVITIES: Miniature golf, fishing, hiking trails, swimming, and tennis. An assortment of programs for both adults and children is offered by a fully qualified staff of recreation directors and naturalists.

INFORMATION: Big Bone Lick State Park, 3380 Beaver Road, Union, KY 41091-9627. Telephone 606-384-3522.

Blue Licks Battlefield State Park

For as long as history has been recorded the salt springs of Blue Licks have been attracting visitors, from prehistoric animals and birds, to Indians, pioneers, settlers, and now vacationers. All came to enjoy the soothing and, some say, medicinal effects of the water. It was in 1782, however, that Blue Licks gained national attention when it became the site of the last major battle of the Revolutionary War fought in Kentucky.

The 150-acre park has 51 modern campsites and several rental cottages, all available year-round, and including hookups, a dump site, three central service stations complete with activities rooms, restrooms and showers, a grocery store, laundry facilities. There are meeting facilities available throughout the year, as well as a museum, a swimming pool, hiking trails, a miniature golf course, picnic facilities, shelters, a playground, and a gift shop.

ACTIVITIES: There's the usual program of planned activities for both adults and children, all supervised by a fully qualified staff.

INFORMATION: Blue Licks Battlefield State Park, PO Box 66, Mt. Olivet, KY 41064-0066. Telephone 606-289-5507. The park is located northeast of Lexington off US 68.

Buckhorn Lake State Resort Park

Buckhorn Lake is a Shangri La hidden away in the middle of the lush forests of the Eastern Kentucky mountains. In this idyllic setting the hustle and bustle of city life can really be left behind. It's a major attraction for the naturalist, the hiker, the fisherman, and for anyone who loves the outdoors.

Buckhorn Lodge, the resort's magnificent 36-room hotel, offers all of its guests a private balcony or patio and a heart-stopping view of the lake or mountains. The dining room can seat up to 210 people for breakfast, lunch and dinner and offers "the finest of Kentucky cuisine and gracious service." The lodge also has a private swimming pool for the exclusive use of lodge and cottage guests.

Although Buckhorn doesn't have the facilities to cater for a large convention, if your party is a small one of around 40 people, the staff will take special care of you in one of its two private dining rooms. The lodge gift shop, too, is a worthwhile experience; it offers a wonderful selection of Kentucky's crafts and souvenirs.

There are also two two-bedroom executive cottages and one three-bedroom executive cottage available year-round. All the necessary equipment is provided to ensure your stay is a comfortable one, including tableware, cooking utensils, and fresh linens on a daily basis.

Watersports enthusiasts will find the 1,200-acre Buckhorn Lake much to their liking. The park marina has two launching ramps, and an assortment of boats available for hire, including fishing boats and pontoons. The fishing is excellent and the lake well-stocked with large-

Cyclists take a break and admire the view

mouth and smallmouth bass, crappie, bluegill, channel catfish, and muskie.

ACTIVITIES: Tennis, shuffleboard, volleyball, horseshoes, miniature golf course, and swimmimg on the public beach, which has a bathhouse. There's also a 1.5-mile nature trail, and the opportunities for hiking in the mountain forests are unlimited.

Finally, there's the usual program of planned activities for both adults and children, all supervised by a fully qualified staff.

INFORMATION: Buckhorn Lake State Resort Park, HC 36, Box 1000, Buckhorn, KY 41721-9602. Telephone 606-398-7510, or you can call toll free for reservations 800-325-0058. Take I-64 east to Mountain Parkway. Exit at Campton and take Kentucky Highway 15 south to Kentucky Highway 28 west, then Kentucky Highway 1833 to the park.

Constitution Square
State Historic Site

On June 1, 1792 Kentucky became the 15th state in the union. Constitution Square is dedicated to commemoration of the 10 constitutional conventions that led eventually to Kentucky's acceptance into the union. Isaac Shelby, a hero of the Revolutionary War, was named as the first governor of the Commonwealth.

Visitors to the site can tour many original buildings, including the first post office west of the Alleghenies, Grayson's Tavern, and replicas of the old jail, the courthouse, and the meeting house.

INFORMATION: Constitution Square State Historic Site, 105 E. Walnut Street, Danville, KY 40422-1817. Telephone 606-236-5089.

Cumberland Falls
State Resort Park

Cumberland Falls is a spectacular, 125-foot wide curtain of water that cascades more than 60 feet into the gorge below. The local people talk of a "whispering mist that kisses the face, and a magical moonbow only visible on a clear night under a full moon." The description is romantic, but it accurately depicts one of Kentucky's finest natural treasures, "The Niagara of the South." The magical moonbow is unique, a phenomenon not found anywhere else in the Western Hemisphere.

Visitors to the park will enjoy a variety of outdoor activities. Hikers and horseback riders have more than 17 miles of hiking trails and bridleways that twist and turn through the surrounding woodlands. There's good fishing on the river, or whitewater rafting starting just below the falls and continuing for several miles. Even better is to take the scenic train excursion through nearby Big South Fork National River and Recreation Area.

Whitewater at Cumberland Falls

Accommodations include a lodge hotel with 72 rooms, dining room, convention center with meeting rooms, gift shop, and staff equipped to meet every need, from a family vacation to a company convention. There are 26 secluded rental cottages available year-round, and 50 campsites available during the summer months. The sites offer hookups, a dump site, three central service stations complete with activities rooms, restrooms and showers, a grocery store, and laundry.

Other facilities include a museum and nature center, and the usual program of planned activities for both adults and children supervised by a fully qualified staff. There's a swimming pool, several tennis courts, and a gift shop.

INFORMATION: Cumberland Falls State Resort Park, 7351 Highway 90, Corbin, KY 40701-8814. Telephone 606-528-4121, or 800-325-0063.

From I-75 take the Corbin exit to US 25W, then to Kentucky Highway 90.

Dr. Thomas Walker
State Historic Site

Contrary to popular belief, Daniel Boone was not the first frontiersman to enter Kentucky. That distinction falls to Dr. Thomas Walker. A physician and surveyor, he led the first expedition through Cumberland Gap in 1750. He named the river "Cumberland Water" and built the one-room log cabin which stands on the site today.

The 12-acre park offers visitors quiet afternoons picnicking under the trees or in one of the shelters. Children can spend time on the playground while parents relax. There's also a concession stand, a miniature golf course, and a gift shop.

INFORMATION: Dr. Thomas Walker State Historic Site, H. C. 83, Box 868, Barboursville, KY 40906-9603. Telephone 606-546-4400.

From Barboursville take Kentucky Highway 459.

Fort Boonesborough State Park

Fort Boonesborough is the site of Fort Boone, Kentucky's second permanent settlement. Daniel Boone and a party of pioneers arrived on April 1st, 1775, and immediately began construction of log dwellings on a site some 60 yards from the riverbank. By the summer it had grown into a full-blown fort with four block houses and 26 log cabins. It was fortunate for the settlers that construction was completed so quickly, for almost immediately the fort suffered a series of Indian attacks, including "The Great Siege of Boonesborough."

For several years the fort was a way station for pioneers traveling westward, but slowly, as civilization came to the area, its population declined, until it was eventually abandoned sometime after the Revolutionary War.

Today, Fort Boonesborough has faithfully been reconstructed. The blockhouses, cabins, and workshops, complete with all the trappings and period furnishings, offer visitors a tiny peek into the everyday life of pioneers in frontier Kentucky.

Reconstructed pioneer cabins

Facilities at the park include 167 campsites, available year-round, offering hookups, a dump site, a central service station, restrooms and showers, a grocery store, and laundry. There's an activities room that can accommodate up to 150 people, a pool, and a sandy beach (for sunbathing only) with a snack bar and bathhouse. There's also a meeting room, and two gift shops.

ACTIVITIES: Miniature 18-hole golf course, hiking the half-mile nature trail, fishing for bluegill, bass, catfish, and crappie on the Kentucky River. There are boat ramps, three picnic shelters, restrooms, and a playground. The staff offers an assortment of activities for all, including tours of Fort Boonesborough and the White Hall State Historic Site, home of abolitionist Cassius Clay.

INFORMATION: Fort Boonesborough State Park, 4375 Boonesborough Road, Richmond, KY 40475-9316. Telephone 606-527-3131.

From I-75, take Exit 95. On I-64, exit at Winchester.

General Burnside State Park

General Burnside is Kentucky's only island park. Named for the Civil War commander with the famous sideburns, Major General Ambrose E. Burnside, the 430-acre island on Lake Cumberland welcomes more and more visitors each year. Burnside and his troops patrolled the Cumberland River in search of Confederate invaders. Today, the park offers a quiet, lakeside retreat with a variety of outdoor activities from fishing to golf.

The park has 94 campsites, available from April 1st through October 31st, with hookups, a dump site, two central service stations complete with activities rooms, restrooms and showers, a grocery store, and laundry. There's also a swimming pool and bathhouse.

Other outdoor facilities include a fine 18-hole golf course with a fully equipped pro shop, where clubs and carts are available for rent. Those who like to spend time on the water will find this area a "perfect playground," with miles of shoreline and some of the best fishing in the state. There's a marina next to the park where you can rent an assortment of fishing boats, ski boats, pontoons, and houseboats. The waters of Lake Cumberland are reputed to contain more bass, walleye, and crappie than any other lake in America.

The day visitor can spend quiet hours by the community pool, playing shuffleboard, or simply relaxing with the family in one of the park's two picnic shelters while the children enjoy themselves on the playground. The park offers the usual planned activities for both adults and children by a fully qualified staff.

INFORMATION: General Burnside State Park, PO Box 488, Burnside, KY 42519-0488. Telephone 606-561-4192.

The park is eight miles south of Somerset on US 27.

General Butler State Resort Park

The General Butler Resort offers one of the most comprehensive programs of outdoor and recreational activities in the state. It boasts the system's only snow ski area with more than 20 acres of ski trails and snow-making facilities. The ski school here offers instruction for all ages and all levels of expertise from novice to expert.

Hilltop Lodge has something for the family vacation or for the company convention. There are 57 rooms, a full-service dining room, and meeting facilities. For something a little different, the park's 23 rustic cottages give you the option to spend a few days out of touch with the rest of the world.

Lovers of the great outdoors will enjoy wandering the woodland trails and the spectacular views of the Ohio River valley, or simply spending lazy afternoons on the lakeside beach enjoying the sunshine and a good book. For active outdoorsmen and women there's a challenging little nine-hole golf course and pro shop, tennis courts, and rental pedal boats and row boats.

For the camper, 111 fully equipped campsites are available throughout the year. There's a miniature golf course, more than two miles of hiking trails, picnic shelters with tables and grills, and a playground. The Park Service offers an assortment of planned activities for both adults and children by a fully qualified staff. Of special interest is the Butler-Turpin House, built in 1859 by a nephew of General William Orlando Butler, for whom the park is named. The old home is filled with fine furnishings, antiques, and family heirlooms that offer visitors a window on the past and a glimpse at what life might have been like in the early 19th century.

INFORMATION: General Butler State Resort Park, Box 325, Carrolton, KY 41008-0325. Telephone the resort office 502-732-4384, Ski Butler toll free 800-456-3284, or reservations toll free 800-325-0078.

The park is 44 miles northeast of Louisville off I-71 at Carrolton.

Isaac Shelby Cemetery State Historic Site

When you visit Constitution Square be sure to take a little extra time to visit the grave of Isaac Shelby, Kentucky's first and fifth governor. Isaac Shelby was born in 1750. It is a testament to his life and times, and to the esteem for his political accomplishments, that counties in nine states are named after him. Shelby died in 1826 after a long and illustrious career, and was buried in the cemetery on his estate, Traveller's Rest.

INFORMATION: Isaac Shelby Cemetery State Historic Site, Danville, KY 40422. Telephone 606-236-5089.

The site is located five miles south of Danville off US 127.

Kincaid Lake State Park

The 850-acre Kincaid Lake State Park is a favorite backcountry retreat for campers, hikers, and fishermen alike. The 183-acre lake has a dock with 38 open slips, a launching ramp, and an assortment of rental boats available by the hour or by the day. The park's large, multi-purpose building is open year-round for meetings and activities, and an assortment of planned activities for both adults and children is offered by a fully qualified staff.

This park offers 84 campsites hookups, a dump site, a central service station with restrooms and showers, a grocery store, laundry, and a gift shop. There's a miniature golf course, paddle tennis, picnic shelters with tables and grills, and a playground for the children.

INFORMATION: Kincaid Lake State Park, Route 4, Box 33, Falmouth, KY 41040-9203. Telephone 606-654-3531.

Levi Jackson Wilderness Road State Park

This 900-acre park is dedicated to the memory of the first judge in Laurel County and to two of the nation's most historic pioneer trails. The Wilderness Road, often said to be "the most significant trail in the westward flow of English colonization," carried more than 200,000 pioneers into Kentucky. Boone's Trace, from Cumberland to the Kentucky River. It was blazed, of course, by Daniel Boone.

Levi Jackson is the perfect place for a stroll

Today, rolling acres of parkland, a working pioneer grist mill, and a fine museum make the park a significant stop on the tourist map.

The park facilities include 15 group camping cabins and 146 campsites, both available year-round. The campsites offer hookups, a dump site, three central service stations complete with activities rooms, restrooms and showers, a grocery store, and laundry. There's a swimming pool and a gift shop.

There's also a miniature golf course and more than eight miles of hiking trails, where you can retrace a few of the steps along original sections of trails taken by early settlers to the region. Alternatively, just sit and relax in one of the picnic shelters while the children enjoy a fine time on the playground. For the vacationer, the park offers an assortment of planned activities for both adults and children by a fully qualified staff.

Several other interesting features at the park include the authentic reproduction of McHargue's Mill on the banks of the Little Laurel River; McNitt's Defeat where, on the night of October 3, 1786, 24 members of the McNitt party died during a bloody Indian massacre; and the Mountain Life Museum, a reproduction of an early pioneer settlement and a tribute to life as it must have been in Laurel County during the 19th century. The buildings that make up the settlement are filled with the artifacts and implements of pioneer Kentucky.

INFORMATION: Levi Jackson State Park, 998 Levi Jackson Mill Road, London, KY 40741-8944. Telephone 606-878-8000.

The park is just south of London, off I-75 at Exit 38.

Natural Bridge State Resort Park

Natural Bridge State Resort Park is in the midst of Daniel Boone National Forest near Red River Gorge Geological Area. The natural sandstone bridge, from which the park takes its name, took millions of years to form, and today it is the focus of one of the most dramatic parks in the Kentucky system. The bridge is some 78 feet long and 65 feet high. Surrounded as it is by the natural pageant of the forest, the bridge takes on a new mantle with each passing season. In winter the snow covers it with a blanket of white; spring brings wildflowers and a riot of pastel color; in the summer everything is green under a golden network of sunbeams filtering through the treetops; and fall brings a cascade of bronze, yellow, and burnished gold. All year round, visitors and hikers can enjoy the rugged scenery of the great stone cliffs, natural arches, and woodlands, either on foot or high in the air from the park's skylift.

The 1,900-acre resort park has a 35-room lodge complete with dining room, meeting rooms, and a full-service convention center. There are 10 rental cottages available year-round, and 95 summer campsites, with hookups, a dump site, a central service station complete with restrooms and showers, and laundry. There's a swimming pool, 18 miles of hiking trails, several tennis courts, a gift shop, and a sky lift.

ACTIVITIES: Visiting the nature center, or taking part in the usual program of planned activities for all the family, supervised by a fully qualified staff.

INFORMATION: Natural Bridge State Resort Park, 2135 Natural Bridge Road, Slade, KY 40376-9701. Telephone 606-663-2214. For reservations call toll free 800-325-1710. The resort is 52 miles southeast of Lexington, off the Mountain Parkway on Kentucky Highway 11.

Old Fort Harrod State Park

An authentically reconstructed frontier fort is the focus of Old Fort Harrod State Park. It was in 1774 that Captain James Harrod established the first permanent settlement in what is now central Kentucky. The fort, set upon 15 acres of some of the state's most spectacular countryside, offers a view of what life must have been like for the pioneers of the late 18th century.

Costumed craftsmen and women perform many of the everyday tasks important to maintaining life on the frontier in a pageant of living history demonstrations that include homemaking, wood-craft, and farming, all incorporating the primitive tools and implements of the times.

Adjacent to the fort is the Lincoln Marriage Temple and the original log cabin where Abraham Lincoln's parents were married on June 12, 1806. The park's Mansion Museum houses a fine collection of Civil War artifacts, Old Kentucky memorabilia, and the Lincoln Collection.

All the excitement and romance of life on the frontier in Kentucky is brought to life in the park's outdoor amphitheater during the months of June, July and August, when local actors play out the "Legend of Daniel Boone," a story of the lives and times of Kentucky's earliest settlers.

INFORMATION: Old Fort Harrod State Park, PO Box 156, Harrodsburg, KY 40330-0156. Telephone 606-734-3314. For more information about the "Legend of Daniel Boone," telephone 606-734-3346.

The park is located 32 miles to the southwest of Lexington on US 68 in Harrodsburg.

Perryville State Historic Site

It was on October 8, 1862, when all the realities of the Civil War were brought home to the people of Kentucky. On that day two mighty armies met in what would be the greatest battle of the war to be fought on Kentucky soil.

Confederate Generals Braxton Bragg and E. Kirby Smith met in Chattanooga, Tennessee, on July 31, 1862 and agreed to invade Kentucky. Smith marched from Knoxville on August 14th with a force of 10,000 men and, after a series of quick victories, had established himself in Frankfort, Kentucky. At the same time Bragg, with 30,000 men, marched into Kentucky from Chattanooga, besieged and won the city of Munfordville. Bragg then moved north toward Louisville, but veered eastward and by September 21st had occupied Bardstown. At this point Bragg split his force and sent Major Generals Leonidas Polk and William J. Hardee to sweep the area southeast of Louisville while he went to Frankfort to supervise the installation of a Confederate State Government.

In the meantime, Union Major General Don Carlos Buell had left Nashville, Tennessee, in pursuit of Bragg and by September 25th he was in Louisville. On October 1st he moved out of Louisville with a force of more than 50,000 men. He divided the army into four columns which fanned out to the east and south and, following separate routes, they all headed for Bardstown and a showdown with the Confederate army. The scattered Union army pushed on through Bardstown and Harrodsville, engaging the Confederate skirmishers in a series of small actions until Buell ordered his forces to converge on Perryville by October 7th. Unfortunately, because of unusually dry weather, only 22,000 of his men were on hand for the conflict that was about to begin.

By October 7th Confederate Generals Polk and Hardee, with a force of only 16,000 men, were centered on Perryville. Bragg arrived on the morning of the 8th and ordered Generals Benjamin F. Cheatham's and Simon Bolivar Buckner's divisions to attack the Union left flank and left center. By mid-day the battle had escalated and was raging, sometimes hand-to-hand, across a wide area. By the end of the day when the fighting ended Union General Alexander McCook's corps had been pushed back more than a mile; and General Charles Gilbert was holding only tenuously to his positions. Buell was determined to resume battle on the morning of October 9th, but by then General Bragg had withdrawn his forces and retired to Harrodsburg. The Federal losses during the one-day battle totaled more than 4,200 killed, wounded, or missing in action; the Confederate casualties some 3,400. The result? General Bragg was severely criticized for his failure to hold Kentucky for the Confederacy, and General Buell, for allowing the Confederate army to escape, was relieved of his command.

The Crawford House at Perryville

Today, the one-time killing fields are a memorial to the soldiers of both armies who gave their lives for their beliefs. The Crawford House, General Bragg's headquarters, and the H.P. Bottom House, both of which were at the center of the battle, are still standing. More than 100 acres of Kentucky parkland, a museum, hiking trails, picnic shelters and playgrounds, offer the visitor an interesting day out.

INFORMATION: Perryville Battlefield State Historic Site, PO Box 296, Perryville, KY 40468-9999. Telephone 606-332-8631.

From Lexington, take US 68 west to US 150 west.

Pine Mountain State Resort Park

Pine Mountain, a beautiful mountain top resort, was established in 1924; it was the first park in the Kentucky system. Overlooking the hills and valleys of Kentucky Ridge State Forest, the 1,500-acre park offers panoramic views of some of the most spectacular mountain scenery in the southeast.

Pine Mountain is a unique place where one can go to get away from the rigors of everyday life and become part of a truly natural environment. It's a place to spend long days lost among the trees on the more than nine miles of woodland nature trails. These walks can be especially refreshing in May, when beautiful mountain laurels bloom, turning the mountain top and valleys below into a riot of color.

The secluded, stone and timber mountain lodge has two lobbies where visitors can spend an hour or two comfortably seated in front of the stone fireplace. Each of the lodge's 30 guest rooms has its own private patio or balcony, and a view of the mountain scenery.

Facilities at the lodge include a fine dining room, with seating for up to 216 people and spectacular views. Meeting rooms are available for groups of up to 150 people, and the modern, full-service convention center located next to the lodge can cater for parties of 50 to 300.

There are 20 rustic cottages; 10 one-bedroom log cabins, each with a stone fireplace and private deck, and 10 two-bedroom units with screened in porches. All 20 cottages are furnished with grills and private picnic areas.

There are 30 primitive campsites available and a central service station complete with restrooms and showers. There's also a swimming pool and a gift shop.

Other facilities include picnic areas, shelters, playgrounds, a gift shop, miniature golf course, a challenging nine-hole golf course complete with pro shop, rental equipment, and golf carts. There's also a nature center, and an assortment of trails and natural mountain features with names like "The Living Stairway," "Honeymoon Falls," and "Hemlock Garden." The daily program of planned activities has something for everyone, adults and children alike, and focuses mostly on the local environment and its inhabitants. The activities are supervised by a fully qualified staff of recreation directors and naturalists.

Of special interest is the Laurel Cove natural amphitheater where the Mountain Laurel Festival is held annually on the last weekend in May. Other events held at the park each year include the "At the Top" 10 K Run in April, and the Great American Dulcimer Convention in September.

INFORMATION: Pine Mountain State Resort Park, 1050 State Park Road, Pineville, KY 40977-0610. Telephone 606-337-3066, or call toll free for reservations 800-325-1712.

The resort is 15 miles north of Middlesboro off US 25E in Pineville.

Waveland State Historic Site

Waveland is a fine example of a Greek Revival mansion. The house was built in 1847 by Joseph Bryan, a descendant of Daniel Boone. It's a stately ante-bellum home, a typical pre-Civil War southern plantation. The site features 10 acres of parkland, a gift shop, and a playground.

INFORMATION: Waveland State Historic Site, 225 Higbee Mill Road, Lexington, KY 40514-4778. Telephone 606-272-3611. The site is located south of Lexington off US 68.

White Hall State Historic Site

White Hall, home of Cassius Marcellus Clay, is located near Fort Boonesborough and is well worth a visit if you happen to be in the area. Clay was a close friend of Abraham Lincoln, a one-time Minister to Russia, a newspaper publisher, and an ardent abolitionist. The 44-room mansion was built in 1799 by Clay's father.

It was remodeled in the 1860s when the central heating and running water were added, and it has been extensively renovated since then. Visitors will enjoy the 13 acres of parkland and gardens. There's a gift shop and a picnic area.

INFORMATION: White Hall State Historic Site, 500 White Hall Shrine Road, Richmond, KY 40475-9159. Telephone 606-623-9178.

The park is located off I-75 at Exit 95.

William Whitley House
State Historic Site

The William Whitley House was the first brick house built in Kentucky. William Whitley was one of the original pioneers in the state. The house, famous for its unusual architecture, became a gathering place for many of the state's most prominent people, including Daniel Boone and George Rogers Clark.

INFORMATION: William Whitley State Historic park, 625 William Whitley Road, Stanford, KY 40484-977. Telephone 606-355-2881.

Take US 127 south from Lexington to US 150 east.

Eastern Kentucky

Breaks Interstate Park

Breaks is unusual in that it is a joint venture established in 1954 by the Kentucky and Virginia state legislatures. More than 4,500 acres of mountain greenery, dense woodland, and rugged river valleys and canyons offer the visitor the opportunity for a memorable outdoor vacation. This is Hatfield and McCoy country. Daniel Boone is said to have traveled the forest trails. There are tales of a vast fortune in silver hidden somewhere in the woods close to the Towers Overlook. Breaks is a land that time forgot, a land of primitive beauty where only the sounds of the swift rushing waters of the Russell Fork River, the gentle breeze in treetops, and the sweet songs of the birds disturb the quiet rhythm of mother nature at her best.

Everything you will need for your recreational enjoyment can be found at Breaks Interstate Park. Rhododendron Lodge offers 34 well-equipped, modern units, a fine dining room and an adjacent banquet room which can accommodate the needs of the corporate convention or the business seminar. There's also an Olympic-size swimming pool, a gift shop, and a modern Visitor Center.

Other accommodations include several two-bedroom, fully-equipped family cottages available throughout the year, and 122 summer campsites, with hookups, a dump site, restrooms, and hot showers.

ACTIVITIES: There are several hiking trails, lake and river fishing, white-water rafting, a boat ramp, picnic shelters, tables, grills, and playgrounds.

INFORMATION: Breaks I-Park, PO Box 100, Breaks, VA 24607. Telephone 703-865-4413, or for Lodge reservations telephone 703-865-4414. The park is 30 miles southeast of Pikeville on Kentucky/Virginia Highway 80.

Carter Caves State Resort Park

This unique resort offers the visitor something a little different. A great labyrinth of underground caverns, galleries, and corridors, some charted and some still unexplored, runs for miles beneath the 1,350-acre state park and surrounding mountains and forests. Visitors can sign up for a guided tour of the cave system and enjoy a strange new underground world, where the stops along the way include Cascade Cave and its underground waterfall, or X Cave with its luminous stone fans, pipes, and spirals that were millions of years in the making. Lighted and unlighted tours are available daily, and special tours for spelunkers, beginners or experienced cavers can also be scheduled by arrangement.

Aside from the unique attraction of the cave system, Carter Cave Resort is an outdoor lover's paradise. More than six miles of trails twist and turn through the mountain woodland. Boating is available on the 45-acre lake, where fishing and rental boats can be hired by the hour or by the day. The lake is well stocked with bass, bream, catfish, crappie, and muskie.

Accommodations at the resort are provided by Caveland Lodge: 28 rooms with full amenities, a fine dining room serving a variety of Kentucky dishes for breakfast, lunch, and dinner, and two meeting rooms close to the lodge, where the staff are well able to cater to all the needs of parties up to 180 people. There are 15 cottages for rent year-round, each in its own private woodland setting and with all the usual equipment provided, including tableware, cooking utensils, and daily linen service. A private swimming pool is available for lodge and cottage guests.

There are 90 campsites offered during the summer months with hookups, a dump site, two central service stations, complete with restrooms and showers, and laundry. There's also a community swimming pool, six miles of hiking trails, and several tennis courts.

Other facilities include a welcome center, a community swimming pool, a gift shop offering a large selection of local crafts and souvenirs, tennis courts, picnic shelters, tables, grills, and a playground for the children.

ACTIVITIES: The usual program of planned activities for all the family, supervised by a fully qualified staff of recreation directors and naturalists. Guided canoe trips on Tygart's Creek are available, too. Special events at the park include a Pioneer Life Week in July, and the Fraley Family Mountain Festival in September.

INFORMATION: Carter Caves State Resort Park, R.R. #5, Box 1120, Olive Hill, KY 41164-9032. Telephone 606-286-4411, or toll free for reservations 800-325-0059. The resort is 30 miles west of Ashland. Take I-64 west to Kentucky Highway 182 north.

Grayson Lake State Park

Grayson Lake is some 25 miles southwest of Ashland in Northeastern Kentucky. It's a land of sheer sandstone cliffs and silent waters where the fishing is excellent and the outdoor experience is one never to be forgotten. As it once was a favorite gathering place for Shawnee and Cherokee Indians, so it is for the harassed city dwellers of today as they head for the open skies and the serenity of Kentucky's silent mountains.

Facilities at the park include 71 year-round campsites, with hookups, a dump site, a central service station complete with restrooms and showers, and laundry facilities. There's a boat launching ramp, hiking trails, a picnic shelter, tables, grills, a rest room, and a playground for the children.

INFORMATION: Grayson Lake State Park, Route 3, Box 800, Olive Hill, KY 41164-9213. Telephone 606-474-9727. Take I-64 west to Kentucky Highway 7 south.

Greenbo Lake State Resort Park

Author and poet Jesse Stuart, a longtime resident of Greenup County, once wrote "If these United States can be called a body... then Kentucky can be called its heart." He was inspired by the beauty of Kentucky's forests, mountains, and deep blue grasslands. You, too, will share that inspiration when you visit the center of Stuart's world at Greenbo Lake. More than 3,000 acres of forest woodland surrounds the secluded lakeland paradise where the fishing is claimed to be "the best anywhere." Largemouth bass of record size have been taken from the quiet waters, and the lake teams with crappie, bluegill, and catfish.

The 36-room lodge offers all the amenities one might expect to find at the best seafront resorts. These include the Jesse Stuart Library and Reading Room, meeting facilities, a gift shop, a dining room where breakfast, lunch, and dinner feature the finest of Kentucky cooking.

The park marina has 65 open slips and an assortment of rental boats for hire by the hour or by the day, including motor boats, pontoons, rowboats, and canoes.

Over 64 campsites are available during the summer months. These come with all the usual utilities including hookups, a dump site, a central service station complete with restrooms and showers, groceries, and laundry. There's a swimming pool, more than nine miles of hiking trails, several tennis courts, picnic shelters, tables, grills, a gift shop, and the usual program of planned activities for all the family, supervised by a fully qualified staff.

INFORMATION: Greenbo Lake State Resort Park, H.C. 60, Box 562, Greenup, KY 41144-9517. Telephone 606-473-7324, or for reservations you can call toll free 800-325-0083.

The resort is on Kentucky Highway 1, 18 miles north of I-64 from the Grayson exit.

Jenny Wiley State Resort Park

Jenny Wiley was a pioneer woman who was taken captive by Indians in 1789. Her brother and children were killed by the Indians but, after more than 11 months of captivity, she managed to escape and make her way to safety through the forests and woodlands, a small part of which became the state park that today pays tribute to her heroism.

The Jenny Wiley Resort Park lies deep in the heart of the Appalachians. Visitors can wander over more than nine miles of mountain trails and along the shores of Dewey Lake where, more than 200 years ago, the great pioneer lady made good her escape. And if hiking over the rugged terrain is a little too much, there's a sky lift which carries its riders to the top of Sugar Camp Mountain, where the air is cool and invigorating, and the views spectacular. Of special interest is the outdoor amphitheater where, during the summer months, professional actors present a program of Broadway plays and musicals.

The resort lodge is a secluded, 49-room mountain retreat offering magnificient views and a wide range of amenities. The gift shop is packed with all sorts of local Kentucky crafts and souvenirs; the dining room can seat up to 224 and features something different in the form of delicious local cuisine; and there's a swimming pool available for the exclusive use of guests at the lodge and cottages. The lodge complex includes two meeting rooms, each capable of seating up to 125 people, and catering facilities for parties, large or small, of up to 800 people.

Seventeen rustic cottages are available year-round, each with all the usual amenities, including tableware, cooking utensils, and daily linen service.

Other accommodations include 117 summer-only campsites, with hookups, a dump site, two central service stations, complete with restrooms and showers, a grocery store, and laundry facilities. There's an Olympic-size swimming pool available to all visitors, more than nine miles of hiking trails, a testy nine-hole golf course complete with pro shop, rental equipment, and golf carts. Picnic shelters, tables, grills, and playgrounds are located throughout the park and campground.

The full-service marina on Dewey Lake has 199 open slips, as well as rental fishing boats and pontoons. The fishing is said to be "the best anywhere," and the lake teams with largemouth, small-mouth and rock bass, bluegill, catfish, crappie, and muskie.

The resort also offers visitors a program of planned activities for all the family, supervised by a fully qualified staff.

INFORMATION: Jenny Wiley State Resort Park, H.C. 66, Box 200, Prestonburg, KY 41653-9799, or telephone 606-886-2711, or toll free for reservations 800-325-0142. Contact the Jenny Wiley Theater by telephone 606-886-9274.

The park is in Prestonburg off US 23/460 on Kentucky Hwy 3.

Kingdom Come State Park

At an elevation of 2,700 feet, high on the crest of Pine Mountain, and named for the popular Civil War novel, "The Little Shepherd of Kingdom Come," by Kentucky author John Fox, Kingdom Come is Kentucky's highest state park.

Spectacular views of the unspoiled wilderness, a mountain lake, a natural sandstone bridge, and some of the most extraordinary rock formations, are only a few of the exceptional features that have made Kingdom Come one of Kentucky's most outstanding tourist attractions.

Other facilities at the park include more than seven miles of hiking trails, including the Little Shepherd Trail; the Cave Amphitheater; primitive camping at the roadside picnic areas; a nine-hole miniature golf course; two picnic shelters with restroom facilities, tables, grills, and playgrounds. The 3.5-acre lake is well stocked with bass, bluegill, catfish, and crappie.

INFORMATION: Kingdom Come State Park, Box M, Cumberland, KY 40823-0420. Telephone 606-589-2479. The park is 50 miles northeast of Middlesboro in Cumberland, off US 25E.

Paintsville Lake State Park

This fisherman's paradise on the shores of spectacular Paintsville Lake is one of Kentucky's newest state parks. Here, in the heart of the mountains, the warm, lazy days and long nights of summer evolve slowly into a riot of autumn color, then to winter when the lake turns into a shimmering sheet of glass and the mountains turn white under a blanket of snow. Spring brings an explosion of life to the "Jewel of the Eastern Kentucky Mountains."

Paintsville Lake is a veritable stockyard of fish, including largemouth and smallmouth bass, muskie, walleye, bluegill, sunfish, catfish, crappie, and list goes on. This watersport extravaganza is supported by a full-service marina complete with 84 open slips, 80 covered slips, a four-lane boat ramp, and a full range of rental boats, including fishing boats and houseboats.

INFORMATION: Paintsville Lake State Park, 150 Staffordsville, KY 41256. Telephone 606-297-1521. The park is four miles west of Paintsville, off Kentucky Highway 40 from US 460.

General Information

Accommodation Rates

LODGE ROOMS: As the room rates at the lodges vary from season to season, and from location to location, it is advisable that you contact the park resort of your choice directly. Typically, though, the rates at Kentucky Dam Village range from $34 per night for one person during the winter season, $49 per night during spring, $49 per night in the fall, and $55 per night in the summer. The two-person rate during the winter is $44 per night, $59 per night in the spring, $59 per night during the fall, and $65 per night during the summer season. At other locations the rate varies by perhaps a dollar or two depending upon the season. Rates, as always, are subject to change, so it is advisable to call or write the park or resort of your choice, or contact the Kentucky Department of Parks, 500 Mero Street, 11th Floor, Frankfort, KY 40601-1974. Telephone toll free 1-800-255-PARK.

COTTAGES: The daily rate for rental cottages varies greatly from season to season, and from location to location. They can be as lowas $57 per night for an efficiency unit at Pennyrile Forrest from November through March. At the other end, it costs $150 for a three-bedroom, two-bathroom, executive cottage at General Butler during the summer (April to October). As the rates vary so much, and because they are always subject to change, it is impossible to go into further detail. For more detailed information it is advisable to call or write to the park or resort of your choice, or to contact the Kentucky Department of Parks, 500 Mero Street, 11th Floor, Frankfort, KY 40601-1974. Telephone toll free 1-800-255-PARK.

CAMPING: Most of Kentucky's State Parks have campgrounds, with the majority open year-round, but some are available only during the summer months. The rates are $10.50 per night for two persons (15% discount for senior citizens), and $8.50 at the primitive sites, plus an extra $1 per person over 16 years of age.

MEETING FACILITIES: Each of Kentucky's State Resort Parks has meeting facilities. There are more than 60 rooms statewide ranging in capacity from 10 to 700 persons. For more information and group reservations call 1-800-255-PARK or 502-564-2172, and ask for group sales.

FOR MORE INFORMATION write to the Kentucky Department of Parks, 500 Mero Street, 11th Floor, Frankfort, KY 40601-1974. Or call toll free 1-800-255-PARK.

Tennessee

Tennessee is a land bounded by the Great Smoky Mountains to the east, and by the mighty Mississippi River to the west. In between, some of the most beautiful scenery in the world welcomes visitors to a state rich in history, resources, and culture.

The misty, blue mountains, and the lush, green forests; the great lakes, rivers, streams, creeks, and spectacular waterfalls; the ancient river gorges, the sandstone bluffs, and the great plateaus; the hiking trails and the bridle paths that wind their ways through the thousands of square miles of unspoiled wilderness; the astonishing variety of plant, bird, and animal life; are all a part of the Tennessee outdoor experience. Add to all that a system of state parks unrivaled anywhere else in the United States, and a visit to Tennessee can be a treasure to remember for a lifetime.

There are more than 50 state parks in the Tennessee system, each unique in its own special way. And, no matter where in the state you might be, there's always one nearby.

The system includes seven resort inns, some of which rival even the finest of those found at the nation's vacation hot-spots, sev-

Tennessee

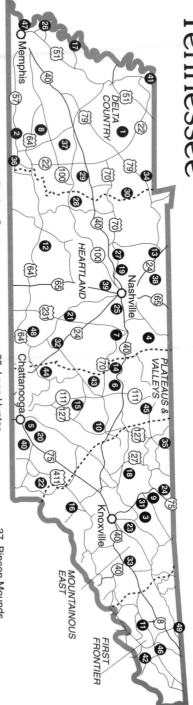

1. Big Cypress Tree
2. Big Hill Pond
3. Big Ridge
4. Bledsoe Creek
5. Booker T. Washington
6. Burgess Falls
7. Cedars of Lebanon
8. Chickasaw
9. Cove Lake
10. Cumberland Mountain
11. Davy Crockett Birthplace
12. David Crockett

13. Dunbar Cave
14. Edgar Evins
15. Fall Creek Falls
16. Fort Loudon
17. Fort Pillow
18. Frozen Head
19. Harpeth Scenic River & Narrows
20. Harrison Bay
21. Henry Horton
22. Hiwassee River
23. House Mountain
24. Indian Mountain

25. Long Hunter
26. Meeman-Shelby Forest
27. Montgomery Bell
28. Mousetail Landing
29. Natchez Trace
30. Nathan Bedford Forrest
31. Norris Dam
32. Old Stone Fort
33. Panther Creek
34. Paris Landing
35. Pickett
36. Pickwick Landing

37. Pinson Mounds
38. Port Royal
39. Radnor Lake
40. Red Clay
41. Reelfoot Lake
42. Roan Mountain
43. Rock Island
44. South Cumberland
45. Standing Stone
46. Sycamore Shoals
47. T. O. Fuller
48. Tim's Ford
49. Warrior's Path

DELTA COUNTRY

HEARTLAND

PLATEAUS & VALLEYS

MOUNTAINOUS EAST

FIRST FRONTIER

Memphis

Nashville

Chattanooga

Knoxville

eral hundred vacation cabins and chalets equipped with all the comforts of home, and more than 2,900 camping sites, most of them fully developed to provide all the modern conveniences.

The state is famous for its hunting and fishing; indeed, the headquarters of the National Sport Fishing Association is in Chattanooga. The great lakes and rivers have become centers for watersports activities on a grand scale, and the vast tracts of wilderness and virgin forest have become a mecca for the dedicated naturalist.

To make things easy for the visitor, the state is divided into five distinct, geographic regions: Delta Country in the west, the Heartland, Plateaus and Valleys, the Mountainous East, and the First Frontier in the east.

Delta Country

Big Cypress Tree State Natural Area

Big Cypress Tree lies on the Middle Fork of the Obion River at Greenfield in West Tennessee. It's a very scenic area with some 300 acres of bottom land and hardwood forests which provide habitats for a wide variety of plant and animal life, including the bald cypress, tupelo, beaver, and fox squirrel.

There are no facilities at Big Cypress Tree, although there are several hiking trails. It's essentially a day-use park where visitors can spend a few hours studying nature, bird watching, or hiking.

INFORMATION: Big Cypress Tree State Natural Area, Kimery Road, Greenfield, TN 38230. Telephone 901-235-2700. The park is located off US 45E.

Big Hill Pond State Park

Big Hill Pond is a nature and recreation center more than 5,000 acres in area. It's a park where man has put his stamp upon the countryside to good effect. The cypress-bordered pond, from which the park takes its name, was formed during the construction of a levy for the Memphis-Charleston Railroad. Today, the park features not only the pond, but the popular McNatt Fishing Lake, and a vast tract of backcountry and scenic wetland. Big Hill Pond offers visitors one of the best opportunities in the state to contemplate nature and the aftermath of man's positive interaction with it.

Facilities at the park include a meeting room for up to 40 persons, 20 full-service camping sites, 10 campsites for tents only, a backcountry primitive camping area, several backpacking, hiking and nature trails, boat launching facilities, lake access for canoes and small boats, picnic areas with playgrounds, and a visitor center, all within the park area. There's also a boardwalk trail which leads visitors deep into the wetland, where they can observe many species of wild birds and animals.

ACTIVITIES: Fishing on McNatt Lake for bass, crappie, and bluegill, hiking, backpacking, nature study, bird watching, photography, camping, and picnicking. Better still, you can join one of the on-going programs of interpretive and educational activities provided by the Park Service staff.

INFORMATION: Big Hill Pond State Park, Route 1, Box 150C, Pocahontas, TN 38061. Telephone 901-992-5523. The park is open during the summer months from 8 AM until 10 PM, and from 8 AM until sundown during the winter.

Big Hill Pond is on State Highway 57, west of Ramer, on the junction of the Tuscumbia and the Hatchie State Scenic Rivers.

Chickasaw State Park

With a total area of more than 14,300 acres, Chickasaw is the third largest park in the Tennessee system. In times before the Jackson

Purchase of 1818 it was a part of a vast area that belonged to the Chickasaw Nation, hence its name. The park is an area of wild beauty with more than 50 miles of fire roads, trails, and back-country paths winding their way through the great forest on some of the highest terrain in western Tennessee. Add to this the still waters of Lake Placid, and you have one of the finest outdoor recreational facilities in the entire state.

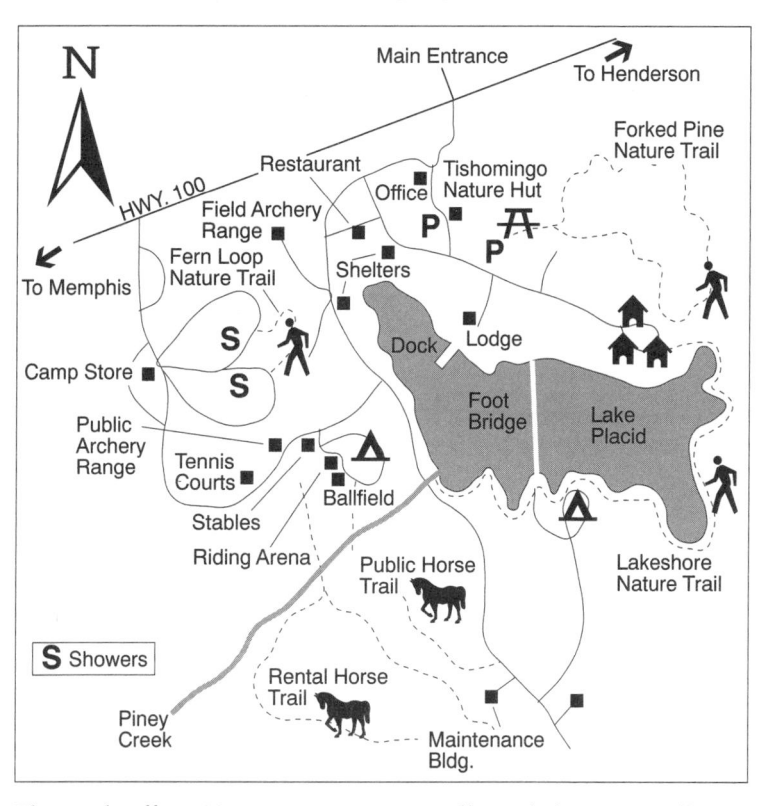

The park offers 13 vacation cottages, all nestled among tall pine trees and within easy access of the lake. Each cabin can accommodate up to six persons, has a fireplace, and is fully equipped for housekeeping.

There are 110 camping sites, 70 of which provide all the usual utilities, including water and electric hookups. Forty of the 70 sites located at the Wrangler Campground have bathhouses as well as water and electric hookups. All sites have picnic tables and grills, and a modern bathhouse provides campers with hot showers and restroom facilities. All sites are available on a first-come, first-served basis.

A fully equipped group lodge with accommodations for up to 40 persons is available the year-round, and has a kitchen for food preparation. There is also a group camping lodge with accommodations for up to 142 persons. It, too, is fully equipped with a dining hall, cabins, bunks, restrooms, and its own swimming area. The dining hall has everything campers might need for an extensive stay, including cooking and serving utensils and equipment. The group camp is open April through October, and reservations are required.

The park also has a fine restaurant with capacity to seat up to 100 persons, where the finest of Southern cuisine is served in a restful atmosphere. The restaurant is open year-round from 4 PM until 10 PM Wednesday through Saturday, and from 11 AM until 10 PM on Sundays.

ACTIVITIES: Swimming from the beach on Lake Placid; there's a modern bathhouse and a concession stand, and there's a lifeguard on duty during swimming hours. Rowboats are available for rent (personal boats are not permitted), fishing on the lake is excellent – there's nothing quite like a fresh-caught, pan-fried, bluegill, crappie, or bass cooked over an open fire. There's also hiking, nature study and bird watching, tennis, basketball, archery, and volleyball. There are seven picnic pavilions and 45 picnic tables and grills conveniently located throughout the park.

Horseback riding, too, is a popular pastime at Chickasaw. During the summer months horses are available for rent, and visitors with their own mounts can wander at will along more than 50 miles of roads and trails within the forest.

The park naturalist and the recreation director together conduct a series of daily programs throughout the summer months, including arts & crafts, hayrides, guided tours, campfire sessions, evening movies, and organized games. Square dancing is held at Sagamore Recreation Lodge during the summer months.

INFORMATION: Superintendent's Office, Chickasaw State Park, Henderson, TN 38340. Telephone 901-989-5141. The park is open from 8 AM until 10 PM, and the camper quiet time 10 PM.

The park is in Chester and Hardeman Counties, 18 miles south of Jackson, on State Highway 100.

Fort Pillow State Historic Park

The Confederate Army built the extensive fortifications at Fort Pillow in 1861 and named them for General Gidion J. Pillow, a somewhat overrated commander who never fully realized his ambitions, either on the battlefield or in politics. His one real claim to fame was his defeat at Fort Donnelson in 1862 and his abandonment of the troops therein.

Fort Pillow eventually fell to the Union Army which occupied it for the rest of the war. Some of the original earthworks still remain and are well preserved. Visitors to the park will enjoy strolling the old fortifications as they try to imagine what life might have been when the fort was a bustling military encampment.

The park is also well know for the surrounding scenery, its wildlife, and its great natural beauty, from Cold Creek to the nearby Hatchie State Scenic River and Chickasaw Wildlife Refuge.

The 1,650-acre park offers 40 acres of river frontage, a meeting room that seats up to 50 persons, 40 camping sites (tents only), backcountry camping sites, a laundromat, a visitors center, a museum, a gift shop, several hiking trails, a boat ramp, and a picnic area with tables and grills and a playground for the children.

ACTIVITIES: Fishing in the creek, by boat or from the river bank, hiking, picnicking, and bird watching and nature study.

INFORMATION: Fort Pillow State Historic Park, Route 2, Box 109A, Henning, TN 38041. Telephone 901-738-5581. The park is open during the summer months from 8 AM until 10 PM, and from 8 AM until sundown during the winter.

The park is located off US 51, and west on State Highway 87.

Meeman-Shelby Forest State Park

Located on the banks of the mighty Mississippi River on the Chickasaw Bluffs, the Meeman-Shelby State Park is a vast hinterland of hardwood forest, oak, cypress, tupelo, soggy bottom land and lakes which provide natural habitats for more than 200 species of wild birds and animals, including beaver, turkey, and deer. The Chickasaw Bluffs, the developed area of this great park, were formed over long years by wind-blown silt and soil. The bluffs and the surrounding bottom lands offer naturalists many unique opportunities for nature study, bird watching, and photography. The park itself is a haven for those who like to spend a few quiet hours, or days, in the wide open countryside.

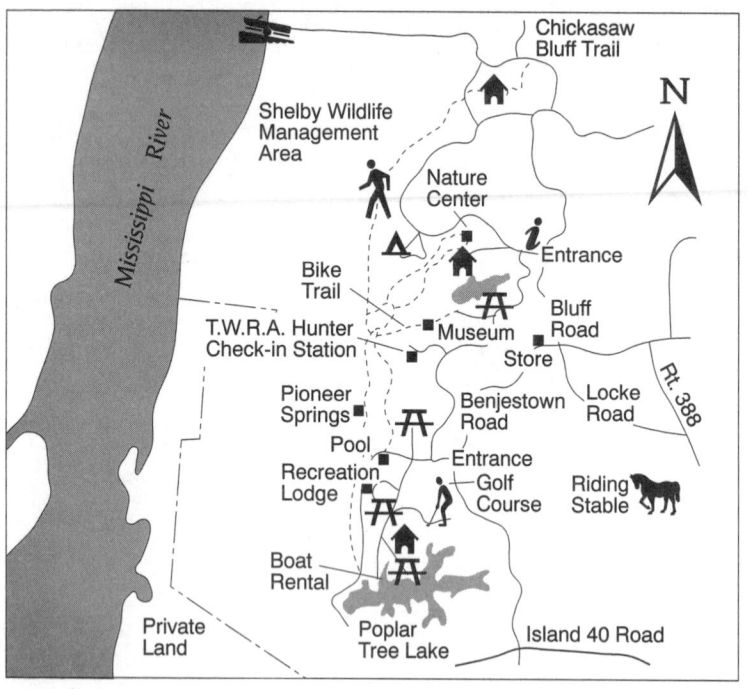

Facilities here include six two-bedroom vacation cabins conveniently on the shores of Poplar Tree Lake in a secluded, wooded section of the park. The cabins are fully equipped for housekeeping. Linens are provided as a part of the service, and each unit can accommodate up to six persons.

The camping ground provides 50 full-service sites with all the usual utilities, including water and electrical hookups, a table and grill, a conveniently located bathhouse with hot showers and restroom facilities, and a dumping station. All sites are available on a first-come, first-served basis.

Two group camps are available from April through October: one has the capacity for up to 120 persons, the other up to 136 persons. They include a large dining hall equipped for food preparation and serving, group cabins, bathhouses with showers and restrooms, and a swimming pool. Linens are not provided. The camps may be rented by the week only during the summer months, and on weekends at other times. Interested parties should contact the park office for availability.

Other facilities include a visitors center, a nature center, a gift shop, boat rentals and a boat cruise, boat launching facilities, an archery range, a recreations center with a swimming pool, a wading pool for the children, a modern bathhouse, and a concession stand where one can purchase light refreshments.

ACTIVITIES: Fishing Poplar Tree Lake for largemouth bass, bream, crappie, bluegill, and catfish. There are more than 20 miles of trails winding through the park and the bottom lands are perfect for hiking, bicycling, and horseback riding (rental horses are available). During the summer months, park naturalists and recreation staff provide a variety of programs, guided tours, organized games, square dances, and living history demonstrations.

INFORMATION: Meeman-Shelby State Park, Route 3, Millington, TN 38053. Telephone 901-876-5215. Park hours are from 8 AM until 10 PM during the summer months, and from 8 AM until sundown during winter. The camper quiet time is 10 PM.

The park is in Shelby County, 13 miles north of Memphis near Millington, off US 51.

Natchez Trace State Park

During the 18th and 19th centuries the Natchez Trace was the wilderness road from Natchez to Nashville. During those years a spur of the trail ran through what is now the Natchez Trace State Park. The Natchez Trace Parkway of today is administered by the National Park Service and has no connection with the State Park.

During the early years of the 20th century, land in the area was abused and eroded to such a degree that it was virtually turned into a wasteland. So much so that by the mid-1930s the sad state of affairs had caught the attention of the US Government. In a desperate attempt to reverse the situation, the US Department of Agriculture bought the land, relocated the occupants, and set up a "Land Use Area" project, the aim of which was to reclaim the wasteland through the application of proper conservation and management practices.

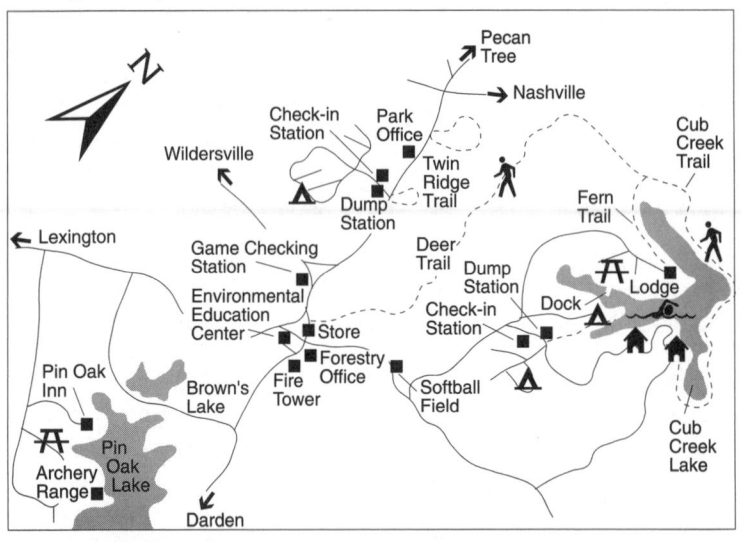

Today, three state agencies, the Tennessee Division of State Parks, the Tennessee Division of Forestry, and the Tennessee Wildlife Resources Agency, share the administration of the park providing the state and visitors with one of the finest outdoor recreational facilities in the country.

More than 14,000 acres of parkland and forest, lakes and rivers, along with some 45 miles of hiking, backpacking, and bridle trails in the center of the Natchez Trace State Forest provide visitors with a unique opportunity to observe the literally hundreds of species of flora and fauna that make their homes in the great forest. Natchez Trace is a naturalist's paradise.

Overnight and recreational facilities at the park are extensive. The modern Pin Oak Lodge, situated in a wooded glade on the shores of Pin Oak Lake, is a 20-room resort hotel. The dining room offers good Southern cuisine and can seat up to 120 persons. Other lodge facilities include a recreation room, a playground, tennis courts, a swimming pool, and a children's pool. Private meeting rooms and dining facilities are available for parties of up to 300 persons.

Other accommodations include 18 rental cabins in the woodlands on the shores of Cub Lake. Each cabin can sleep up to four persons and is fully equipped for housekeeping, including utensils for food preparation and service. All have fireplaces, air conditioning, and daily linen service.

The camping ground provides 143 full-service sites, all with tables, grills, water and electric hookups, and access to modern bathhouses with hot showers and restrooms. There's also a park store and service station, where visitors can purchase groceries, ice, and picnic and camping supplies.

Other facilities include softball courts, an archery range, basketball courts, croquet courts, and volleyball courts. There are a number of picnic sites with tables and grills conveniently located in the woodland glades, along with drinking fountains, playgrounds, and picnic shelters.

ACTIVITIES: Fine fishing on four lakes for bluegill, crappie, bream, and bass. Hikers will enjoy the many miles of trails that wind their way through the woodlands, along the lake shores and the river banks, within the boundaries of the 45,000-acre Natchez Trace State Forest.

During the summer months park recreation directors and naturalists offer a full program of activities, including arts & crafts, movies, slide shows, archery instruction, horseback riding, hay rides, and square dancing. Weekly activity schedules are available from Pin Oak Lodge, the recreation center, and the park office.

INFORMATION: Natchez Trace State Park, Route 1, Box 265, Wildersville, TN 38388; telephone 901-968-8176. The park is open during the summer months from 8 AM until 10 PM, and from 8 AM until sundown during the winter. The camper quiet time is 10 PM.

The park is 40 miles northeast of Jackson on I-40, between Nashville and Memphis at Exit 116.

Nathan Bedford Forrest State Park

The 3,000-acre Nathan Bedford Forrest State Park, set on the western shores of Kentucky Lake, and the 741-foot-high Pilot Knob, overlook the Civil War battlefield of Johnsonville. Pilot Knob, so named because it was an important point of reference for the riverboat captains plying the Tennessee River, offers visitors to the park one of the outstanding views in the state. A monument to the great Civil War cavalry commander from whom the park takes its name is located next to the visitors center. The park is also home of the Tennessee River Folklife Museum.

Facilities offered here are extensive. They include 38 full-service camping sites with all the usual utilities, including water and electric hookups, 15 tent-only camping sites, several backcountry camping sites, a group lodge with accommodations for up to 64 persons, a bathhouse with showers and restroom facilities, a visitors center, a gift shop, a museum, boat launching facilities, several picnic areas with tables and grills, miles of hiking and nature trails, and a playground for the children.

ACTIVITIES: Fishing on the river, boating, waterskiing, swimming, nature study and bird watching, and hiking the woodland trails.

INFORMATION: Nathan Bedford Forrest State Park, Eva, TN 38333. Telephone 901-584-6356. The park is open during the summer months from 8 AM until 10 PM, and from 8 AM until sundown during the winter.

The park is north of I-40, near Camden on State Highway 191.

Paris Landing State Park

Paris Landing State Park, set on the western shores of Kentucky Lake, was named for the important steamboat and freight landing on the Tennessee River that was in heavy use during the early to mid-1800s. Today, the 841-acre park has become famous as one of Tennessee's premier outdoor recreational facilities.

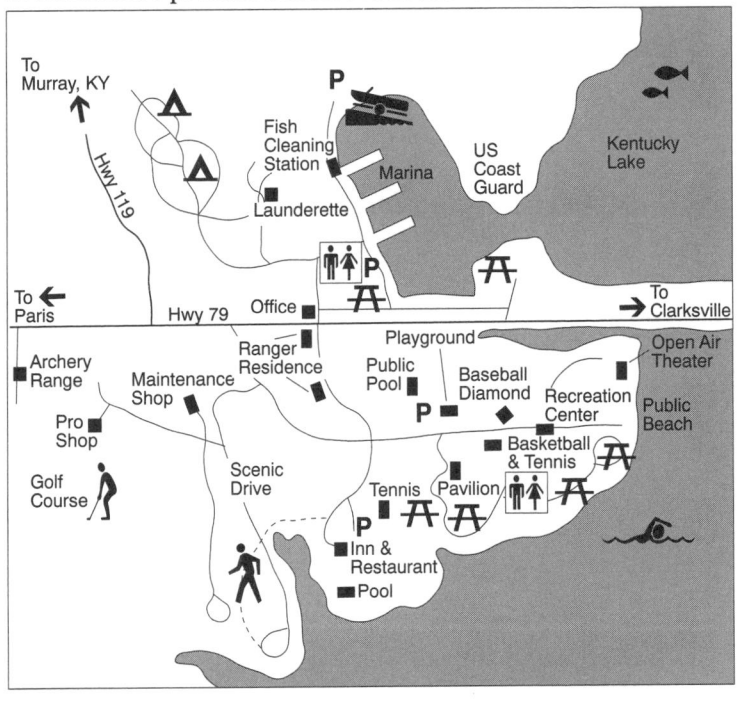

The Park Service at Paris Landing has literally turned the park into a vacation resort that rivals even the finest of beachfront resorts on either the east or the west coast. The 100-room Paris Landing Inn provides a spectacular view of Kentucky Lake and the surrounding countryside, while its restaurant offers seating for up to 385 persons and the very finest of Southern cuisine. The restaurant is famous across the state for its winter fare of buffalo steak and roasts.

The Paris Landing camping ground provides its visitors with 46 sites, all with tables and grills, as well as water and electrical hookups. There's a conveniently located bathhouse with hot showers and restroom facilities, a launderette, snack bars, a gift shop, and a dumping station.

There is a full-service marina, equipped to handle craft of all sizes, a refueling dock, ice service, fishing and boating supplies available at the marina store, and rental boats as well. The park also has boat launching facilities, tennis courts, hiking trails, picnic areas with tables and grills, and a playground for the children.

Best of all, though, is the magnificent, 18-hole golf course – claimed to be one of the most beautiful and challenging in the state. A full-time golf pro is on duty during playing hours; there's a driving range, a practice putting green, and a snack bar. Golfing equipment and carts can be rented at the pro shop.

ACTIVITIES: Yachting, sailing, cruising, waterskiing, swimming, and fishing. Kentucky Lake is famous for its largemouth, smallmouth, and white bass, as well as for its crappie, bluegill, catfish and sauger.

During the summer months park recreation directors and naturalists offer a full program of activities, including guided walks, cave tours, arts & crafts, movies, slide shows, pontoon boat rides, and much more. Special outdoor entertainment is provided on Saturday evenings in the park's outdoor theater. Weekly activity schedules are available at the Paris Landing Inn and the park office.

INFORMATION: Paris Landing State Resort Park, Route 1, Buchanan, TN 38222. Telephone 901-644-7359. The Resort Inn telephone number is 901-642-4311. The marina and park store are open during the summer months from 6:30 AM until 8 PM. The inn is open 24 hours, the restaurant from 7 AM until 9 PM, the golf course is from sunup to sundown, and day-use hours are from sunup to 10 PM. The camper quiet time is 10 PM to 6 AM.

The park is located 16 miles northeast of Paris on US 79.

Pickwick Landing
State Resort Park

Pickwick Landing is a 1,390-acre resort park nestled on the shores of the scenic Pickwick Lake. With more than 9,500 acres of deep blue waters, the park is a watersportsman's paradise. The surrounding countryside is a broad, backcountry terrain of rolling parkland and densely wooded forests. Hiking trails and woodland paths meander through the park, the adjacent land, and along the many miles of lakeshore. The broad open vista of the lake, the cool clean air, and the secluded location of the park, all make for an unforgettable outdoor experience.

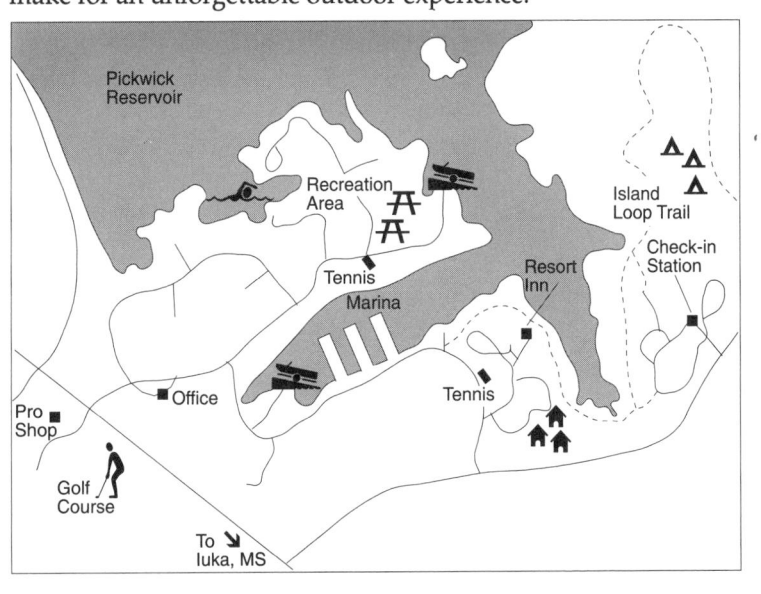

The park's modern inn provides 75 single and double guest rooms, along with three luxury suites and spectacular views overlooking the water. The main dining room can seat up to 135 persons, with additional capacity for 320 in a separate, private dining room. There are also three large rooms for meetings and conventions, and the dining staff offers the finest in Southern cuisine. The inn's private recreational facilities – adult and children's pools, a playground, and lighted tennis courts – ensure visitors will enjoy a pleasant vacation without having to go too far afield for their outdoor entertainment.

Other accommodations here include 10 two-bedroom luxury cabins, each overlooking the lake, and each fully equipped for housekeeping, food preparation, and serving. They both have central heating and cooling, a television, patio, and a fireplace. Cabin guests also enjoy all the privileges available at the inn.

The wooded camping ground offers 48 sites, each with a picnic table, grill, and water and electrical hookups. There's a conveniently located bathhouse with hot showers and restroom facilities, and there's also a dumping station nearby for self-contained trailer rigs.

The park's full-service marina is equipped to handle craft of all sizes. The marina store stocks an extensive range of boating and fishing equipment for sale, and rental boats are available by the hour or by the day. There are three public boat launching facilities. The lake is well stocked with fish, and is famous for its largemouth, smallmouth, and striped bass, as well as for its crappie, bluegill, sauger, and catfish.

For the golfer, Pickwick Landing's 18-hole, par 72 course offers a challenging, yet enjoyable day's sport. The pro shop provides an assortment of rental equipment and golf carts, and there's a full-time pro ready to offer a little friendly advice when it's needed.

ACTIVITIES: Sailing, skiing, and fishing. There are more than two miles of swimming beach on the lakefront providing ample room for sunbathing and picnicking. Picnic tables and grills are conveniently located around the park, and all are accessible to restrooms, water fountains, and playgrounds.

Across the Lake Bruton Branch Primitive Area, a 347-acre area of primitive parkland, provides a swimming beach, a boat launching ramp, primitive camping sites, and a modern bathhouse with all the usual facilities.

INFORMATION: Pickwick Landing State Resort Park, PO Box 15, Pickwick Dam, Tennessee 38365. Telephone 901-689-3129, or call the inn at 901-689-3135. The park is open from 6 AM until 10 PM year-round. The camper quiet time is 10 PM. The marina and the resort inn provide 24-hour service.

The park is located just south of Pickwick Dam, at the intersection of State Routes 57 and 128. It is 13 miles south of Savannah, and 20 miles north of Corinth, Mississippi.

Pinson Mounds
State Archaeological Park

Pinson Mounds was, in prehistoric times, an important Indian religious and ceremonial center. The 1,086-acre park is a showcase; a mixture of archaeological research and the pristine natural beauty of the area. Research is still being conducted on-site, and visitors to the park will enjoy viewing the scientific operations as they progress. The park's museum, the self-guided trails, and an elevated boardwalk along the banks of Forked Deer River, all ensure the best possible view of whatever might be going on. The signature piece of the park is a ceremonial center containing the second highest Indian mound in the United States.

Facilities here are mostly limited to day use, but there is a small group camp that accommodates up to 32 people. There's also a visitors center and a museum.

INFORMATION: Pinson Mounds State Archaeological Park, 460 Ozier Road, Pinson, TN 38366. Telephone 901-988-5614. The park is in Pinson, just off US 45.

Reelfoot Lake State Park

Reelfoot is Tennessee's only natural lake. It was created by a series of cataclysmic earthquakes during the winter of 1811-12. Large areas of land were displaced as the earth moved. Some was pushed upward, while still larger areas sank. One of those areas filled with water, forming the great lake we now know as Reelfoot.

Today, Reelfoot is one of the finest fishing and hunting preserves in the nation. The waters and surrounding woodlands provide habitats for a variety of wild birds, plants, and animals. As the seasons change, naturalists, botanists, and nature lovers from around the country converge on Reelfoot to study and enjoy all that this wild and wonderful backcountry area has to offer.

The facilities provided at the park are extensive. The Airpark Inn and Restaurant offers its guests 20 well-appointed rooms, including eight luxury suites, along with a five-unit motel located at the Reelfoot spillway. The dining room can seat up to 100 persons, and offers good Southern cooking.

For those who like to fly, the park provides a 3,500-foot, lighted, all-weather landing strip adjacent to the inn.

Reelfoot has two camping grounds, providing a total of 120 sites. Each site is fully equipped with a picnic table and grill, and with water and electric hookups. Modern bathhouses with showers and restroom facilities are conveniently located at both campgrounds, and dumping stations are provided for self-contained camping rigs.

Reelfoot also has a 400-seat, air-conditioned auditorium with a full-service kitchen available for banquets and conventions year-round. There's a visitors center where one can view a variety of exhibits that provide insight into the natural and cultural history of the area. Exhibits include an earthquake simulator and a variety of audio-visual programs.

Recreational opportunities at Reelfoot are well-known across the state. Few outdoorsmen and women have not heard of the great natural area situated in the northwest corner of Tennessee. Anglers will enjoy fine sport fishing on the well-stocked lake for largemouth bass, crappie, bream, bluegill, and walleye.

ACTIVITIES: Scenic boat rides on the lake, swimming, hiking, nature study, bird watching, wildlife photography, and picnicking at one of 200 secluded spots around the park.

During the winter Reelfoot is host to some very famous visitors of another kind. From December to March the park is a wintering ground for a growing population of bald eagles. Throughout the season park naturalists conduct daily eagle tours. On weekends they offer a variety of eagle-related programs, including slide shows, guest lectures and bus tours. Eagle watching is a popular pastime, so it's advisable to contact the Park Service well in advance to make reservations.

INFORMATION: Superintendent's Office or the Airpark Inn, Reelfoot Lake State Resort Park, Route 1, Tiptonville, TN 38079. Telephone 901-253-7756. The park is located off State Highway 78, 10 miles north of Tiptonville.

T. O. Fuller State Park

T. O. Fuller is named for the prominent clergyman and educator, Dr. Thomas Oscar Fuller, and was one of the first four parks established by the Department of Conservation. Construction of the park by the Civilian Conservation Corps began in 1938 and continued on through 1940, when excavations of a proposed swimming pool uncovered evidence of a prehistoric Indian settlement. It was soon realized that the site was an important one, and work began on reconstruction of the village. Today, Chucalissa Indian Village, now under the management of Memphis State University, along with some of the original preserved excavations and an interpretive museum, offer visitors a window on the past.

Besides being an important historic site, T. O. Fuller is a major recreational facility, not only for the people of Memphis, but for out-of-state visitors as well.

Overnight facilities at the park are limited to 52 modern camping sites, each furnished with a table and grill, and with water and electrical hookups. The campground is served by a modern bathhouse offering hot showers, a laundromat, and restrooms.

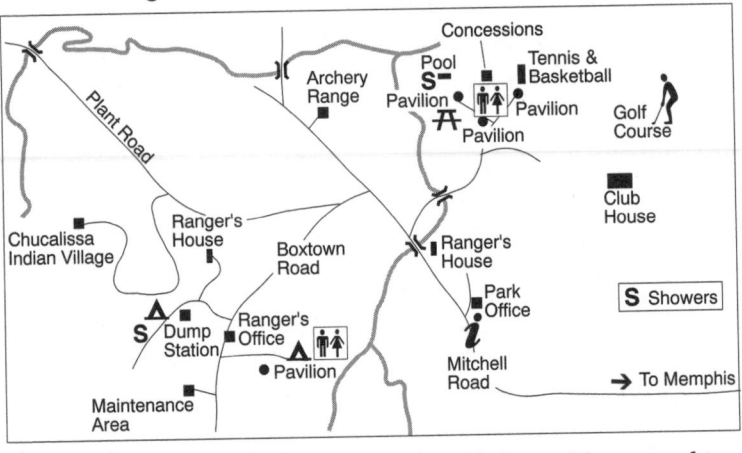

The park also has a visitors center, a snack bar, a 20-acre archery range with 14 practice and 24 tournament targets, a swimming pool with plenty of room for sunbathing, several tennis courts, public restrooms, a group pavilion, and lots of picnic areas throughout, all with tables and grills. There is also a formidable 18-hole, USGA-sanctioned golf course open daily from April through December. Clubs and carts are available for rent.

INFORMATION: T. O. Fuller State Park, 1500 Mitchell Road, Memphis, TN 38109. Telephone 901-543-7581, or the golf course 901-543-7771. The park is open from 8 AM until sundown, and the camper quiet time is 10 PM.

The park is on Mitchell Road, west of US 61, 11 miles from downtown Memphis.

The Heartland

Bledsoe Creek State Park

The Bledsoe Creek State Park covers 164 acres of park and woodland and is on the shores of Old Hickory Lake, near the 1780s settlement of Cairo in Sumner County. The park offers its visitors many unique recreation opportunities in an area of scenic beauty seemingly far away from, but easily accessible to, the big city environment of one of the nation's entertainment capitals: Nashville, Music City USA.

The atmosphere here is one of quiet solitude, silent waters, and backcountry seclusion, where one can wander more than six miles of hiking and nature trails through some of Middle Tennessee's most picturesque countryside.

Facilities and accommodations at the park include 110 full-service camping sites, all with water and electrical hookups, picnic tables and grills, along with bathhouses where hot showers, restrooms, and a laundry room are available for park guests. There are boat launching facilities at the lake, picnic areas with tables, grills, and playgrounds for the children.

ACTIVITIES: Fishing the well-stocked lake for bass, crappie, bluegill, and catfish, waterskiing, camping, backpacking and hiking, nature study and bird watching, and guided boat cruises on the lake.

NEARBY ATTRACTIONS: Nashville, the Homes of the Country Music Stars in Nashville, Cedars of Lebanon State Park, Long Hunter State Park, and the historic sites of Wynnewood, Cragfront, Rock Castle, and Fort Bledsoe.

INFORMATION: Bledsoe Creek State Park, 400 Zieglers Fort Road, Gallatin, TN 37808. Telephone 615-894-3706. The park is open during the summer months from 8 AM until 10 PM, and from 8 AM until sundown during the winter.

Bledsoe Park is located off State Highway 25 at Gallatin.

Cedars Of Lebanon State Park

Cedars of Lebanon State Park is named for the distinctive tree that once existed in great forests in the Biblical land of Lebanon. The tree is not actually a true cedar, rather a close cousin, the juniper. It was valuable to the area around the turn of the century for its use in the pencil industry, for railroad cross-ties, and for its cedar oil. The area was replanted by the Civilian Conservation Corps in the 1930s, and is now the largest remaining red cedar forest in the United States.

Of the 8,887 acres that make up the park, only 831 acres are used for recreational purposes, the rest is operated by the State Parks Division as a natural area, and by the Forestry Division as a State Forest.

Facilities at the park are extensive, and include nine modern, two-bedroom cabins, each fully equipped for housekeeping, and available by reservation year-round.

The park has 119 camping sites, all with picnic tables and grill, and 89 sites have electric and water hookups. Three bathhouses provide campers with hot showers and restroom facilities. There's also a camp store, a souvenir shop, a laundromat, and a dumping station. The campground is open the year-round, and all sites are available on a first-come, first-served basis.

A modern group lodge offers sleeping for up to 40 persons, with private restrooms and showers, and a full-service kitchen with facilities for food preparation and serving. The lodge is available year-round, but reservations should be made well in advance.

Other facilities at the park include horseshoe pits, a lighted softball field, an archery range, a volleyball court, 125 picnic tables, 11 picnic pavilions, numerous drinking fountains, several restrooms, playgrounds, and soft drink machines located throughout the park. There's also an Olympic-size swimming pool with ample room for sunbathing, more that eight miles of hiking and nature trails, 12 miles of horseback riding trails, stabling for horses (sorry, no rentals), and a nature center.

ACTIVITIES: The park naturalist and the recreation director conduct a series of daily programs throughout the summer months, including arts & crafts, hayrides, guided tours, campfire sessions, evening movies, and organized games.

INFORMATION: The park is open during the summer months from 8 AM until 10 PM, and from 8 AM until 8 PM during the winter. For more information, contact the Superintendent's Office, Cedars of Lebanon State Park, Lebanon, TN 37087. Telephone 615-443-2769.

The park is located approximately 31 miles east of Nashville in Wilson County, six miles south of I-40 on US 231.

David Crockett State Park

In 1817, Davy Crockett moved from Limestone, Tennessee to Lawrence County, where he served as justice of the peace, colonel of the state militia, and as state representative. It was while he was living in Lawrence County that he established himself in business, building along the banks of Shoal Creek a powdermill, a gristmill, and a distillery. Unfortunately, all three businesses were lost to floodwaters in 1821. So, plagued by financial difficulties, Crockett moved to west Tennessee, where he was elected to Congress. Crockett died in 1836, along with Jim Bowie and Colonel Travis, at the Alamo during Texas' fight for independence from Mexico.

David Crockett State Park, dedicated to the honor and memory of one of Tennessee's most famous sons, is on the banks of Shoal Creek.

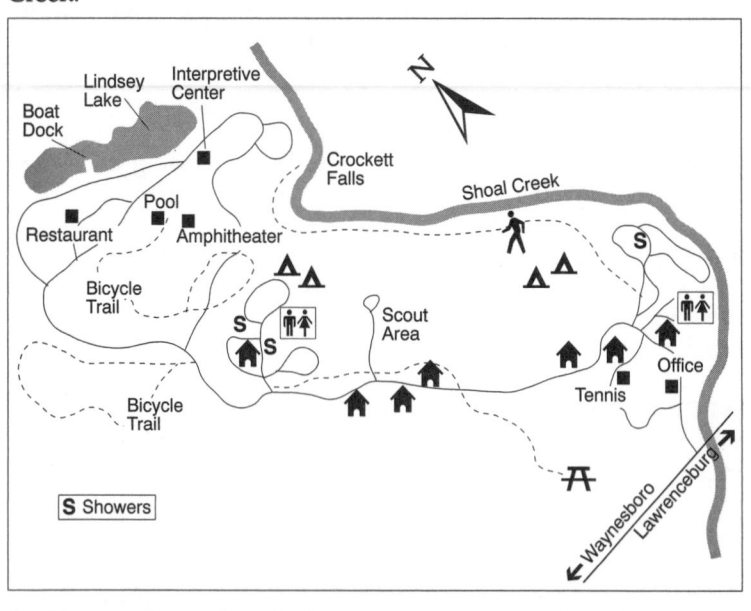

Facilities at the park include two camping grounds with a total of 107 sites, each equipped with a picnic table and grill, and all the usual utilities, including water and electrical hookups, a modern bathhouse with hot showers, restrooms, and a dumping station.

The park restaurant, which seats 240 persons, is set on a hill overlooking Lindsey Lake. It offers visitors to the park some of the finest southern cuisine. The restaurant also has two private dining rooms available year-round for group functions.

There's an Olympic-size swimming pool with a modern bath-house and a concession stand, ample space for sunbathing, a chil-dren's pool, and a lifeguard on duty during swimming hours. Other facilities include a visitors center, a museum, a gift shop, snack bars, several picnic areas with tables and grills, boat rent-als, an archery range, a paved bicycle trail, hiking trails, a 35-acre lake, tennis courts, a softball field, a volleyball court, and a play-ground.

ACTIVITIES: The park naturalist and recreation director conduct a series of daily programs throughout the summer months, in-cluding arts & crafts, hayrides, guided tours, campfire sessions, evening movies, and organized games.

INFORMATION: Park Manager's Office, David Crockett State Park, Lawrenceburg, TN 38464. Telephone 615-762-9408. The park is open year-round from 8 AM until 10 PM, and the camper quiet time is 10 PM.

David Crockett State Park is on US 64 in Lawrence County, one-half mile west of Lawrenceburg.

Dunbar Cave State Natural Area

Dunbar Cave State Natural Area is one of those unusual places where time seems to have passed by, leaving behind great natural beauty and a deep sense of local history. The 105-acre area is riddled with caves and sinkholes, the most important of which is Dunbar Cave. Archaeologists have determined that the cave was occupied by man for thousands of years.

The large area at the mouth of the cave has been the site of many a country music concert, radio show, square dance, and big band concert. Its most famous owner was country music star, Roy Acuff who, during his time of ownership, organized country mu-sic shows starring the legends of the Grand Ole Opry.

Facilities at the park include a 15-acre lake where fishing is permitted, a visitors center and museum, a picnic area, and a playground for the children.

ACTIVITIES: Organized cave hikes and environmental programs are presented by the Park Service staff throughout the year.

INFORMATION: Dunbar Cave State Natural Area, 401 Old Dunbar Cave Road, Clarksville, TN 37043. Telephone 615-648-5526. The park is open during the summer months from 8 AM until 10 PM, and from 8 AM until sundown during the winter.

Dunbar is located south of US 79.

Harpeth Scenic River & Narrows Historic Area

The 200-acre park known as the Harpeth Scenic River Complex is an area of great historical importance, famous for its many unique feats of engineering, including a 100-yard-long tunnel, hand-cut through solid rock, that is today an industrial landmark on the National Register of Historic Places. The complex also includes the 100 Bridge, the 1862 Newsom's Mill ruins, McCrory Lane Bridge at Hidden Lake, the Narrows of the Harpeth which provide upstream and downstream river access, Bell's Bend 5-mile float, and a unique 1/4-mile portage.

ACTIVITIES: Group interpretive tours, hiking, horseback riding, and picnicking.

INFORMATION: Harpeth Scenic River and Narrows Historic Area, Kingston Springs, TN 37082. Telephone 615-797-9052. The park is open during the summer months from 8 AM until 10 PM, and from 8 AM until sundown during the winter.

The complex is located off US 70 in Davidson County.

Henry Horton State Resort Park

Henry Horton State Park is set on the banks of Duck River on what was once the estate of the 36th Governor of Tennessee, Henry H. Horton. The park is well known for its fine resort inn, its scenic golf course, and for the Duck River itself, the longest free-flowing stretch of river in Tennessee and home of a thriving freshwater pearl industry.

Horton Inn, the signature piece of the park, provides 72 well-appointed rooms, including four suites complete with kitchenettes. Each room features two double beds, air conditioning, a television, and a telephone.

The restaurant at Henry Horton tempts the visitor with good country cooking and can seat up to 350 persons. It also offers three separate dining rooms suitable for group meetings, receptions, and private banquets.

In addition to the resort inn, there are four modern rental cabins, each providing accommodations for six persons, and all fully equipped for housekeeping, food preparation and serving. Each cabin is air conditioned, and has a fireplace, television and telephone.

There are 75 camp sites situated along the banks of Duck River. Twenty-one of the sites are recommended for tent camping only, while the other 54 are fully equipped with picnic tables, grills, and water and electric hookups. There are two modern bathhouses with showers and restroom facilities, and a convenient dumping station.

The park has an Olympic-size swimming pool with plenty of space for sunbathing and a concession stand where visitors can purchase snacks and soft drinks. There's also a wading pool for the children with lifeguards on duty during swimming hours.

There are 83 picnic sites at attractive intervals along the riverbank, all with tables and grills, restrooms and playgrounds. Playing fields are conveniently located nearby.

For the golfer, there is Buford Ellington 18-hole, par 72, championship golf course. It is claimed to be one of the finest in the entire Southeast. Certainly the course provides one of the most challenging rounds of golf you will ever encounter. The pro shop here is a full-service operation with dressing rooms, rental clubs, carts, a driving range, a practice green, and a full line of equipment for sale. A golf professional is always on duty, and the course is open year-round.

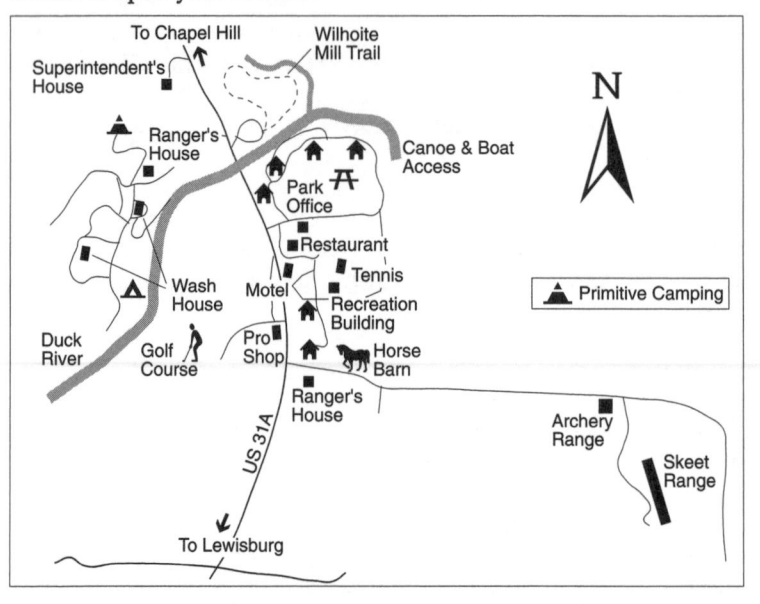

ACTIVITIES: Park recreation directors offer a range of organized activities during the summer months, including arts & crafts, movies, slide shows, archery instruction, horseback riding, hay rides, and square dancing. Weekly activity schedules are available at the Horton Inn, the recreation center, and at the park office.

INFORMATION: Henry Horton State Resort Park, PO Box 128, Chapel Hill, TN 37034. Telephone 615-364-2222. The park is open during the summer months from 8 AM until 10 PM, and from 8 AM until sundown during the winter. The camper quiet time is 10 PM.

The park is located near Chapel Hill on US 31A.

Long Hunter State Park

Long Hunter, close to Nashville on the shores of Percy Priest Lake, is a 2,400-acre tract of unspoiled natural beauty set aside for day-use recreation. The park provides its visitors with access to a diverse selection of plant and animal life, including an unusual cedar glade which is home to small woodland animals and birds.

Attractions at the park include the more than 14,000 acres of Percy Priest Lake, a visitors center, a gift shop, boat launching facilities, several hiking and nature trails, and a picnic area with tables and grills, and a playground. There is no overnight camping.

ACTIVITIES: Fishing the deep, still waters of the lake for bass, crappie, bluegill, walleye, and catfish, hiking the 28 miles of backpacking and nature trails, bird watching and nature study, swimming and boating, and picnicking.

NEARBY ATTRACTIONS: Grand Ole Opry and Opryland itself, the General Jackson Riverboat, and much more, all in nearby Nashville.

INFORMATION: Long Hunter State Park, 2910 Hobson Pike, Hermitage, TN 37076. Telephone 615-885-2422. The park is open during the summer months from 8 AM until 10 PM, and from 8 AM until sundown during the winter.

Long Hunter State Park is located off Interstates 40 and 24 on State Route 174.

Montgomery Bell State Park

As with many of Tennessee's state parks, Montgomery Bell is founded upon what was once a thriving industrial complex. In this case that industry was iron. In the late 1700s Dickson County and the surrounding hills and valleys was a land rich in iron ore, so rich in fact, that astute men like General James Robertson, who established the Cumberland Ironworks, and Montgomery Bell, for whom the park is named, saw great opportunities for profit.

Bell traveled south from his native Pennsylvania to establish an extensive iron works in the area upon which the state park now stands.

Today, The Laurel Furnace, built in 1810, the old ore pits, and some of the original workings are still very much in evidence. More than just a testament to area history and tradition, Montgomery Bell has become one of the premier resort parks in the state, with extensive recreational and outdoor facilities, including a resort inn and restaurant, vacation cabins, and full-service camping grounds.

The 37-room Montgomery Bell Inn, a blend of contemporary architecture and native stone in a natural setting of unrivaled beauty, is a convenient watering hole for travelers, where comfort, service, and fine dining are just as much a part of the overall ambiance as the woodland setting, magnificent Acorn Lake, and the acres of rolling parkland.

There are also eight two-bedroom cottages available year-round, just a short walk across a rustic wooden bridge. They are fully equipped for housekeeping and food preparation, and they provide all the comforts one might expect for a relaxing, backcountry vacation.

Secluded cabin at Montgomery Bell

A large and spacious camping ground, open year-round, provides 120 sites, 92 of which are fully equipped with water and electric hookups, picnic tables and grills, a dumping station, and three bathhouses with showers and restroom facilities. There's also a group camp, open from May through September, with accommodations for up to 120 persons.

For the golfer, the Frank G. Clement Golf Course offers a testy 18-hole experience. It also has a full-service pro shop, rental equipment and carts, and a concession stand.

The swimming beach on Acorn Lake offers sunbathing and a two-story bathhouse with a vending station and a recreation facility. A lifeguard is on duty during swimming hours.

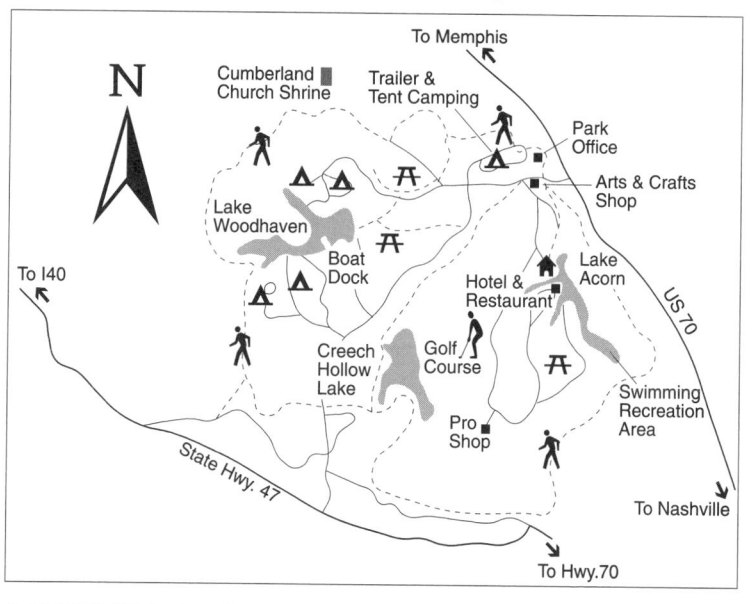

ACTIVITIES: Rowboats and paddleboats are available for rent. There's a boat dock and launching facilities on the lake, and 120 picnic tables and grills, as well as drinking fountains and restrooms, all conveniently located at scenic spots around the park. For the family there are three picnic pavilions, public restrooms, lighted tennis courts, a playground for the children, an archery range, basketball courts, croquet fields, volleyball courts, and shuffleboard courts.

An experienced naturalist and a park recreation director conduct a variety of programs throughout the summer season, including guided tours, campfire programs, and organized games.

INFORMATION: Superintendent's Office or the Inn, Montgomery Bell State Park, PO Box 39, Burns, TN 37029. Telephone the Visitor Center 615-797-9052, or the Inn 615-797-3101 for

Cabin, Group Camp, and Shelter reservations. Park hours are from 8 AM until 10 PM during the summer months, and from 8 AM until sundown during the winter. The camper quiet time is 10 PM.

The park is located seven miles east of Dickson, on US 70. Turn north from the I-40 Montgomery Bell exit and follow the signs to the park.

Mousetail Landing State Park

Mousetail Landing, so called for the great exodus of the little creatures from a burning tannery during the Civil War, is a 1,200-acre park on the banks of the Tennessee River, south of the Land Between the Lakes, near Perryville. Though it's not quite as well known or as popular as some of its contemporaries, the Tennessee River, its many tributaries, and over 50 small lakes scattered around the area provide the best boating, fishing, and other watersports in the vicinity.

Facilities at the park include 20 camping sites, opportunities for primitive and backcountry camping, a gift shop, boat launching ramps, picnic areas, and playgrounds.

ACTIVITIES: Swimming during the summer months, hiking, fishing the Tennessee River and its tributaries, picnicking and camping.

INFORMATION: Mousetail Creek State Park, Route 3, Box 280B, Linden, TN 37096. Telephone 615-847-0841. The park is open from 8 AM until 10 PM during the summer months, and from 8 AM until sundown during the winter. The camper quiet time is 10 PM.

The park is located north of Perryville on State Highway 50.

Old Stone Fort Archaeological Park

Old Stone Fort is a quiet, out-of-the-way park on the banks of Duck River. The ancient earthworks were built by local Indians more as a religious center than for protection. Old Stone Fort, though quite well known, seems to be one of those rare places where one can find seclusion outdoors under a blanket of lush green foliage, with the only sound the rushing waters of a nearby waterfall. For the naturalist, the park is a wonderland of wildlife and rare plants; for active outdoorsmen and women, it's a place to walk for miles in one of Tennessee's most pleasant environments.

Facilities at the park include 51 camping sites, a visitors center, a museum, a gift shop, picnic areas, a playground, and a nearby golf course.

ACTIVITIES: Fishing, hiking, nature study and bird watching, photography, and picnicking.

INFORMATION: Old Stone Fort Archaeological Park, Route 7, Box 7400, Manchester, TN 37355. Telephone 615-723-5073.

The park is on US 41, some 1.5 miles from I-24.

Port Royal State Historic Park

Port Royal once was a bustling little community and an important trading center for the area. Today, the 34-acre park, the smallest in the Tennessee State Park System, offers its visitors a unique opportunity to take a step back to a time when life was, though often hard, much simpler. The sights and sounds of everyday life in the old settlement are long gone now, but the quiet beauty of the park and the Red River with its covered bridge provide a small oasis of quiet seclusion beyond the stress and strains of the modern, high-tech world.

Facilities at the park are limited to day-use, but there is a museum and a visitors center, a boat launching ramp into the Red

River, access for canoes, and a hiking trail along the riverbank. Park Service staff will provide interpretive walks and talks on request.

INFORMATION: Port Royal State Historic Park, 3300 Old Clarksville Highway, Adams, TN 37010. Telephone 615-358-9696.

The park is located near Adams on State Route 76.

Radnor Lake State Natural Area

Radnor Lake, a 957-acre natural area, provides an extensive biological, geological, and environmental experience. The 85-acre lake for which the park is named was impounded in 1914 by the Louisville and Nashville Railroad Company to furnish water for steam locomotives and livestock at nearby Radnor Railroad Yards. It was also intended that the site would provide a private hunting and recreational facility for L&N railroad executives. In 1923, however, L&N stopped all hunting and fishing and, at the request of the Tennessee Ornithological Society, declared the site a wildlife sanctuary. During the years that followed the site changed hands several times, and attempts were made to develop the area for housing. Fortunately, public outcry and opinion put paid to such ideas. In 1973, the Tennessee Department of Conservation, with financial assistance from the Federal Government and many concerned citizens, purchased the site which was to become the state's first natural area.

Today, Radnor Lake Park provides an outstanding outdoor experience, both for the casual visitor and the dedicated naturalist. It is a region of diverse habitats and scenic areas, streams, hillocks, and woodland. Here, a variety of wild animals and plantlife make their homes, including geese, herons, hawks, coots, salamanders, frogs, snakes, lizards, turtles, mosses, fungi, ferns and wildflowers.

ACTIVITIES: Six walking trails wind their through the park, providing access to almost all the different habitats found here. The trails range in length from an easy quarter-mile stroll to a more strenuous 1.5-mile hike.

As Radnor Lake is not recreation-oriented, the facilities at the park are limited to a visitors center, a museum, and the six trails.

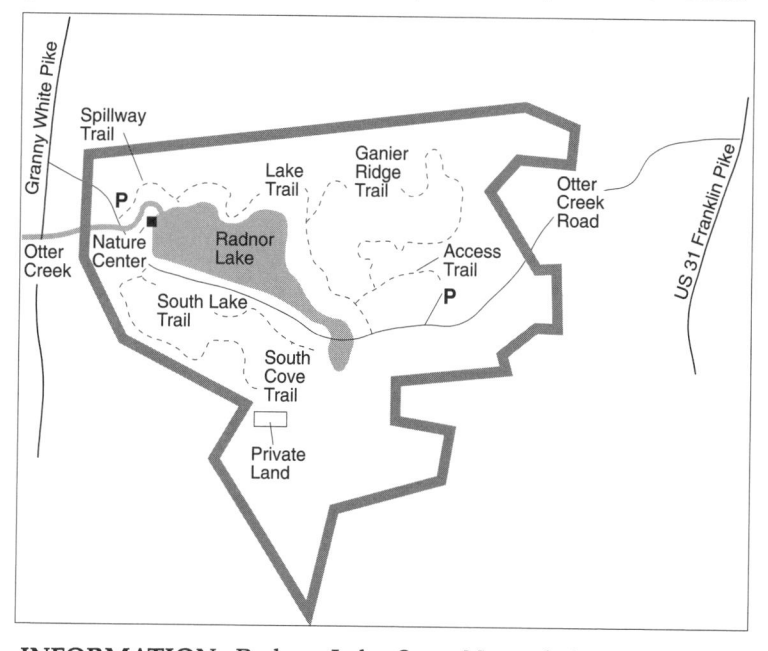

INFORMATION: Radnor Lake State Natural Area, 1050 Otter Creek Road, Nashville, TN 37220. Telephone 615-373-3467. The park is open from 7 AM until sundown during the summer months, and from 8 AM until sundown during the winter.

The lake is in Nashville, on Otter Creek Road a half-mile east of Granny White Pike, and 1.5 miles west of Franklin Road (US 31).

Tim's Ford State Park

Tim's Ford is a pleasant 400-acre park on the edge of the Cumberland Plateau in South Central Tennessee. Set among rolling hills and wooded valleys, the park is a major center for outdoor recreation. The vast reservoir, a product of the Tennessee Valley Authority's ever expanding hydroelectric program, is regarded as one of the top bass fishing lakes in the Southeastern United States.

Overnight facilities at Tim's Ford include 20 luxury vacation cabins situated on the wooded slopes of the lake. Each two-bedroom cabin is fully equipped for housekeeping, including cooking and serving utensils, and linen service. Each cabin has a fireplace and balcony.

The park also offers 50 camping sites, all with tables, grills, and water and electrical hookups. Conveniently located bathhouses provide campers with hot showers, a laundromat, and restrooms there's a dumping station for those campers with self-contained trailer rigs. There's also a restaurant, a gift shop, an L-shaped swimming pool (one of the largest pools in the Tennessee State Park System), a full-service marina where rental boats are available, boat launching facilities, five miles of paved trails for hiking and bicycling, 50 picnic tables with grills, two picnic shelters with fireplaces and tables, public restrooms, and a playground.

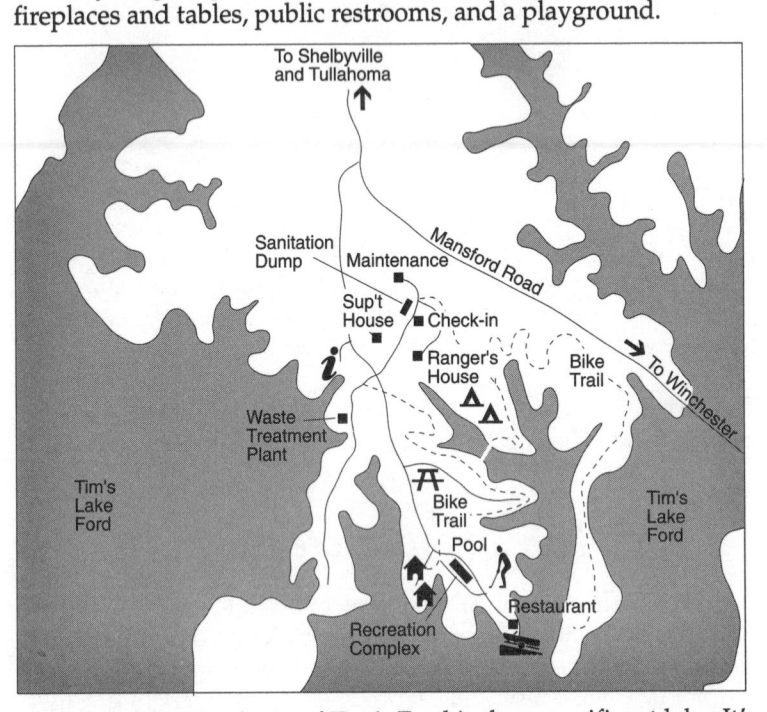

ACTIVITIES: The focus of Tim's Ford is the magnificent lake. It's no wonder that most activities here are water-related. The fishing is regarded as the best in the state, providing outstanding catches of largemouth, smallmouth, striped, and white bass, crappie, bluegill, catfish, and walleye. However, if fishing is not for you, then you might enjoy strolling the paved trails, a game of badminton or basketball, or simply spending a few quiet hours taking it easy at the poolside where there's plenty of room for sunbathing, and a lifeguard on duty during the swimming hours.

INFORMATION: Tim's Ford State Park, Route 4, Winchester, TN 37398. Telephone 615-967-4457. Park hours are from 8 AM until 10 PM during the summer months, and from 8 AM until sundown during winter. The camper quiet time is 10 PM.

Tim's Ford Park is located approximately 11 miles west of Winchester, off State Highway 50.

Plateaus & Valleys

Booker T. Washington State Park

This park is just north of Chattanooga and is named for the famous educator, Booker Taliaferro Washington. Sited on the shores of the Chickamauga Reservoir, the 353-acre park is something of a get-away for the citizens of the nearby city. The great lake is only one of the Scenic City's tourist attractions offering fine boating and fishing.

Although there are no individual camping sites at the park, the other facilities are extensive. These include a swimming pool, playgrounds for the children, several picnic areas with tables and grills provided, and a group camping site. There is also a concession building where one can purchase refreshments as well as camping and picnicking supplies. Boats may be rented and there's a boat-launching ramp. A group lodge is available the year-round, with a fully equipped kitchen, and it is large enough to accommodate up to 40 persons. All this is set among acres of rolling fields, hiking trails, nature trails, and country walks.

NEARBY ATTRACTIONS: Tennessee Aquarium, Hunter Museum of Art, Tennessee Railroad Museum, Chattanooga Choo-

Choo Resort Complex, Falling Water Falls on Signal Mountain, the Southern Belle Riverboat, Lookout Mountain National Battle-field Park, Cloudland Canyon State Park, Raccoon Mountain Caverns, Ruby Falls on Lookout Mountain, Rock City (also on Lookout Mountain), Harrison Bay State Park, Red Clay State Park, and Chickamauga National Battlefield.

INFORMATION: Booker T. Washington State Park, 5801 Champion Road, Chattanooga, TN 37416. Telephone 615-894-4955. The park is off State Highway 58 north of Chattanooga.

Burgess Falls State Natural Area

Burgess Falls is an area of great natural beauty on the edge of the Upper Cumberland Plateau. The 155-acre park is a small tract of backcountry, rolling hills, forests, woodlands, and river set aside by the state for all to enjoy. It's a place where only the sounds of rushing water and nature are heard. The main feature of the park is, of course, Burgess Falls, but there's much more to it than that. A stream-side nature trail winds its way through several miles of lush, green woodlands, slowly descending the scenic limestone cliffs, past cascading falls, and the ruins of historic waterworks, to the waters of Center Hill Lake.

Facilities are limited. There are no overnight accommodations, but there is a boat-launching ramp, several hiking trails, and picnic tables.

INFORMATION: Burgess Falls State Natural Area, 400 Falls Drive, Sparta, TN 38583-8456. Telephone 615-432-5312. The park is open during the summer months from 8 AM until 10 PM, and from 8 AM until sundown during the winter.

Burgess Falls is eight miles south of I-40, near Cookville off State Route 135.

Cumberland Mountain State Park

With more than 1,700 acres and located some 2,000 feet up on the Cumberland Plateau, Cumberland Mountain State Park offers the outdoor vacationer something different. Up here on the mountain, far away from the pollution of big cities, the air is always sweet, the breeze always cool, and the waters of the lake always refreshing. Cumberland Plateau is claimed to be the largest forested plateau in the United States and the Tennessee Park Service, along with the Forest Service and the Tennessee Department of Wildlife, has made the most of this wild and scenic area. Hiking trails, nature trails, and backpacking trails interlace the surrounding forests. One of the largest Civilian Conservation Corps Projects ever undertaken in the State of Tennessee, a seven-arch sandstone bridge spanning Byrd Lake is located at Burgess Falls.

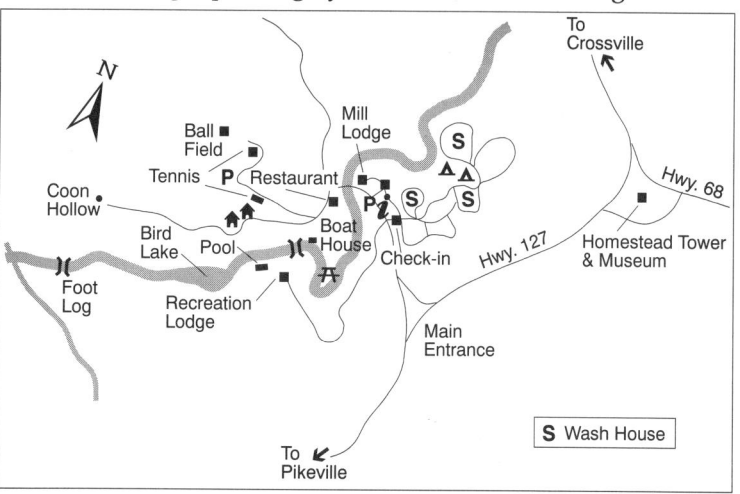

Facilities at the park are extensive. The 37 rustic cabins, complete with all modern conveniences, offer the finest in family accommodations, while 147 camp sites include water and electric hookups, a camp store, and a dumping station. A group lodge is perfect for large families or small groups of up to 16 persons. There's also an Olympic-size swimming pool, dozens of picnic tables and grills, and several pavilions. Restrooms and drinking fountains are scattered about the park.

Cumberland Mountain Restaurant has the capacity to seat up to 250 persons with three additional meeting rooms for parties, banquets, and other private functions of up to 300.

ACTIVITIES: Experienced park naturalists and recreation directors are available during the summer months. They conduct a series of daily programs including arts & crafts, hayrides, guided tours, campfire sessions, slide shows, and organized games.

INFORMATION: Park Manager's Office, Cumberland Mountain State Park, Route 8, Box 322, Crossville, TN 38555. Telephone 615-484-6138. The park is open from 8 AM until 9 PM during the summer months, and from 8 until sundown during the winter. The camper quiet time is 10 PM, and the restaurant is open from 11 AM until 8 PM.

Cumberland Mountain State Park is four miles south of Crossville, on US 127, off I-40.

Edgar Evins State Park

Center Hill Reservoir – "reservoir" is a clinical term that belies one of Tennessee's most picturesque lakes – is the result of a great dam constructed by the Corps of Engineers to supply electricity to middle Tennessee, and the site of the magnificent 6000-acre Edgar Evins State Park.

Set among the rolling hills of middle Tennessee, in the heart of the Caney Fork River Valley, Edgar Evins offers its visitors an outdoor experience of unusual proportions. Ever since its inception, the park has been attracting boaters, fishermen, campers, and naturalists from around the state. Its great natural beauty, fresh clean air, spectacular sunsets, deep clear waters, and magnificent views of the surrounding countryside, all are well known in Tennessee. Edgar Evins, truly, is a jewel in the crown of the Tennessee State Park System.

Facilities at the park include a 34-unit cabin village, where each one-bedroom unit is fully equipped for housekeeping, with linen service, appliances, and cooking and serving utensils. There are 60 platform-style camping sites, all built on the slopes of Center

Hill Lake and equipped with tables and grills, plus water and electrical hookups. This unusual campground is further served by three modern bathhouses, all with hot showers and restrooms, and a dumping station.

There are four picnicking areas with tables and grills, three picnic pavilions perfect for large groups and family reunions. Each pavilion is equipped with a fireplace and grill, and there are restrooms and playgrounds for the children. There's also a swimming pool open to the general public, a scenic three-mile hiking trail that meanders through the woods and around the edge of the lake, and an easy half-mile trail for those who like to walk but are not up to the more strenuous hike along the lakeshore.

ACTIVITIES: Fishing, boating, and waterskiing are popular here. Record catches have been made at Center Hill, and the lake is well known for its largemouth and smallmouth bass, as well as for its walleye, crappie and bluegill.

INFORMATION: Superintendent's Office, Edgar Evins State Park, Route 1, Silver Point, TN 38582. Telephone 615-858-2446. The park is open during the summer months from 8 AM until 10 PM, and during the winter from 8 AM until sundown.

Edgar Evins is in DeKalb County, 20 miles north of Smithville and 20 miles west of Cookville, easily accessible from I-40 at Exit 268 and State Highway 141.

Fall Creek Falls State Park

Fall Creek Falls offers one of the most spectacular views in the State of Tennessee, if not in the nation, and with more than 16,000 acres of rolling countryside it's the largest park in the Tennessee system. Visitors often stand and stare, awe-struck, from the observation platform across the gorge at the mighty falls tumbling more than 250 feet to the pool below. More than half of this spectacular park is designated a Natural Wilderness Area providing habitats for hundreds of species of bird and animal life. The park's Nature Center houses a variety of interesting exhibits which interpret the local ecology, the plantlife, and the animals that inhabit Fall Creek Falls.

Cascading water at Fall Creek Falls

Facilities at the park include a resort inn with 73 well-appointed rooms, 20 cabins, two group lodges with accommodations for 100 and 40 persons respectively, two group camps with capacities for groups of 144 and 96 persons, 227 camping sites and a camp store, backcountry camping facilities, a visitors center, a restaurant, a gift shop, several snack bars and picnic areas with tables and grills, boat rentals, bicycle rentals, tennis courts, and playgrounds for the children.

There's also a challenging 18-hole, championship golf course that's listed as one of the top public courses in the United States. The golf course has a pro shop which offers everything the dedicated golfer might need for a fine day of sport.

There are several hiking and nature trails, a bicycle trail, and, of course, a 345-acre lake where the fishing is said to be excellent.

ACTIVITIES: Golfing, nature study, bird watching, and wildlife photography, hiking, bicycling, swimming, and fishing.

INFORMATION: Superintendent's Office, Fall Creek Falls State Park, Route 3, Pikeville, TN 37367. Telephone 615-881-5241. The park is open during the summer months from 8 AM until 10 PM, and from 8 AM until sundown during the winter.

Fall Creek Falls is in Pikeville, Tennessee, off State Highway 111 and State Highway 30.

Harrison Bay State Park

Harrison Bay is the result of Tennessee Valley Authority's recreation demonstration site project of the 1930s; it's located just a few miles north of Chattanooga. The 1,200-acre park, along with more than 40 miles of Chickamauga Lake shoreline, provides some outstanding recreational opportunities in a setting of quiet isolation, deep still waters, and spectacular sunsets. It's no wonder that Harrison Bay, with its wooded parklands and magnificent lake, has become a popular attraction.

With 190 tent and trailer camping sites, 135 of them with water and electrical hookups, and all with picnic tables and grills, the park is one of the largest and most popular camping areas in Tennessee. There are several bathhouses conveniently located in the campground that provide hot showers and restroom facilities. There's also a dumping site and a camp store where, during the summer months, one can purchase camping and fishing supplies.

A group camp provides accommodations for up to 144 persons, and is complete with a dining room and a kitchen, both fully equipped for food preparation and serving. Accommodations at the group site include group cabins, a bathhouse with hot showers and restrooms, a recreation shelter, and a large playing field. The group camp is available during the summer months and can be rented on a weekly basis only.

A full-service marina, in one of the best protected harbors on Chickamauga Lake, provides 140 boat slips and several boat launching ramps; marine supplies, fuel, fishing supplies, bait, and skiing equipment. Boat rentals are all available at the marina store. There is ample parking for visitors' cars and boat trailers.

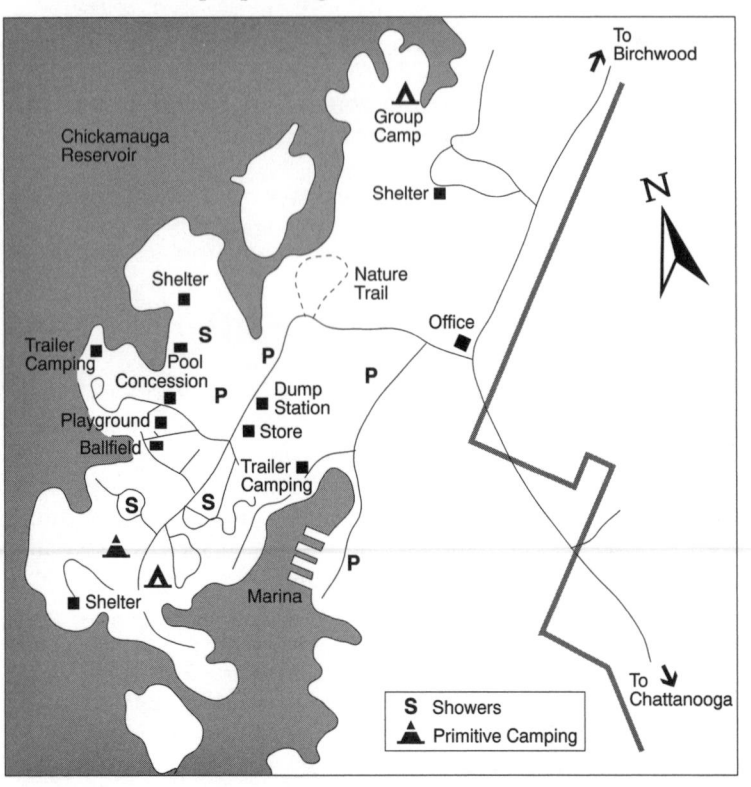

ACTIVITIES: Fishing the year-round for largemouth bass, striped bass, crappie, bream, bluegill, and catfish. There's a swimming pool with adequate space for sunbathing, a children's pool, a public bathhouse, a concession stand, a recreation shelter, and a playground. There are a number of well-shaded picnic areas conveniently located around the park, all with picnic tables and grills. There's also a pavilion perfect for group get-togethers.

NEARBY ATTRACTIONS: Tennessee Aquarium in Chattanooga, Falling Water Falls on Signal Mountain, Hunter Museum of Art in Chattanooga, Tennessee Railroad Museum, Chattanooga Choo-Choo Resort Complex, the Southern Belle Riverboat, Lookout Mountain National Battlefield Park, Cloudland Canyon State Park on Lookout Mountain, Raccoon Mountain

Caverns, Ruby Falls on Lookout Mountain, Rock City, Harrison Bay State Park, Red Clay State Park, and Chickamauga National Battlefield.

INFORMATION: Harrison Bay State Park, 8411 Harrison Bay Road, Harrison, TN 37341. Telephone 615-344-6214. The park is open from 8 AM during the summer months, and from 8 AM until sundown during winter. The camper quiet time is 10 PM.

The park is eight miles north of Chattanooga on US 58.

Pickett State Park

Picket State Park is 11,752 acres of the most beautiful parkland in the upper Cumberland Mountains. The park and the surrounding forests posses "a combination of scenic, botanical, and geological wonders found nowhere else in Tennessee." The most interesting features in the park are the uncommon rock formations, natural bridges, and the caves which once were the homes of pre-historic Indians.

The park's remote location means that it's not high on everyone's list of vacation hot-spots; it's more a place of seclusion where one might go to spend a few days in fresh air far away from the hectic life of a big city. The lush green woodlands, rolling acres of parkland, and limpid waters of the lake, make Pickett a once-in-a-lifetime outdoor experience.

Facilities at the park include five chalets, five rustic stone cottages, and five wooden cottages, all fully equipped for housekeeping, including appliances, cooking and serving utensils, and linens.

There are 40 camping sites equipped with tables and grills, 31 of them with water and electrical hookups, and there's a modern bathhouse with hot showers and restroom facilities. There's also a group camp with sleeping cabins, a bathhouse, and a kitchen fully equipped for food preparation and serving.

More than 58 miles of hiking and backpacking trails meander through the woodlands and rhododendron groves, past the caves, the waterfalls, the great rock formations, and on into the surrounding countryside.

On Arch Lake the sandy swimming beach provides a pleasant spot to catch the sun or enjoy a quiet picnic. The lake itself is well stocked with fish, and small boats are available for rent (private boats are not permitted).

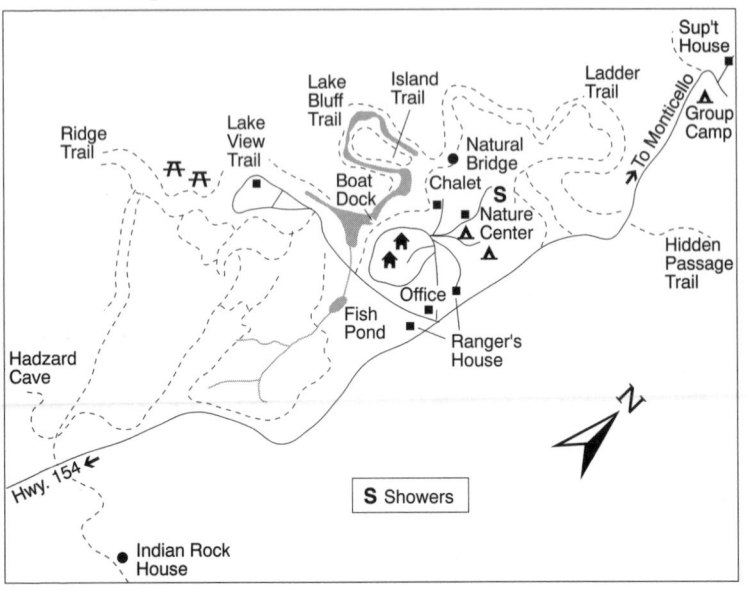

ACTIVITIES: Archery, badminton, tennis, volleyball, and an assortment of nature related activities, including guided tours with a qualified naturalist, demonstrations, and campfire programs.

NEARBY ATTRACTIONS: Colditz Cove State Natural Area, Lone Mountain State Forest, Obed National Wild and Scenic River, Big South Fork National Recreation Area, and historic Rugby.

INFORMATION: Pickett State Park, Polk Creek Route, Box 174, Jamestown, TN 38556. Telephone 615-879-5821. The park is open during the summer months from 8 AM until 10 PM, and from 7:30 AM until 4 PM during the winter. The camper quiet time is 10 PM.

Pickett State Park is 12 miles northeast of Jamestown on State Highway 154.

Red Clay State Historic Park

Red Clay is a 260-acre park dedicated to the memory of the Cherokee Indians who died on the infamous Trail of Tears. Red Clay, after the Cherokees were banned from their nearby capital of New Echota, became the site of the last Tribal Councils before the exodus to reservations in Oklahoma and North Carolina. Today, the park is a quiet sanctuary of rolling green fields, sparkling streams, and lush parkland; a place where one can spend a few quiet hours on a sunny afternoon.

Woodland trails at Red Clay

Facilities at the park are limited to day use only so there are no overnight accommodations. There is, however, a visitors center, a museum and gift shop, a picnic area, and several hiking trails.

NEARBY ATTRACTIONS: Tennessee Aquarium in Chattanooga, Falling Water Falls on Signal Mountain, Hunter Museum of Art, Tennessee Railroad Museum, Chattanooga Choo-Choo Resort Complex, the Southern Belle Riverboat, Lookout Mountain National Battlefield Park, Cloudland Canyon State Park on Lookout Mountain, Raccoon Mountain Caverns, Ruby Falls, Rock City, Harrison Bay State Park, Hiwassee State Scenic River and Ocoee River, and Chickamauga National Battlefield.

INFORMATION: Red Clay State Historic Park, 1140 Red Clay Road SE, Cleveland, TN 37311. Telephone 615-478-0339.

The park is located off US 60, about 10 miles south of Cleveland, close to the Georgia state line.

Rock Island State Park

The 883-acre Rock Island State Park is in one of Tennessee's most scenic natural areas. The wooded park is dominated by Great Falls on the Caney Fork River, and by the river gorge itself with its spectacular scenic overlooks, waterfalls, woodland trails, and rock pools. The park is situated on Crater Hill Lake which offers fine fishing, lakeside trails, and a sandy beach with plenty of room for sunbathing, swimming, and picnicking. Along with its many recreational facilities, Rock Island also has some interesting historic features, including a 19th century textile mill and one of Tennessee's earliest hydroelectric plants.

Although Rock Island is a day-use-only facility without any substantial overnight accommodations, some backcountry camping sites are available for visitors who like to do it the primitive way. Other than that, the park provides a visitors center and a museum, a gift shop, boat launching facilities, tennis courts, hiking trails, several picnic areas, and a playground.

ACTIVITIES: Hiking the woodland trails, nature study and bird watching, picnicking, and fishing on Center Hill Lake for large-mouth bass, crappie, bluegill, bream, and catfish.

INFORMATION: Rock Island State Park, Route 2, Box 20, Rock Island, TN 38581. Telephone 615-686-2471.

The park is located near Center Hill Dam on US 70S.

South Cumberland Recreation Area

South Cumberland Recreation Area is unique in the Tennessee State Park System in that its more than 30,000 acres are spread across a 100-square-mile section of the Cumberland Plateau. This vast system within a system includes seven separate park areas, five of which are natural areas. The system is a diverse wilderness tract of dense forests, winding rivers, sparkling streams and creeks, mysterious caves, spectacular natural bridges, shaded woodland trails, and scenic lakes. It's an area where one might spend several weeks in the great outdoors exploring one breathtaking location after another. Hikers and naturalists will find this a totally new and refreshing experience.

Grundy Lakes State Park provides its visitors with opportunities for swimming, fishing, and picnicking. It was the original site of the Lone Rock Coke Ovens where, a long time ago, coal was mined and converted into coke using convict labor. The operation closed down in 1896, but the old ovens still remain, an interesting reminder of those tough times.

The Grundy Forest State Natural Area includes a tract of dense woodland some 200 acres in size. Grundy Forest is the northern access point to the famous Fiery Gizzard Trail, one of the nation's outstanding hiking trails, which meanders through the woodland park, past scenic waterfalls and magnificent sandstone formations, until it eventually emerges from the forest at the spectacular Foster Falls.

Foster Falls is a small area managed jointly by the Tennessee Valley Authority and the Tennessee Division of State Parks. The park, the culmination of the Fiery Gizzard Trail, provides its visitors with picnic facilities, including tables and grills, and some limited overnight camping facilities.

Sewannee Natural Bridge at South Cumberland

The Sewanee Natural Bridge State Natural Area is only a short walk from a parking lot off State Highway 56. The great stone bridge is a classic example of its type. You can walk across the bridge high inside the lush, green canopy of the forest, and then descend by way of a series of natural stone steps, to the woodland floor, where you can explore the unusual rock system and surrounding forest.

Carter State Natural Area, a section of an 18,000-acre natural sink-hole known as Lost Cove, is only a couple of miles from Sewanee Natural Bridge. Visitors can enter the area via the Buggytop Trail. The trail winds its way through the woods for almost two miles to the entrance of Lost Cove Cave, one of the most spectacular cave entrances in the state.

Hawkins Cove State Natural Area is the latest addition to the South Cumberland System. The Cove is a 244-acre area set aside in 1985 to protect the rare and endangered Cumberland Rosin-weed. It's a remote and undeveloped area of dense forest without trails or facilities – an area ideal for outdoor expeditions and exploration.

The Savage Gulf State Natural Area is a vast hinterland of virgin timber forests. The 11,500-acres are a maze of more than 55 miles of backcountry trails, bridleways, woodland paths, and primitive camping grounds. True lovers of the great outdoors will find Savage Gulf to be an outstanding experience.

South Cumberland Park visitor center serves as the headquarters of the recreation area. Visitors to the system would be well advised to begin their tour at the center, where they will find everything they need to make the visit a memorable one: local hotel/motel and restaurant information, maps, trail information, directions to all the park areas, as well as an interesting display of interpretive exhibits depicting the region's ecology, its natural history, and its cultural resources.

For the visitor who might prefer a little comfort along with the outdoor experience, South Cumberland Recreation Area is liberally served by an assortment of cafes, restaurants, and motels.

INFORMATION: South Cumberland State Recreation Area, Route 1, Box 2196, Monteagle, TN 37356. Telephone 615-924-2980.

The visitor center is located between Tracy City and Monteagle on Highway 56.

Standing Stone State Park

Standing Stone, a 1,055-acre park, is named for an eight-foot-tall rock which once served as the boundaryline between Indian nations. Today the remote, densely forested park provides its visitors, not only with an outstanding recreational facility, but also with some of the finest scenery in the state.

More than 15 miles of hiking and backpacking trails wind through the woodland glades, and the hills and dales that surround the park. The 65-acre Standing Stone Lake provides quiet days of fishing or row-boating, while nearby Dale Hollow Lake offers opportunities for a variety of watersports, including waterskiing, sailing, cruising, and fishing for largemouth, smallmouth, spotted, and white bass, lake trout, rainbow trout, bluegill, crappie, bream, catfish, muskie and walleye.

Overnight facilities at Standing Stone include 23 vacation cabins, all equipped for housekeeping, including appliances, cooking and serving utensils, and linen service. There's a group lodge with accommodations for up to 50 persons, and 35 modern, full-service camping sites with tables, grills, water and electric hook-ups, and a modern bathhouse with hot showers and restrooms. Backcountry camping is also available for those who really like to get away from it all.

Other facilities at Standing Stone include a snack bar, picnic areas with tables and grills, several hiking trails, and a playground.

ACTIVITIES: Fishing (either on Standing Stone Lake or Dale Hollow Lake), boating (non-powered boats only on Standing Stone), picnicking, hiking, camping, nature study and bird watching.

INFORMATION: Standing Stone State Park, 1674 Standing Stone Park Highway, Hilham, TN 38568. Telephone 615-823-6347.

The park is close to the Tennessee/Kentucky state line, off State Highway 52.

The Mountainous East

Big Ridge State Park

Big Ridge is one of Tennessee's finest state parks, offering visitors a wide range of recreational activities and more than 3,600 acres of scenic and heavily forested parkland where it's easy to escape, if only for an hour or two, into the natural refuge of the great outdoors without ever leaving civilization too far behind.

The park was developed as one of five joint ventures between the Tennessee Valley Authority, the National Park Service, and the Civilian Conservation Corps, for public recreation on the shore of TVA lakes. Big Ridge State Park lies on the southern shore of TVA's Norris Lake.

Facilities here are extensive and include a variety of overnight and long-stay accommodations. There are 19 rustic vacation cabins available April through October; each able to accommodate up to six persons with two double beds and a hide-a-way sofa bed, all in one large living area. All cabins have fireplaces, screened porches, and are equipped for light housekeeping with linen service, and cooking and dining utensils provided. And, because Big Ridge is supposed to provide a genuine opportunity for solitude, you will not find televisions or telephones in any of the cabins.

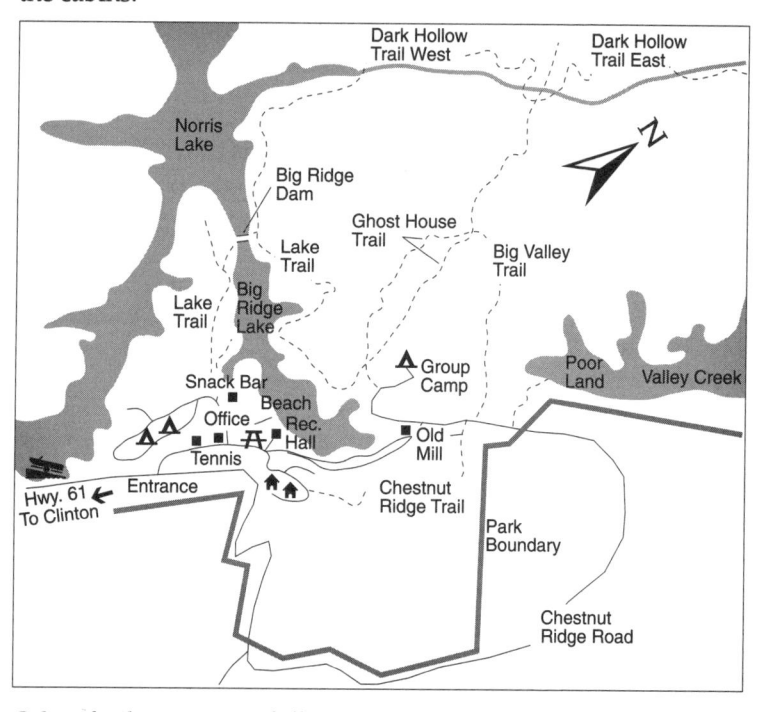

Other facilities are 56 full-service camping sites on the shores of Norris Lake, all with water and electrical hookups, a picnic table and a grill. The campground is served by two nearby bathhouses with hot showers and restrooms. There's also a group camping site with accommodations for up to 120 persons in 18 bunk houses, each sleeping six to eight people. The group site also has two bathhouses and a large kitchen complete with utensils and all equipment necessary for preparing and serving meals. The park also offers tennis courts, boat launching ramps, snack bars, a gift shop, a visitors center, and a park laundry.

Picnicking facilities are provided at three separate sites, all with tables, grills and playgrounds for the children. There are three pavilions, also with tables and grills, available for large groups. The pavilions may be reserved through the park office.

The park features some 15 miles of backpacking, hiking and nature trails which meander through the park and surrounding woodlands. They offer an opportunity to observe many species of wild birds, native plants, wildflowers, and animals.

ACTIVITIES: Nature study, bird watching and photography. And, for the visitor who might need a little help and instruction, the Park Service has a variety of planned daily activities for all the family, including guided hikes, arts and crafts, nature programs, sports, and campfire programs, all available during the summer months. You can also fish and boat on Norris Lake. Canoes, paddleboats, and flat-bottomed rowboats are available for rent, and visitors may use their own electric trolling motors. Gasoline powered outboards are not permitted. There's a large sandy beach for swimming and sunbathing, open from Memorial Day through Labor Day, and a concrete-bottomed, shallow-water area is set aside for the children. There's also a diving area with two diving stands: one at three meters high, the other one meter high. Lifeguards are on duty during swimming hours.

INFORMATION: Superintendent's Office, Big Ridge State Park, Maynardville, TN 37807. Telephone 615-992-5523. The park is open during the summer months from 8 AM until 10 PM, and from 8 AM until sundown during the winter.

Big Ridge State Park is approximately 25 miles north of Knoxville on State Highway 61, 12 miles east of I-75.

Cove Lake State Park

Located in a beautiful mountain valley on the eastern edge of the Cumberland Mountains, 673-acre Cove Lake State Park is arguably one of the most picturesque parks in the Tennessee system. It's a vast area of rolling parklands, open grasslands, and densely forested woodlands where amateur and professional naturalists alike will find more than enough to see and do during their vacations.

In the winter months, when the forest has stripped off its cloak of green, the park provides a lakeshore haven and feeding ground for several hundred Canada geese. All through the park hiking trails and bike trails wind their way across the grasslands and the woodlands providing access to natural habitats of a wide assortment of bird and animal life.

Facilities at the park include 210-acre Cove Lake, 97 camping sites, a park restaurant, a gift shop, a snack bar, several picnic areas with tables and grills, boat rentals, boat launching ramps, an archery range, several tennis courts, and a playground for the children.

ACTIVITIES: Swimming and sunbathing, fishing for bass, crappie, and bluegill, hiking, bicycling (bike rentals are available), nature study and bird watching, wildlife photography, camping, and archery.

INFORMATION: Superintendent's Office, Cove Lake State Park, Route 2, Box 108, Caryville, TN 37714. Telephone 615-562-8355. The park is open during the summer months from 8 AM until 10 PM, and from 8 AM until sundown during the winter.

Cove Lake is located off I-75, on US 25W.

Fort Loudoun State Historic Park

The 1,200-acre Fort Loudoun State Historic Park is the location of one of the earliest British fortifications on the western frontier. The original fort was built in 1756 near some of the principle villages of the Cherokee Nation, including Tenase, from which the state derives its name, and Tuskegee, the birthplace of the great Sequoyah, one of the Cherokee Nation's most famous members.

Today, the fort and the Tellico Blockhouse overlook Tennessee Valley Authority's 16,500-acre Tellico Reservoir, and the foothills of the Great Smoky Mountains far away to the east.

This is a day-use-only park. Facilities include a visitors center which offers historical and interpretive programs, a museum, a gift shop, a picnic area, boat launching facilities into Tellico Lake, and several hiking trails.

ACTIVITIES: These center mainly around Tellico Lake and include all sorts of watersports – fishing for bass, crappie, bluegill, and walleye, swimming, waterskiing, boating, sailing and canoeing.

INFORMATION: Fort Loudoun State Historic Park, 338 Fort Loudoun Road, Vonore, TN 37885. Telephone 615-884-6217. The park is open during the summer months from 8 AM until 10 PM, and from 8 AM until sundown during the winter.

Fort Loudon is located at Vonore, off US 41.

Frozen Head State Natural Area

Frozen Head is an 11,869-acre wilderness area near the peak of one of the Cumberland Mountains for which it's named. It's a vast, backcountry region of unspoiled mountain splendor, where the true outdoorsman and woman can disappear into the forests, far away from civilization, and enjoy, for a few days at least, one of the few remaining tracts of the once boundless "Cumberland Wonderland."

In the winter, the peak of Frozen Head becomes a winter wonderland of ice and snow, where frozen crystals hanging in the trees gleam and sparkle in the early morning sunshine. In the spring, wildflowers bloom and bring new life to the mountains. In summertime, the air is always a little cooler on the mountain tops, and then, when fall arrives, the hills and valleys flame under a canopy of yellow, gold and bronze.

More than 50 miles of hiking, backpacking and nature trails wind through the forests, providing opportunities for observing the abundance of plant and animal life. Of special interest is a fire tower, accessible by one of the trails, which offers spectacular views of the surrounding mountains.

Facilities at the park include some 20 camping sites (tents only), several backcountry sites, a gift shop, a snack bar and a camp store (open during the summer months), a picnic area with tables, grills, and a playground.

ACTIVITIES: Swimming, fishing, hiking, backpacking, primitive camping, nature study and bird watching, photography, and picnicking.

NEARBY ATTRACTIONS: Lone Mountain State Forest, Obed National Wild and Scenic River, Big South Fork National Recreation Area, and historic Rugby.

INFORMATION: Frozen Head State Natural Area, 964 Flat Fork Road, Wartburg, TN 37887. Telephone 615-346-3318. The park is open during the summer months from 8 AM until 10 PM, and from 8 AM until sundown during the winter.

Frozen Head is at Wartburg, off State Highway 62.

Hiwassee State Scenic River And Ocoee River

The Hiwassee was the first river managed in the Tennessee State Scenic River Program. It comprises a 23-mile stretch of river from the North Carolina state line to US 411 just to the north of Benton. This part of the river, though famous for its trout fishing, offers a

Breathtaking scenery at Hiwassee

variety of watersports, including canoeing, and boating. Hikers and photographers, too, will find the huge tract of great natural beauty a haven where they can observe wild animal and plantlife. There are numerous public sites along the riverbank which offer boat ramps, as well as a number of picnic and swimming areas.

The Ocoee River, from the North Carolina state line to the Ocoee Dam near Reliance, Tennessee, is one of the premier whitewater rivers in the Southeast. The fast-running river winds its way down Copper Basin, high on the mountain, through Cherokee National Forest and a scenic natural gorge, passing along the way a number of public access sites, picnic areas, swimming beaches, until finally it widens, becomes tranquil, and enters the great Parksville Lake just above Ocoee River Dam, 10 miles east of Cleveland.

INFORMATION: Hiwassee State Scenic River & Ocoee River, PO Box 255, Delano, TN 37325. Telephone 615-338-4133. The park is open during the summer months from 8 AM until 10 PM, and from 8 AM until sundown during the winter.

House Mountain
State Natural Area

The 525-acre House Mountain State Natural Area is a limited day-use park with very few facilities, but that doesn't meant it's not well worth a visit. The park, only a few miles from downtown Knoxville, has an elevation above 2,000 feet and offers fine views of the surrounding terrain: the hills and valleys of Eastern Tennessee and the Great Smoky Mountains far away in the distance. The rocky sandstone peak of House Mountain, with its stands of chestnut oak, mountain pine, and pitch pine, provide natural habitats for a variety of wild birds and animals. In the spring, as the area bursts with new life and wildflowers, it becomes a naturalist's dream.

Facilities at the park are limited to hiking trails and a playground.

NEARBY ATTRACTIONS: Knoxville, Knoxville Zoo, Fort Loudoun State Historic Site, Knoxville Sunsphere, the campus at the University of Knoxville, Great Smoky Mountain National Park, Dollywood, Gatlinburg, James White Fort, and riverboat rides of the Tennessee River at Knoxville.

INFORMATION: House Mountain State Natural Area, 3903 Idumea Road, Corryton, TN 37721. Telephone 615-933-6851. The park is open during the summer months from 8 AM until 10 PM, and from 8 AM until sundown during the winter.

The park is located off US 11.

Indian Mountain State Park

Indian Mountain is a small area of parkland in the Cumberland Mountains. It is on the Tennessee/Kentucky state line, within the city limits of Jellico, among the lush, green hills and valleys of the great Cumberland Plateau. The park, on land reclaimed from strip mining, offers visitors an opportunity to enjoy a little peace and quiet in an area where tourism hasn't yet become an over-developed industry. At Indian Mountain one can spend a few hours hiking among the trees of the surrounding woodlands, or simply picnicking with the family on a quiet, sunny afternoon.

Facilities at the park include 49 camping sites, a camp store, boat rental during the summer months, hiking trails, a picnic area, and a playground.

ACTIVITIES: Camping, fishing in two small lakes and the Elk Fork, boating, hiking, and picnicking.

INFORMATION: Indian Mountain State Park, Jellico, TN 37762. Telephone 615-784-7958. The park is open during the summer months from 8 AM until 10 PM, and from 8 AM until sundown during the winter.

The park is in Jellico, off I-75 at Exit 160.

Norris Dam State Park

Norris Dam is a 4,000-acre park on the shores of the great Norris Lake Reservoir, a hydro-electric utility project of the US Corps of Engineers begun in 1933 to provide electricity to the local area. The park is a lush land of scenic hills and valleys, woodland and forest, mysterious caves and sparkling waters – a place where history and technology have come together to provide one of Tennessee's outstanding outdoor experiences. The Lenoir Pioneer Museum features an 18th-century, water-powered grist mill, a threshing barn, and a shop featuring authentic Tennessee Crafts. The massive Norris Dam at the head of the lake towers above the river and, from its summit, offers spectacular views of the surrounding parkland.

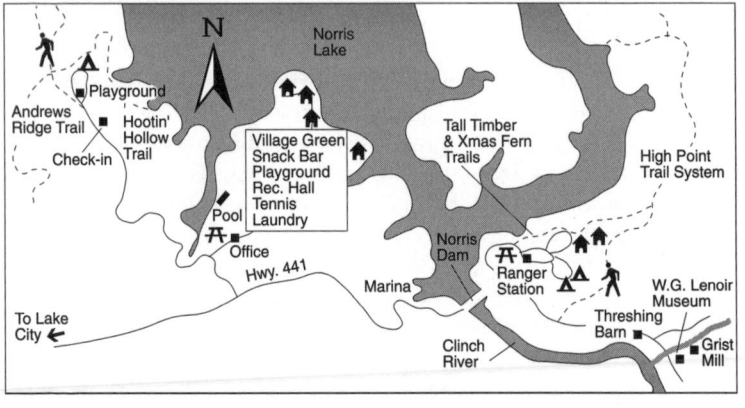

As one might imagine, facilities at the park are extensive. Nineteen rustic vacation cabins and 10 three-bedroom luxury cabins provide guests with all the modern amenities, including electrical appliances, cooking and serving utensils, and bed linens.

Norris Dam has two camping areas: one on the eastern side of the park with 40 sites, and another to the west with 50 sites. Most of the sites are fully equipped with water and electrical hookups, picnic tables and grills, while modern bathhouses provide campers with hot showers and restrooms. There's a laundromat conveniently located near the park village green complex, a recreation center, and an Olympic-size swimming pool.

The waters of Norris Lake provide opportunities for visitors to enjoy all sorts of water-related sports and activities: waterskiing, boating, sailing, swimming, and, of course, fishing. The lake is well stocked with bass, bream, bluegill, crappie, and walleye. There's also a nearby commercially-operated marina.

For the hiker and naturalist, many miles of woodland trails thread their way among the forests, rolling hills and valleys of the adjacent lands.

The park recreation center provides all sorts of recreational activities, including archery, badminton, and volleyball. At the pool a lifeguard is on duty during the swimming hours, and there's a concession stand where you can purchase refreshments.

ACTIVITIES: During the summer months park recreation directors and naturalists offer a full program of activities, including guided walks, cave tours, arts & crafts, movies, and slide shows. Weekly activity schedules are available at the recreation center and at the park office.

INFORMATION: Norris Dam State Park, Route 1, Box 500, Lake City, TN 37769. Telephone 615-426-7461. The park is open during the summer months from 8 AM until 10 PM, and from 8 AM until sundown during the winter. The camper quiet time is 10 PM.

Norris Dam is about 20 miles northwest of Knoxville and accessible from I-75 at both the Lake City and Norris exits.

Panther Creek State Park

Panther Creek, 1,440 acres of parkland just six miles west of Morristown, is named for the nearby Panther Creeks Springs, a landmark of pioneer times. The signature feature of the park is a 1,460-foot-long ridge which provides a spectacular panoramic view of the East Tennessee Ridge and Valley region. The park is a hot-spot for naturalists and bird watchers, and rightly so, for the ridge provides an unparalleled vantage point from which to observe a variety of wild birds, including several species of birds of prey and migrating waterfowl.

Facilities at the park include 15 vacation cabins, all equipped for housekeeping with appliances and cooking and serving utensils, 50 fully-equipped camping sites with water and electrical hook-ups, a camp laundry, and a gift shop. There's also a picnic area with table and grills, public restrooms, tennis courts, hiking trails, boat launches at the nearby lake, and a playground for the children.

ACTIVITIES: Nature study and bird watching, wildlife photography, fishing, swimming, and boating on the lake, hiking the many miles of backcountry trails, camping and picnicking.

INFORMATION: Panther Creek State Park, 2010 Panther Creek Road, Morristown, TN 37814. Telephone 615-723-5073. The park is open during the summer months from 8 AM until 10 PM, and from 8 AM until sundown during the winter. The camper quiet time is 10 PM.

Panther Creek is west of I-81, off US 11E.

The First Frontier

Davy Crockett Birthplace State Park

Davy Crocket was born on the banks of Nolichuckey River near the mouth of Limestone Creek in 1786. In the mid-1950's, spurred on by the lately generated enthusiasm for the famous backwoodsman in the TV series, "King of the Wild Frontier," the Davy Crocket Birthplace Association built and furnished a replica of the log cabin Crocket was born in and developed the three-acre area into a park. In 1973, the association presented the park to the State of Tennessee. Historical inaccuracies, among other things, however, caused the Department of Conservation to dismantle the cabin and rebuild it. The new construction is a more accurate reflection of the type of cabin Davy Crocket would have lived in during those turbulent times.

In 1976 more land was added to the already popular park, and today, there's a fine visitors center, a camping ground with 73 modern sites, all with water and electrical hookups, a bathhouse, public restrooms, and a dumping station. There are also three picnic pavilions, many scenic picnic areas with tables and grills, boat access to the river, a hiking trail, a swimming pool, and the Davy Crocket Birthplace Cabin.

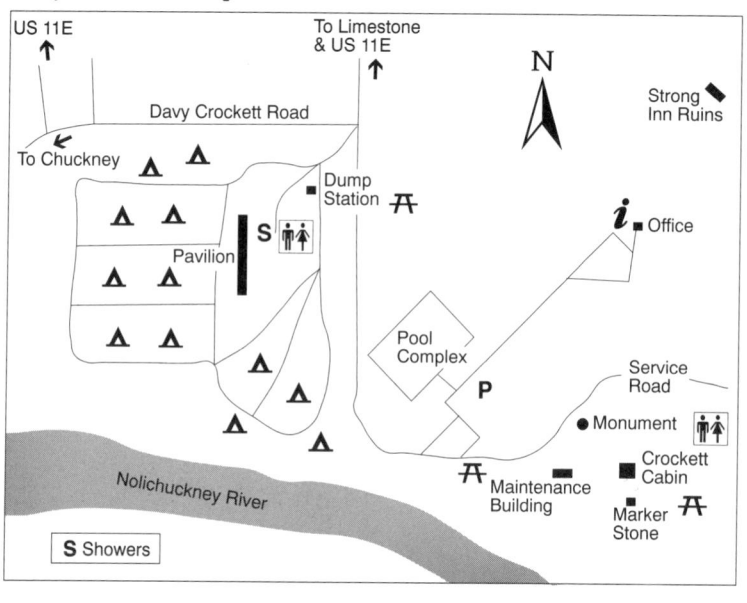

INFORMATION: Davy Crocket Birthplace, Route 3, Box 103A, Limestone, TN 37681. Telephone 615-257-2167. The campground is open May through October from 8 AM until 10 PM, and November through April from 8 AM until 6 PM. The Historical Cabin is open from 8 AM until 10 PM.

The park is about 3.5 miles off US 11E near Limestone, Tennessee.

Roan Mountain State Park

At an elevation of more than 6,200 feet, Roan Mountain is one of the highest peaks in the Eastern United States. The state park is surrounded by the great Cherokee National Forest, more than 700,000 acres of dense, unspoiled woodland in East Tennessee.

Roan Mountain's signature attraction is its 600-acre rhododendron park high atop the mountain. During early summer the garden sets the entire mountain top ablaze with color. It's a natural spectacle that must be seen to be believed.

Facilities at the park include 20 vacation cabins, each with accommodations for up to six people, and fully equipped for housekeeping, including appliances, cooking and serving utensils, and linen service. There are 87 modern camping sites on two campgrounds, each with a table and grill, and water and electric hookups. There are 20 more camping sites for tent campers only. All the sites are well served by three bathhouses, each of which provides hot showers and restroom facilities. There's also a dumping station for those campers with self-contained rigs. The park restaurant can seat up to 50 persons and is open for breakfast, lunch, and dinner.

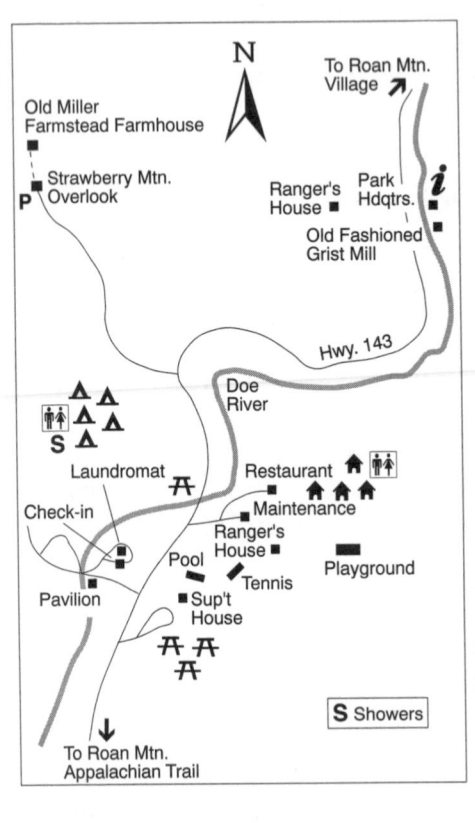

Roan Mountain also has a visitors center and museum, a gift shop, tennis courts, several picnic areas with tables and grills provided, and a fine playground for the children. More than four miles of hiking and backpacking trails of varying difficulty meander around the park. Some trails lead upward to the peak of the mountain, others follow the streams and the banks of Doe River.

ACTIVITIES: Hiking the mountain trails, nature study and bird watching, picnicking and camping, and, especially during the rhododendron flowering season, photography. Cross-country skiing is also a popular activity during the winter months. There are three well-developed ski trails of varying difficulty. During the summer months a qualified park naturalist offers a variety of programs and activities, including guided tours, campfire programs, slide shows, and demonstrations.

Annual special events at the park include the Carter County Wildflowers Tours and Bird Walks in May, the Rhododendron festival in June, and the Roan Mountain Naturalist Rally in September.

INFORMATION: Roan Mountain State Park, Route 1, Box 236, Roan Mountain, TN 37687. Telephone 615-772-3303. The park is open the year-round 8 AM until 10 PM. The camper quiet time is 10 PM.

The park is on the Tennessee/North Carolina border, off US 19E on State Highway 143.

Sycamore Shoals
State Historic Park

Sycamore Shoals is a small, 47-acre historic park on the outskirts of Elizabethton in Northeast Tennessee. The main feature of the park is its museum and a reconstruction of the frontier fort Watauga. The museum and fort provide visitors with an interpretation of the area's history and of life as it must have been in the 18th century – an area once known as the State of Franklin. It was here at Fort Watauga that the mountain men gathered together in September, 1780 before the battle of Kings of Mountain. Also of interest is the monument on the lawn of Carter County Courthouse in Elizabethton. It marks the spot where the pioneers here formed the Watauga Association in 1772. Their constitution was the first to be adopted by independent Americans, and it united the people of eastern Tennessee during the War of Independence.

The facilities are limited to day use only, but they include the visitors center and museum, a gift shop, boat launching facilities on the nearby Watauga River, a hiking trail, and a picnic area.

NEARBY ATTRACTIONS: Covered Bridge Park on the banks of the Doe River, the 18th-century Carter Mansion, Roan Mountain State Park, and Watauga Dam and Lake.

INFORMATION: Sycamore Shoals State Historic Park, 1651 West Elk Avenue, Elizabethton, TN 37643. Telephone 615-543-5808.

The park is just outside Elizabethton. From Johnson City take US 321.

Warrior's Path State Park

Warrior's Path, on the shores of Fort Patrick Henry Lake in Upper-east Tennessee, is perhaps one of the most scenic recreation areas in the state system. The park is named for the ancient war paths and trading trails used by Cherokee Indians in pioneer times. Today, Warrior's Path provides its visitors with a memorable outdoor experience. Activities are, for the most-part, water related, but more than nine miles of hiking trails wind through the scenic woodland glades, and up Holston Buffs to the Devils Backbone for breathtaking views of the surrounding countryside. The neighboring forests, rolling hills and valleys provide habitats for a wide variety of woodland creatures and plantlife.

Overnight facilities include 95 modern camping sites with tables, grills, water and electric hookups, a modern bathhouse, a snack bar, and a camp store, where groceries, camping, picnic, and recreational supplies are available.

ACTIVITIES: There's a recreation center, an 18-hole golf course, a full-service marina on Lake Fort Patrick Henry, boat launching, tennis courts, overnight boarding for horses, and hiking trails, bicycle trails, and bridleways.

The fishing at Warrior's Path is claimed to the best in upper-east Tennessee, and many fine catches of largemouth, smallmouth, and white bass, rainbow trout, crappie, bluegill, catfish, muskie, and walleye have been recorded at Fort Patrick Henry Lake.

INFORMATION: Warrior's Path State Park, PO Box 5026, Kingsport, TN 37663. Telephone 615-239-8531. The park is open from 8 AM until 10 PM and the camper quiet time is 10 PM.

The park is on State Route 36. From I-81 take Exit 59.

General Information

For information and brochures, contact the Tennessee Department of Environment & Conservation, Bureau of Parks & Recreation, 7th Floor L&C Tower, 401 Church Street, Nashville, TN 37243-0446 or telephone 1-800-421-6683, or 615-532-0001, Monday through Friday, from 8 AM until 5 PM.

Activities Fees

CAMPING: Fees for camping depend upon the individual parks but generally range from $9.50 to $14 per night for RV sites, and from $6.25 to $9.50 per night for tent sites. A non-refundable deposit of $5 may be required in order to reserve a campsite. Camp sites may be reserved by telephoning the park of your choice directly.

RESORT HOTELS: For rates and reservations call the resort of your choice directly. At Pickwick Landing the room rates range from $55 to $57 per night. At Fall Creek Falls, Tennessee's most expensive state park, a single room on weekdays, in season, costs $51.19, and $53.46 on weekends. Rates for a double room are $62.56 on weekdays, and $64.84 at weekends; add $6 per night per extra adult (16 and older). Children aged 15 and under stay free. There is an off-season rate, December 1 through February 28, of $44.36 on weekdays, and $46.64 on weekends (single or double) with a charge of $5 per extra person.

MODERN CABINS, RUSTIC CABINS: For rates and reservations call the resort of your choice directly. At Pickwick Landing the rates range from $60 per night, plus tax, during the week, and $80 per night, plus tax, on the weekends, with a two-night minimum stay. At Fall Creek Falls the rates for a cabin range from $73.94 per night, including tax, to $96.69 per night, with a two-night minimum stay. A deposit equal to one night's rent is required upon making a reservation. Charges may made by personal check or by Visa or Mastercard.

GOLF: Golf at Fall Creek Falls - for unlimited play the fee is $16. The fee for nine holes is $9. Cart rental costs $9 per 9 holes, and clubs may be rented for $2.50. Pull cart rental is $2. Most state park courses require you reserve a tee-time for weekend play. An annual, state-wide, golf permit, good for play the year-round at any of Tennessee's state parks costs $600; senior citizens aged 62 or older may purchase the same state-wide permit for only $300.

FISHING: Fishing at all Tennessee state parks is free for park guests. The daily rate for day-use visitors is $1.50. A valid Tennessee fishing license is required. These can often be purchased at the park store.

BOAT RENTAL: Fishing boat rentals are available at most parks where water dominates the activities. Fees range from $4.50 per half-day to $14.50 per full day, depending upon the park. Canoe, rowboat, and paddleboat rentals range upward from $3 per hour.

INTERPRETIVE EVENTS are usually free of charge, although in some cases there may be a nominal charge.

SWIMMING: Fees vary from park to park and range from $1 to $2 per day.

PICNIC SHELTERS: Reservations must be made directly with each park, or may be used on a first-come, first-served basis. The daily fees charged vary from park to park. At Fall Creek Falls a picnic shelter with water and electric utilities, grills, picnic tables, and room for 50 to 100 persons rents for a daily rate of $40.78.

GROUP LODGE: Reservations must be made directly with each park. The fee depends upon location, size, and number of accommodations available. Prices range upward from $4.50 per person per night with a minimum daily rate which also varies from park to park; at Fall Creek Falls the minimums range from $130 for a 40-person lodge to $190 for a 104-person lodge.

TENNIS: Tennis is free at all Tennessee state parks.

PARK FEES: There are no admission fees at Tennessee state parks.

SENIOR CITIZENS: Senior citizens residing in Tennessee aged 62 and older are eligible for a 50% discount on camping facilities, 10% at the inns, and can golf free (green fees only) on Mondays, except for holiday weekends.